THE ALMANAC OF
QUOTABLE QUOTES
FROM 1991

D1047728

Ronald D. Pasquariello

PRENTICE HALL
Englewood Cliffs, New Jersey 07632

Prentice-Hall International (UK) Limited, *London*
Prentice-Hall of Australia Pty. Limited, *Sydney*
Prentice-Hall Canada, Inc., *Toronto*
Prentice-Hall Hispanoamericana, S.A., *Mexico*
Prentice-Hall of India Private Limited, *New Delhi*
Prentice-Hall of Japan, Inc., *Tokyo*
Simon & Schuster Asia Pte. Ltd., *Singapore*
Editora Prentice-Hall do Brasil, Ltda., *Rio de Janeiro*

© 1992 *by*

Ronald D. Pasquariello

10   9   8   7   6   5   4   3   2   1

Library of Congress Cataloging-in-Publication Data

The Almanac of quotable quotes from 1991 / [compiled] by Ronald D. Pasquariello.
   p. cm.
   Includes index.
   ISBN 0-13-031717-9
   1. Quotations.   I. Pasquariello, Ronald D.
PN6081.A54   1992
081–dc20   90–25345
                                                                        CIP

ISBN 0-13-031717-9

PRENTICE HALL
Business Information & Publishing Division
Englewood Cliffs, NJ 07632
Simon & Schuster. A Paramount Communications Company

Printed in the United States of America

DEDICATION

To

Sean Sammon, Ph.D.

for his incredible goodness and generosity

ACKNOWLEDGMENTS

Ginny is a real estate agent in Walnut Creek, California. About once a month an envelope would arrive in the mail with carefully clipped pages and highlighted quotes, often with a sage or wry comment in the margin. Ginny induced her sisters, Kootchie and Sheila, to also make brief contributions.

Roy is the founder and director of "Your Personal Best," a fitness training center in San Francisco. He faithfully supplied me each week with two or three magazines from his apparently huge subscription portfolio. He always went out of his way to deliver the issues personally, or saw to it that they were brought to me by any one of a number of his clients who might be passing my way.

Andrew Nichols is the head writer for "The Tonight Show," starring Johnny Carson. He marshalled the resources of the six writing teams, and had the tapes of many shows reviewed to collect a dozen pages of jokes as Johnny Carson used them.

Daniel McGroarty, Deputy Director of Speechwriting for President Bush, did the same thing for the president's speeches, helping me locate a number of quotes that were given in public addresses, but not fully reported by the press.

My special thanks to them. It's their contributions that make this book shine. And special thanks also to Carol Lewis for her help in inputing the quotes into my database.

"Many are picked, but few are chosen," we were reminded this year by an advertisement for C & W frozen peas. Well, when it comes to writing quote books, many pledge to help, but few deliver. Of all my many good-intentioned friends who loved last year's volume and promised to pass along some quotes this year, only a few carried through. Yes, I still love them all, but my special thanks go to Ginny Hawley, Roy Cameron, Daniel McGroarty of the White House, and Andrew Nichols of "The Tonight Show."

This book could never have happened without the support of Paul Caruso, who took on many extra burdens so that I could find time to do the incredible amount of reading and rewriting this type of book demands. My unceasing thanks to him.

INTRODUCTION

The only thing that limited the number of quotations included in this book was the finite number of trees in the world. The more than two thousand quotations here could have just as easily numbered over four thousand, or even outweighed *Harlot's Ghost,* Norman Mailer's new 1300 page novel about the CIA.

What this volume proves, like last year's, is that we are eminently quotable. Most of us drop a well-worded line as easily and as often as we turn on the TV.

Each quote here represents more than one decision by the quote collector—about whether or not it should be included, under what heading it should be included, whether it represented the best that can be said on the issue at hand. Each quote was required to first pass the test of relevance to 1991, that is, it had to be said in 1991 and had to be related to a 1991 event or personage or mood or atmosphere.

And the events vary in substance, from the provocative Gulf War, which merited a chapter, to the compelling nomination of Clarence Thomas, to the curious arrest of Pee-Wee Herman, to the intriguing nuptials of Liz Taylor, to the mundane publishing of new health guidelines by the Department of Agriculture.

In the chapter on the Gulf War, you find some of the words of the President, the Major, the tyrant, and a host of comments from armchair generals. But you will also read touching descriptions of the struggles in the sand from the real heroes, the women and men who did battle for us.

In addition, you'll hear Liz Taylor say that she was "signed up all over the world" in response to a question about her bridal registry. And you might chuckle at Eddie Fisher's (wry?) comment that this was the first time that she married a laborer.

There are poignant statements throughout, like Bob Hope's stirring remark on the death of Danny Thomas—that he heard it on the best authority that God said "Make Room for Danny."

Of course, the unexpected testimonies at the nomination of Clarence Thomas to the supreme court generated a whole passel of statements about sexual harassment, many of which were included in a special section in the chapter on "work."

There are some sayings that get you to think, like this from moralist Daniel Callahan: "The fact that some people want to live to be 100 does not mean we have to shape public policy to meet that goal." And some that get you to wonder about the speaker: "I always had a good sense of humor...I realize that may not be apparent to other people" (Alexander Haig).

There were some serious notes sounded last year: That poverty is increasing, that income is declining among the middle class, that breast cancer in increasing (one in nine women now), that lung cancer has surpassed breast cancer as a cause of death among women, that the father's sperm can be guilty in fetal alcohol and drug syndrome.

And the beat goes on. Here you will hear from and about the Bushes, the Reagans, Dan Quayle, Cher, Gorbachev, Madonna. You will find out such interesting things as the average statistics for Playboy's Playmate over the past three decades, Esquire's measurements for the optimal '90s male, and who the highest paid athletes are (boxers, it turns out). You will catch some of the promises of politicians, be flabbergasted by some of the outrageous things (mostly sexist) that have been said, and learn about progress in health, science, and technology. You get a chance to peruse some of the headlines from the tabloids ("Grieving Hubby: I Ate Shark That Ate My Wife") and some creative permutations of the proliferating 1-900 numbers (1-900-XXX-SUDS, for an update on the soap operas).

What you will end with is a picture of who we were in 1991. What our likes were, what our dislikes were, what and how we thought about ourselves, and the events that shaped the year. You will find the volume thought-provoking and entertaining, a continuous source of enjoyable reading and conversation.

CONTENTS

Introduction   vii

Chapter 1: People   1

Chapter 2: The Gulf War   29

Chapter 3: The Nation   53

Chapter 4: The World   81

Chapter 5: Business   95

Chapter 6: Health   109

Chapter 7: The Written Word   129

Chapter 8: Sports   153

Chapter 9: Entertainment   179

Chapter 10: Religion   195

Chapter 11: Science and Technology   213

Chapter 12: Society   233

Chapter 13: Work   259

Chapter 14: Signs of the Times   287

Chapter 15: Far Out   301

Index   317

1

PEOPLE

You can't always expect a certain result, but you can expect to do your best.

Anita Hill

According to the polls, a majority of the American people believed that President Reagan did know...And now, five years later, I am even more convinced: President Reagan knew everything. Ronald Reagan knew of and approved a great deal of what went on with both the Iranian initiative and private efforts on behalf of the Contras, and he received regular, detailed briefings on both.

Ollie North
in his new book, Under Fire

I bet I prepared a couple of hundred thousand pages of memoranda that went up the chain of command and laterally to the Vice President's office. I don't believe anybody has said he (George Bush) wasn't aware of at least a good measure of what was going on [regarding the Contras].

Ollie North

There are two kinds of people in the world—those who walk into a room and say, "There you are"—and those who say, "Here I am!"

Abigail Van Buren

1

First of all, let me say that because of the HIV that I have obtained, I will have to retire from the Lakers today. . . . I think we sometimes think only gay people can get it; it's not going to happen to me. And here I am saying that it can happen to anybody, even Magic Johnson.

Basketball great Magic Johnson
announcing that he had contracted the AIDS virus

If we've learned anything in the past quarter century, it is that we cannot federalize virtue.

President George Bush

Most of our greatest responsibilities confront us not in the government hearing rooms but around dinner tables, on the streets, at the office. If you teach your children and others how to hate, they will learn. And if you encourage them not to trust others, they'll follow your lead. And if you talk about compassion but refuse to help those in need, your children will learn to look the other way.

President George Bush

I catered to him and that gave me a great deal of pleasure, just that very act itself...I don't think we ever had a fight. And he was very Republican; I was way left of center...I really did love him and I was determined that it was going to work. I'm sure Spencer worked at it too, some; but he didn't have to work much because I really made it work.

Katharine Hepburn
on her longterm relationship with Spencer Tracy

If it was such a big deal, how come I could hide everything with my hands?

Burt Reynolds
on his 1973 centerfold in "Cosmopolitan"

I thought it was funny. I have a sense of humor about the shoe situation. It helped me in the end. When they opened the closet, the nice part was they found shoes, but thank God there were no skeletons.

Imelda Marcos
on her collection of 1,060 pairs of shoes

I asked myself, "How many more conquests do you need before you're satisfied you're not a homosexual?" Finally, Geraldo the boy became Geraldo the man, and for the last four years I've been the best husband in America.

Talk show host Geraldo Rivera

A smile isn't any good unless you aim it at someone.

Dennis the Menace

Never lose sight of the fact that the most important yardstick of your success will be how you treat other people—your family, friends, and coworkers, and even strangers you meet along the way.

Barbara Bush

There's too much chance for error, too many flaws, too great a possibility for misuse. If you're going to place the ultimate [death] sentence in the name of the people, sooner or later you will execute an innocent person, and that's too high a price to pay. The sad part about it is, there's a lot of people out there who say that if one's innocent and we kill him, it's still a better way to get the ones who are guilty.

Randall Adams
an innocent man who had spent 13 years as a
convicted murderer on death row

As long as you believe in yourself, others will.

Cynda Williams

A secure and stable America, not justice and fair play, is the real reason Blacks and Whites must learn to live in harmony. The national security depends on it.

Arthur Fletcher
chairman of the United States civil rights commission

I can't figure out why some record company hasn't come to me. I still sing beautiful. My hand still moves over those piano keys very spiffily and my music means something to today's generation.

Rock star Little Richard

Mozart may have been poisoned by mercury and antimony used by doctors treating him for depression and fever.

*According to **Dr. Ian James***

Love is the most ambiguous, delirious, illogical emotion there is...I want to be romantic forever. I want to be cryonically frozen with a box of chocolates under my arm and some flowers, and thaw me out in 200 years so I can propose to someone.

*Actor **Sylvester Stallone***

I have it on great authority that God said: "Move over—make room for Danny."

Bob Hope
on the recently deceased Danny Thomas

She's first of all a wife. That's the reason she's there.

Nancy Reagan
on the primary duty of the First Lady

Our main problem is that most people don't think we have a problem. They think their kids are learning, they think their schools are good, everything's fine.

Education secretary Lamar Alexander

One of the most common fallacies about change is the conclusion that if something is bad, its opposite must out of necessity be good.

Paul Watzlawick

I'm not afraid to show my feminine side—it's part of what makes me a man.

Actor Gerard Depardieu

The fans prevented me from suffocating at parties in Europe, where everyone drinks and smokes and where there's no air-conditioning. And also, you can avoid bad photos—it's a very helpful thing.

Designer Karl Lagerfeld
on why he carries folding fans

Money is not an issue when you believe in what you're doing.

New York hairdresser **Roger Thompson**

I see things in this country today that frighten me terribly. I'm talking about a divisiveness—a self-centeredness—that I'm not sure we've seen before. I have come to the conclusion that good times are not good for the human race. I'm serious about this.

Management consultant **Peter F. Drucker**

Over the years I have learned that what is important in a dress is the woman who is wearing it.

Designer **Yves Saint Laurent**

The net worth (in billions) of the wealthiest people in America:

1. John Kluge, 77, Metromedia	$5.9
2. Sam Walton, 73, Wal-Mart	$4.4 each
John Walton, 46	
Jim Walton, 47	
Alice Walton, 42	
S. Robson Walton, 47	
3. Warren Buffett, 61, Stocks	$4.2
4. Henry Hillman, 72, Industries	$3.3
5. Richard DeVos, 65, Amway	$2.9 each
Jay Van Andel, 67, Amway	

According to **"Forbes"**

After careful consideration, the Jackson family has decided not to dignify La Toya's allegations with a response. We know, and we hope all our friends and fans know, that her ongoing statements are a pack of lies and any comment from us would only add fuel to the fire.

Joseph and Katherine Jackson
on their daughter's accusations of childhood abuse

Self-recommendation is no recommendation at all.

Maxi Priest

He didn't want women around. He's a pompous man, given to moralizing, fourth-rate commentary. He's so impressed with himself, and he kind of lets the audience know that every time he does a piece. He's from the "aren't-I-smart?" school of journalism.

Liz Trotta
former TV reporter, on commentator John Chancellor

He wanted people to know he had died of AIDS. He wanted to reach out to all other families afraid to come forward...From what I've heard, there are other (stars) who are living secret lives.

Susan Bluestein
wife of actor Brad Davis who died of AIDS

If all you have to offer is a look that is supposed to be appealing, then you are going to be paid attention to about a tenth as long as you would be if when you speak you are interesting.

Actress Julia Roberts

When you're with someone who's supportive and adores you, it can't help but make you feel—and look—younger.

Model Cheryl Tiegs

There will be obstacles; you may not have all of your dreams satisfied. But through a lot of hard work and believing in yourself you'll reach the more important of your dreams.

Susan Williams
the first Native American woman graduate
of Harvard Law School

Robin is funny, cultured, and kind, and it took me a long time to find someone like him. That's because it took me even longer to grow up.

Actress Joan Collins
on her current relationship

We live in troubled times, but you are the solution. You must help find the answers and the cures.

Singer Dionne Warwick
in a commencement address

Sometimes we think we have to express our feelings in order to feel better. But sometimes you don't have to touch your suffering a lot. You should have a reserve of refreshing images to counterbalance the suffering within you.

Thich Nahat Hanh

Don't search for opportunities in a distance until you have exhausted the advantages of those right where you are.

Jerry L. Jones Sr.

Men may deny it, but I think their motivation to succeed, to be incredibly powerful and opulent and to maintain an overwhelming, titanic status in the community is for women...Power. That's what women are drawn to.

Actor Sylvester Stallone

A successful man is one who makes more money than his wife spends. A successful woman is one who can find such a man.

Actress Lana Turner

They would tell me, for example, that although Hoover served under 18 attorney generals, none of them knew he had installed a burglary school in the attic of the Department of Justice, that the whole building was bugged, that even Bobby Kennedy's elevator, the one place where he felt safe to talk, was wired, and that a pornographic theater had been built in the basement where Hoover and his aides watched movies.

Curt Gentry
author of J. Edgar Hoover: The Man and The Secrets

Education is what happens to the other person, not what comes out of the mouth of the educator.

Miles Horton

Customer to bookseller: "I'd like to buy a book on chutzpah and I'd like you to pay for it;" and "assertive insistence on first-class status among our peers."

Alan M. Dershowitz
Two definitions of chutzpah offered by Chutzpah author

For seven years, I have said the same thing. I have no plans to run for President and no plans to make plans.

New York governor Mario Cuomo

Before Christ came into my life, the realities of the materialistic world had the priority in my daily living.

Born-again Christian Manuel Noriega

While people are internally forgetful of favors done for them, they rarely forget the favors they have done others. Politicians don't make it to the top doing favors; they make it there by letting other people do them favors.

Christopher Matthews

The things that make a woman beautiful—moving with grace, accepting yourself, the ability to enjoy life—are timeless. I don't think elaborate rituals make a woman beautiful.

Actress Winona Ryder

I'm embarrassed to be a goddamn celebrity. I just don't get it. American people know more about me than they know about the guy who runs the country.

Actor Bruce Willis

I tell you, I find fan mail really real depressing. I mean, the grammatical errors, the spelling errors I see, and I'm not being a stickler about this.

Actress Bebe Neuwirth

My greatest fear was that if I didn't drink, I was going to lose my friends; nobody's going to want me around. But one of the amazing things is I'm having just as much fun. I'm laughing just as much and I still have the same friends. I guess we'll just share a juice.

Pat Sommeral
Recovering alcoholic

It's never too late—never too late to start over, never too late to be happy.

Actress Jane Fonda

If you shoot for the stars and hit the moon it's okay. But you've got to shoot for something. A lot of people don't even shoot.

Robert Townsend

I'm surprised the world is still here. I thought that it had powdered off somewhere. I'm really happy to see a tree, hear an airplane, hear an automobile. I am amazed and baffled.

Edward Austin Tracy
Released American hostage

My mother used to say, "Watch yourself. The higher you are, the farther you can fall. Never let pride be your guiding principle. Pride itself. Let your accomplishments speak for you."

Actor Morgan Freeman

I sometimes think that the more reckless among us may have something to teach the careful about the sort of immortality that comes from living fully every day.

Melvin Conner

The future belongs to the [political] party that knows the health of the people precedes the health of the state.

Bill Moyers

In June, we're going to start trying to conceive. Roseanne had her tubes cut in her previous marriage, so we have to do in vitro fertilization. We've already done my part at the hospital.

Tom Arnold
Roseanne Barr's husband

You were born with your looks. You can either abuse them or improve them. And you can either worry about them...or you can worry about being happy with yourself.

Model Kim Alexis

[George] Wallace says he'd like to be remembered as someone who "turned out to be one of the best friends that Black people had in Alabama and the South." That's not likely. But George Wallace does deserve to be remembered as a man who repudiated his segregationist views and spent his last years trying to undo some of the harm he had done.

Journalist DeWayne Wickam

I know there's still discrimination in the world. But youth has to deal with it. A lot of them feel that their race will hinder them. But with hard work, determination, and commitment, they can accomplish their goals.

Marjorie Judith Vincent

These "artists" who have their minds in the gutter are free to do what they want to with their own time and their own money, but don't ask John Q. Public to pay for it.

Senator Jesse Helms

To see and find baby toys at Playboy Mansion West is so delicious...Now when you find baby oil here, there's a baby around!

Hugh Hefner

Don't trust anyone. Your loyal secretary is the first one who is going to rat on you. Many women have come to me with the source of information being their husband's secretary. A secret shared is a secret nonexistent.

Divorce lawyer Raoul Felder

What is this fascination with Ed McMahon? Every tabloid and magazine seems to think the public is interested in this old womanizer. Give us a break!

Karen A. Tokarz

Spend more time with older women. I happen to think women get better-looking as they get older.

Actor Robert Redford

Somebody's got to do it. It's a dirty job, being ridiculous, but I'll do it.

Cher

I had no idea what I was saying. But I do know that I was at [President] Bush's table, and [Sylvester] Stallone was at Quayle's.

Actress Teri Garr
on dinner at the White House

I believe that was the most comprehensive introduction I have ever received. You omitted perhaps one thing—that in 1974 I had a hemorrhoidectomy.

Alabama Sen. Howell Heflin
on a lengthy introduction

Struggle and survival, losing and winning, doesn't matter. It's entering the race that counts. You enter, you can win, you can lose...but it's all about entering the race.

Pam Grier

Racism does affect us all, but it doesn't affect us all equally. Some have more defenses against racism. It's like bad weather. All of us are affected by it, but some have boots and rain gear and some are naked to the elements.

Columnist William Raspberry

I have been driving for 30 years without incident. I am grateful I did not hurt anybody and will take whatever punishment is dictated.

Actress Tyne Daly
on being charged with drunk driving

The satisfaction derived from money does not come from simply having it. It comes from having more of it than others do.

Alan Durning

People are dying who never died before. It's getting lonely at the top of the tree.

Dorothy Donegan
68-year-old jazz pianist

I look forward to being older when what you look like becomes less and less the issue and what you are is the point.

Actress Susan Sarandon

It's time for us to turn to each other, not on each other.

Jesse Jackson

It reminds me of President Jimmy Carter and brother Billy. I'm no president and she's not Billy, but, nonetheless...there's a sense of constan: embarrassment which you must somehow endure.

Actress Lynn Redgrave
on sister Vanessa Redgrave

Graham Greene will never die...Graham Greene has always been the man at the dizzying brink of things where faith waivers, spies become double agents, love turns subtly into sadism, and anything can happen.

Marie Francoise Allain

I am perfectly capable of enjoying a human being without sleeping with them. Of course, I have slept with some leading ladies, but the necessity is pretty much out of my system.

Actor Nick Nolte

I think to be a good wife you have to be prepared to sacrifice your "self" to become one with another person, and I'm not willing to do that. I think there is something else I'm suppose to do, and I want to stay on that road.

Talk show host Oprah Winfrey

Racism is a bacterium, potentially curable but presently deadly; anti-Semitism is a virus, potentially deadly but presently contained.

Letty Cottin Pogrebin

When *Back to the Future* first made it big, I kept a picture of John Belushi on my living room wall. That was to remind me what could happen if I lost my head and my values over this fame thing.

Actor Michael J. Fox

My mother was a tyrant. If you did anything that outraged her, she would wrap on more punishment...It was really a bad situation for a teenager to be in.

88-year-old Dr. Benjamin Spock

You're no bigger than the things that annoy you.

Jerry Bundsen

I'm no good at marriage. My energy gets directed elsewhere...I am a much better boyfriend than a husband.

Talkshow host Larry King

I can go home again. I often do. In many important ways I never left.

Dan Rather
on his Texas homeland

May you live an extra-long life and suffer.

William Smart
father-in-law of Pamela Smart, who was given life without parole
for arranging her husband's murder

Sex is the ultimate gift a woman can give a man, and the thought of being vulnerable and intimate with a man is very appealing to me...But sex is meant for procreation, and I want to consummate a relationship with a man who's going to be the father of my children.

Actress Brooke Shields

She's sort of the pitbull of journalism. When she gets into something, she sinks her teeth into it and doesn't let it go.

Reporter Jay Grelen
on reporter Wendy Bergen

In the brain, age is like a good wine—it gets better. But age below
the brain isn't like wine at all—it get's worse down there.

Singer Julio Iglesias

We were happily married for eight months. Unfortunately, we were
married for four and a half years.

Pro-golfer Nick Faldo
on his former marriage

He's a great man, a natural man, which is rare. I've been with a lot
of men and I've known a lot of men. And you know I've had romances
with what you'd call famous men, and none compares to Sam in terms
of maleness.

Actress Jessica Lange
about the great love of her life, Sam Shepard

He's won so much acceptance that its made him weary. It's as if he's
afraid we'll fall out of like with him.

James Wolcott
on Jay Leno

Wise people are not always silent, but they always know when to be.

Martha J. Beckman

The only good advice is a good example. You don't tell them a whole
lot of anything. You show them by doing. You teach values by making
choices in their presence. They see what you do and they make judgments
on it.

Actor Ossie Davis

We have a stake in educating and socializing our children. But if we
really expect to see a change in the current situation, men have to get
involved in that process, because it takes a Black man to prepare a
Black boy for whatever he's going to face out there.

Dr. D. R. Spencer Holland

Age should never be a barrier to full participation in life. A good diet's important. Exercise is important. But what's most important is to enjoy life to its fullest, to do things for others, and to never, ever be afraid to stretch your limits!

65-year-old Sister Mary Martin Weaver
winner of 44 medals in a varitey of athletic events

You have to be more than good, you've got be better.

Marjorie Kimbrough

I'm afraid to ask girls out. I think too much about it. My friends say I'm the biggest "girl waster" because I'm always afraid to make that first move.

Actor John Stamos

This is no time for fun.

This is no time for play.

Dr. Seuss is no more

It's a sad, sad, sad day.

He taught us, he teased us; he redrew our world.

And it tickled and pleased us through a 50-year whirl.

Brian Gallagher

We may not agree on what a good society is, but...we will never have one until we realize that the public we complain about is us.

Columnist Kenneth L. Woodward

My life is so full now. I don't want to work full-time anymore. I've got a country house and horses. And I'm going to be made a grandmother by one of my horses in May—life is really good.

Actress Mary Tyler Moore

It's my personal view that we've always had quotas in America. It's just that the quotas were 95 or 96 percent in favor of whites.

Claude Lewis

I'm very against violence. I was forced to do those movies. You see, I came into this country with a bad accent—so I showed my chest and legs.

Actor Jean-Claude Van Damme

The good that Martin Luther King, Jr. did remains undiminished...He was great precisely because, like other heroes, he did not allow human weakness to deter him from doing great works.

Carl McClendon

Generally speaking, no one is going to give you anything because you are Black but a hard time and unmitigated hell—though often subtle, covert and insidious. Such is the inevitable character, logic, and nature of racism.

Samuel DuBois Cook

Brownie pledge, I swear I've never, never, ever tried drugs.

Actress Brooke Shields

People need to feel better about themselves, to feel that, yes, they can do it. First you think highly of yourself; then you accelerate.

Janet Norflett

Messing up is what I did best. My life was in chaos. I destroyed my marriage. I got arrested. I was always living on the edge. There were times when I felt that this world would be better off without me. I know why all this happened. I am an adult child of an alcohlic.

Actress Suzanne Somers

My real assets have always been acting and just being pleasant.

Actress Sally Field

It is better to travel well-dressed than to arrive on time.

Neil Bartlett

You're born and dealt a hand of cards and have no choice but to play them. Multiple sclerosis doesn't affect me because I don't allow it to.

Stephanie LaMotta

No wonder people go into politics. You're able to work when you want to, answer to no one, vote yourself a raise, no review, nothing.

Marjorie Williams

Go home, you parasites, and watch it on the news.

Murder suspect John Riccard
to gawkers as he perched on a 10th-floor windowsill

Maybe [Merv Griffin] lusts after both sexes. Who knows, darling? Frankly, I always thought that Merv was too old and fat to make love at all. The press is making him out to be a sex maniac. Look at him. This is not a sexy man. And God knows, I know what sexy is.

Zsa Zsa Gabor

The best thing about being 15 is dating. It's fun. The worst thing is acne.

Model-actress Milla Jovovich

There are some women who don't need as much [attention]. My mother does not need as much. Maria is high maintenance.

Arnold Schwarzenegger
on wife Maria Shriver

I've always had a good sense of humor...I realize that may not be apparent to other people.

Alexander Haig
Former Secretary of State

To succeed in any endeavor takes relentless belief in yourself. We have to be committed. We can determine our destiny.

Willye B. White

The thing that everybody finds out about me once they really get to know me is just how terrifically boring I am, and how I aspire to being boring...My dream in life is to wear sweats and go to a mall.

Actress-director Jodie Foster

It's like living in a zoo. He's a tiger sometimes. He's a lamb sometimes. He's a monkey on occasion and a fair amount of time he's a jackass.

Norris Church
on her husband, Norman Mailer

You need a strong, unified family base to allow you to have courage to go out there and take risks that you probably wouldn't have taken had you not had the strong foundation to fall back on.

Rapper L.L. Cool J

We outlived the loss of Cro-Magnon man, Neanderthal man, and who knows what others. The only species that we may not outlast is Modern man.

Don Keeley

There's a stereotype in Hollywood of no butt, large breasts, and a pretty face—and not many people are born that way. Someone gave me a hug recently and said, "Wow, real breasts! That makes a nice change." I guess he has been in the business too long and forgotten what it was like.

Actress Emma Samms

We have been here for four centuries. And in every century...from 1619 to 1991, we have made the contribution. We've made the downpayments, paid the interest, spilled the blood. The mortgage is paid up in full. This is home.

Mayor Sharon Pratt Dixon
on being Black in America

The defendant is not a first offender. He has simply been caught and convicted for the first time.

Judge Thomas Penfield Jackson
resentencing former D.C. mayor Marion Barry

The men Americans most admire:
1. George Bush
2. Mikhail Gorbachev

3. Ronald Reagan
4. Pope John Paul II
5. Billy Graham
6. Nelson Mandela
7. Jesse Jackson
8. Donald Trump
9. Jimmy Carter
10. Lech Walesa

The women Americans most admire:
1. Margaret Thatcher
2. Barbara Bush
3. Mother Teresa
4. Nancy Reagan
5. Oprah Winfrey
6. Elizabeth Taylor
7. Cher
8. Elizabeth Dole
9. Jaqueline Onassis
10. Corazon Aquino

According to a recent Gallup Poll

A lot of people have said to me: "It seems you've always been in the right place at the right time." But what they don't realize is that I was prepared to be there. If luck comes and if you're not ready to take advantage of it, it may just as well not have come.

Gordon Parks

If [cripples] were satisfied to be held up for compassion, to be infantilized on telethons, we would discover that this America has a great deal of time for us...What we invariably discover is that our true self, our inner lives, have been auctioned off so that we can be palatable rather than real.

Leonard Kriegel
former Muscular Dystrophy poster child, on the Jerry Lewis telethon

We are the sum of our efforts to change who we are. Identity is no museum piece sitting stock-still in a display case, but rather the endlessly astonishing synthesis of the contradictions of every day life.

Eduardo Galeano

Only you can incarcerate your minds...To be free on the outside, you have to be free on the inside.

Rev. Rabboni Sellah

A gambler...is someone who wages unfavorable odds. A poker player...is someone who wages favorable odds. The one is a romantic, the other is a realist.

Anthony Holden

She took us out in the yard one day and asked us if we knew the price of eggs, of apples, of bananas. Then she asked us to put a price on clean air, the sunshine, the song of birds—and we were stunned.

Consumer advocate Ralph Nader
on his mother, Rose Nader

I've hit 755 home runs, and I did it without putting a needle in my arm or a whiskey bottle in my mouth.

Hank Aaron

If doing things for your children...helping them through life, if that is considered being a stage mother, then, yes, I'm guilty.

Wanda Webb Holloway
convicted of hiring a hit man to kill the mother of her
daughter's cheerleading rival

Education remains the key to both economic and political empowerment. That is why the schools which are in charge of educating African Americans have, perhaps, the longest, the greatest, the deepest challenges of all...to get into the minds of young African Americans so that they who recognize opportunity will come to those who are prepared.

Barbara Jordan

I can't afford to die. I'm booked. I'd lose a fortune.

Comedian George Burns
on his 95th birthday

People keep asking me how it feels to be 95, and I tell them I feel just as good as I did when I was 94.

Comedian George Burns

He's the only man I know who could look at the swimsuit issue of "Sports Illustrated" and complain because the bathing suits weren't flame-retardant.

Secretary of State James Baker
on Michael Dukakis

In 1988, fighting Dukakis, I said that I "would strip the bark off the little bastard" and "make Willie Horton his running mate." I am sorry for both the statements: the first, for its naked cruelty, the second because it makes me sound like a racist, which I am not.

Lee Atwater
George Bush's presidential campaign manager,
in a written apology

Margot Fonteyne was a ballerina of crystal, just as others are ballerinas of steel or of velvet. Everything about her was elegance, refinement.

Sylvie de Nussac

Performing with [Margot Fonteyne] was intoxicating, and it has been my greatest piece of good fortune to have met her and become her friend as well as her partner...She was the greatest dancer of our epoch. Because of her, dance is better.

Dancer Rudolph Nureyev

NO! I've never taken hormones to maintain my high voice. NO! I've never had my cheekbones altered in any way. YES! One day in the future I plan to get married and have a family.

Michael Jackson

I don't think I'm ever totally happy. I am one of the hardest people to satisfy, but at the same time I'm aware of how much I have to be thankful for.

Rock singer Michael Jackson

KITTY KELLEY'S UNAUTHORIZED BIOGRAPHY OF NANCY REAGAN

It's been like a terrible four-year pregnancy.

Kitty Kelley

I hope the next time she is crossing a street, four blind guys come along driving cars.

Frank Sinatra

I think its trash and fiction.

Barbara Bush
on Nancy Reagan: The Unauthorized Biography

There is an old saying in the journalism business that once you have shot, hanged, stabbed, drawn and quartered the person you are writing about, you do not also have to drown him or her. Obviously, no one told this to Kitty Kelley.

Joe Queenan

Anyone who thinks that Kitty Kelley has damaged the reputation of the Reagans has it wrong. It's the press that has been soiled by this affair.

Columnist Richard Cohen

Yes I am Frank Sinatra's love child, I admit it. I guess he did it his way.

Ron Reagan, Jr.

The only right reason to buy this book is to burn it.

John S. Perkins

Oh, I hope so!

First Lady Barbara Bush
when asked if similar tales might be written
about her one day

One thing Nancy Reagan's hair dressers knew for sure is that she's never had a "nooner" with anyone—she'd never mess up her hair in the middle of the day.

Robin Weir
former hairdresser for Nancy Reagan

On the scale of wasted energy, 900,000 people reading Kelley's book ranks right up there with the Kuwaiti oil fires.

William K. Kozel, Jr.

I feel Kitty's [litter] should be buried with all her other books—6 feet deep.

Gloria Grinta

While I am accustomed to reports that stray from the truth, the flagrant and absurd falsehoods cited in a recently published book clearly exceed the bounds of decency. They are patently untrue—everything from the allegation of marijuana use to marital infidelity to my failure to be present at the birth of my daughter, Patti.

Former President Ronald Reagan

The fun here lies not in discovering alleged secrets that are never explained but in trying to sort out, as Kelley never does, America's fascination with this Tinkertoy couple. Watching Nancy Reagan attempt to be the next Jackie Kennedy, and failing miserably, and crying publicy about it is alone worth the (paperback) price of admission.

Reviewer Patricia Holt

A serious examination of Nancy Reagan's intrusion into the presidential office would show how "Mrs. President" satisfied her own power needs— more executive than advisory—behind Reagan's back. Her flagrant dominance of the White House staff made the aging president, at his most vulnerable during the Iran-Contra scandal, appear to be wimpish and ineffectual.

William Safire

[Readers will] learn that there's no speaker more forthright than the one who hides behind anonymity or is quoting the dead. Or who knows that no denial will be issued because what's said doesn't deserve a reply....Truly, nobody deserves this.

A New York Times editorial

You can see that something is right about this book. It is disturbing too many powerful people not to be taken seriously.

Kitty Kelley

MICHAEL LANDON

Remember me with smiles and laughter,
for that is how I will remember you all.
If you can only remember me with tears,
then don't remember me at all.

*From a poem read by Michael Landon's daughter
Leslie, at his funeral*

Somebody should tell us, right at the start of our lives, that we are dying. Then we might live life to the limit, every minute of every day. Do it! I say. Whatever you want to do, do it now! There are only so many tomorrrows.

Actor Michael Landon

I love you all, but go downstairs now. I want to be alone with Cindy.

*Michael Landon's
last public utterance*

The basic tenets of Michael Landon's legacy—the value of a good life, of a good home, the value of family relationships and the value of your own belief in yourself—will not diminish.

Kent McCray

He taught us how to live and he taught us how to die.

Michael Bacon

PEE-WEE HERMAN

Children's television star Pee-wee Herman was arrested for allegedly exposing himself inside an adult theater.

Associated Press

The case is unutterably stupid. Being arrested for masturbating in an X-rated theater is like being arrested for urinating in a rest room. Pornography exists to provoke sexual fantasies. Is this some kind of big news?

Columnist Jon Carroll

It's almost like Donald Duck flashing in a public park.

A Los Angeles newscaster

Pee-wee, get a VCR.

Comedian Robert Klein

You have a squad of folks sitting around with nothing to do. Instead of having them sit around for the rest of the evening, that's when they go to the adult theaters.

Sarasota County Sheriff Geoff Monge

Poor little Pee-wee. Well, I guess if parents call their son a name like that, something is bound to happen. There is a lesson for us to learn from little Pee-wee: wait until it comes out on video.

Comedian Barry Humphries

The fact that Paul Reuben's actions in an adult cinema dominated the radio and newspapers for seven days—and earned two full pages in "Newsweek"—is far more disheartening and weird than anything ever presented on "Pee-wee's Playhouse."

Robert Stanley

A top-grossing bottle-blond female performer whose act includes miming masturbation on a bed before thousands of people tours to widespread acclaim. A male performer who has hosted one of TV's most creative and entertaining children's shows does the real thing in the relative privacy of an adult-movie theater and his career is cut short. Am I missing something?

Robert D. Ruplenas

Pee-wee toys are like wine; they're getting better with age when it comes to dollar value.

John Lancaster

Let my Pee-wee go!

T-shirt

It seems to me X-rated adult movie houses exist for exactly this sort of behavior, but it is indeed a comfort to know that in Florida—where violent drug crime is rampant—they can waste taxpayers' time and money to keep three cops "on the job" in the place where Herman was arrested.

Columnist Liz Smith

To masturbate is human. To spy in a dark theater is fascist. I support Pee-wee Herman.

Marge Leeds

Regardless of what may have occurred in that theater, he was irresponsible for being there in the first place. Pee-wee is an unsuitable role model for kids. I say good riddance.

J F. Fountain

Merchants report Pee-wee Herman dolls with the actor's likeness are becoming collectors items, going for as much as $125, compared with $25 before Reubens' arrest. Pee-wee lunch boxes go for as much as $25, up from $9.

Thomas D. Elias

RONALD REAGAN

An actor knows two important things—to be honest in what he is doing and to be in touch with the audience. That's not bad advice for a politician either.

Former President Ronald Reagan

What hindsight shows us is that after he has left the room, after he has left the White House, after he has left our national life and gone off to retirement, the charisma goes with him and we realize how seduced we were.

Edmund Morris
Ronald Reagan biographer

I'm saying, "Listen, stop. That's not what I want." He was really forceful. You know he's very tall, very strong. I was very lightweight. It was just a battle that, I'm sorry to say, I lost. It was absolutely against my will and it was over in two minutes.

Former actress Selene Walters
describing an alleged 1951 sexual encounter
with Ronald Reagan

When I told him I was pregnant, he said he didn't want to have anything to do with me anymore. He just ran out on me.

Former actress Jacqueline Park
recalling an early relationship with Ronald Reagan

JOHN SUNUNU

I gather that [John] Sununu has palms on both sides of his hands.

William Blatz

I won't say he flew a lot. But he won't start a cabinet meeting until the seat backs and tray tables are locked into the upright position.

Senator Robert Dole
on White House chief of staff John Sununu

DONALD TRUMP

Marla Maples says she won't need a prenuptial agreement if she marries Donald Trump because "our relationship is built on trust." And she's right...If you can't trust the married man you've been running around with, who can you trust?

Johnny Carson

She shouldn't give it back—he walked out on her. If she walks out on him, she gives back the ring. If it's mutual, she offers it to him and he says, "No, you keep it."

Letitia Baldrige
on Marla Maples' engagement ring

I am a private guy. The newspapers shouldn't be doing a story a day on Donald Trump. There are other developers out there, and they're getting killed much worse than I am.

Donald Trump

2

THE GULF WAR

THE PRESIDENT, GEORGE BUSH

But unless you withdraw from Kuwait completely and without condition, you will lose more than Kuwait. What is at issue here is not the future of Kuwait—it will be free, its government will be restored—but rather the future of Iraq.

President Bush
in a letter to Saddam Hussein on January 12

I'm plenty fed up with Saddam, but there are no threats, just determination. I'm confident he doesn't want to fight. I don't think it will come to that.

President Bush
on Iraq's flouting U.N. cease-fire terms

January 15 is a disastrously conceived deadline...Mars will be setting right over Kuwait at the time of the eclipse and will be lined with the fixed star Alcyone, the Weeping Maiden of the Pleiades. If one asks of this day, is this a good time for aggression? Alcyone responds, there will be much to weep for...Astrologers are dismayed.

Astrologer Caroline Casey

29

Just two hours ago, allied air forces began an attack on military targets in Iraq and Kuwait. These attacks continue as I speak. . . . This conflict started August 2nd when the dictator of Iraq invaded a small helpless neighbor. Kuwait—a member of the Arab League and a member of the United Nations—was crushed; its people, brutalized. Five months ago Saddam Hussein started this cruel war against Kuwait. Tonight, the battle has been joined.

President George Bush

While the world waited, Saddam Hussein met every overture of peace with contempt. While the world prayed for peace, Saddam prepared for war.

President George Bush

I am convinced not only that we will prevail, but that out of the horror of combat will come the recognition that no nation can stand against a world united. No nation will be permitted to brutally assault its neighbor.

President George Bush

Each of us will measure within ourselves the value of this great struggle. Any cost in lives—any cost—is beyond our power to measure. But the cost of closing our eyes to aggression is beyond mankind's power to imagine. This we do know: Our cause is just; our cause is moral; our cause is right.

President George Bush

From the moment Operation Desert Storm commenced on January 16th until the time the guns fell silent at midnight one week ago, this nation has watched its sons and daughters with pride—watched over them with prayer. As Commander in Chief, I can report to you our armed forces fought with honor and valor. As President, I can report to the Nation aggression is defeated. The war is over.

President George Bush

The liberation of Kuwait has begun.

White House Press Secretary Marlin Fitzwater
announcing the beginning of Operation Desert Storm

Reasons advanced by President Bush at various times for his intervention:

To punish aggression in violation of international war

To restore the Emir of Kuwait to power

To support the United Nations

To preserve the world's access to Middle Eastern oil at a reasonable price

Putting an end to recurring hostilities involving Muslims, Christians, and Jews

James J. Kilpatrick
as reported by the columnist

We have before us the opportunity to forge for ourselves and for future generations a new world order, a world where the rule of law, not the law of the jungle, governs the conduct of nations.

George Bush
addressing the nation after war began

You may think the President is all-powerful, but he is not. He needs a lot of guidance from the Lord.

Barbara Bush

When I need a little free advice about Saddam, I turn to country music.

President George Bush

In the wake of victory in the Persian Gulf, George Bush has received the highest approval rating of any president in polling history. 89% of Americans approve of the way Bush is handling his job as president.

According to a Gallup Poll

Kuwait is liberated. Iraq's army is defeated. Our military objectives are met.

President Bush
February 27, 1991

As commander in chief, I report to you: our armed forces fought with honor and valor. As president, I can report to the nation, aggression is defeated. The war is over.

George Bush
proclaiming victory in the Gulf War to a joint session of Congress

When you left, it was still fashionable to question America's decency, America's courage, America's resolve. No one, no one in the whole world, doubts us any more.

President Bush
welcoming home Desert Storm forces

Another thing that Vietnam and Kuwait have in common is that Dan Quayle supported both wars and fought in neither.

California Assemblyman
John Burton

Can it be that BUSH stands for Beat Up Saddam Hussein?

Roger Tan

THE MEN, THE WOMEN, THE BATTLE

The conviction and courage we see in the Persian Gulf today is simply the American character in action.

President George Bush

The brave men and women of Desert Storm accomplished more than even they may realize. They set out to confront an enemy abroad, and in the process, they transformed a nation at home.

President George Bush

Many of those fighters are in uniform because poverty and discrimination restricted civilian opportunities. It is immoral to ask them to put their lives on the line for the rest of us while at the same time refusing to support a civil rights act that protects their rights when they reenter civilian life.

John E. Jacob
National Urban League president

How can we have an invasion when the troops storm ashore and then change their minds?

Entertainer Bob Hope
on women in combat

I'm scared to die, but you don't think about that. I think once I've had training and know what I'm facing, I'll be less afraid.

Troy St. Onge
21-year-old enlistee

I wonder if some part of Desert Storm's overwhelming triumph was a result of our soldiers' clear heads, thanks to the absence of alcohol and drugs.

Jeanne Hewitt

In the desert, the mother-soldiers waving to their children are not a reminder that women have gotten more than we bargained for but [that] we have gotten so much less.

Ellen Goodman

We have a lot of computers and you can bring together the tens of thousands of details and work them together in what we call a common air-tasking order and it provides a sheet of music that everybody sings the same song off.

Lieutenant General Charles A. Horner

It's time to get back to work and stop treating us like heroes. Sure, we did disrupt our lives. We did go over there without kicking and screaming and did what we had to do for our country. But we were not that big of a hero.

Petty Officer Marianne Sandoz

Items to send to the troops in Saudi Arabia:

1. Bungee cords, 24" to 30", to secure tents.
2. Wet wipes.
3. Pantyhose, to cut up and to wrap weapons. Keeps sand out and yet allows items to breathe.

Compiled by the Marine Corps League

Women give life, sustain life, nurture life; they can't take it.

Retired Gen. Robert Barrow
on women in combat

They couldn't have drugs, alcohol, or women. During that time they had no alternative but to listen to the Christian message.

Billy Graham
on why many soldiers in the Persian Gulf War found Christ

I don't want to die for my country. I'd rather that some Iraqi die for his country.

Jeff Shapiro
21-year-old enlistee

I reached back with my hand to grab my legs. All I felt was a hole. They [my thighs] were both gone. Another guy I know, he had a funny look on his face. I looked down and he didn't have any legs. I just put my arms across his chest and pulled him as close as I could to the wall, so he wouldn't be so close to the fire. I wanted to be able to help so bad. But he died.

Army PFC Anthony Drees
describing the aftermath of a Scud attack

I am like a prisoner. My stomach is sick. I live unhappy, alone, all day long. May God make this problem easy. May it be solved quickly.

From the diary of an Iraqi soldier
on the day the ground war began

I felt the bullets hit me. It felt like someone was tugging on me. It didn't hurt on initial impact. I fell out and I started cussin'. I was angry. I was extremely pissed. That's probably what helped me get through.

Private Frank Bradish
describing his war injury

It's always sad when a 10-year-old gets drawn into a war.

Matt Groening
creator of "The Simpsons," commenting on Defense Secretary Dick Cheney's flaunting of a Bart Simpson doll in camouflage

A lot of people looked at us like we are heroes, but I feel the ones who died are the true heroes.

Army specialist Jonathan Alston

There's nothing to this. It's like a nature hike. They jump up like squirrels to surrender.

*An American solider
on Iraqi forces*

With war raging in the Persian Gulf, sperm banks in California are reporting an increase in deposits from military men who fear they may be killed or maimed in battle.

UPI

Goodnight, Steve. I miss you. I love you. You're a hero.

*Carol Bentzlin
in a letter she wrote just before her husband
was killed in the Gulf War*

Many of the women warriors' men back home say, in interviews, that they are dumbstruck at how hard it is to work and run a household simultaneously.

Writer Anne Bernays

If there's a bullet out there with my name on it, that's OK—it's my time. It's the ones that say 'To whom it may concern' that worry me.

*Army recruit Rob Fields
of Albany, Ore., on going to war*

Sometimes you have to disassociate how you feel personally about the prospect of going into war and, you know, possibly see the death that's going to be out there. But...this is the moment that everybody trains for—that I've trained for—so I feel ready to meet the challenge.

Maj. Marie Rossi

Army policy allows women to be shot first, but they can't be the first to shoot. The logic eludes me.

Congresswoman Patricia Schroeder

When Jane [Maj. Jane Fisher] got home, we made passionate love for three hours...Then we let go of the doorknob and put the suitcases down.

Henry Fisher
describing the return of his wife from the Gulf War

You're coming down the pike, hauling the mail [going fast] with your nose down 45 to 60 degrees, and you're staring at the bad boy [enemy targets], and you roll in and hit the pickle [drop the bombs] and get outa Dodge, damn and you keep climbing, checking your six, and then you see a big part of the ground go boom, and they hit it, light up the sky with triple-A, and your heart is going 100 miles an hour, and you're eyes are as big as golf balls. And you think, man, this shit's serious. I should have been a banker, maybe a dentist.

Marine pilot Capt. Mike Beguelin

They get relaxed. There are no girls. There's no one around to kiss. So they use their toothbrush to clean their rifle.

Maj. Harold McAdoo
on why so many soldiers have trench mouth
from not brushing their teeth

Nearly one in four American GIs killed during the Persian Gulf War were felled by errant fire [Friendly Fire—when a missle fired by an American plane hits an American target] originating from other U.S. forces.

According to the Pentagon

Being in battle is not glorious. Not even thinking about it later. All you do is run around scared thinking about going home and staying alive.

Sergeant Neftali Rivera Jr.

The brothers and sisters in the Persian Gulf are safer tonight than we are on the streets of Chicago.

Rev. Jesse Jackson

This war will do for women what World War II did for Black Americans in terms of providing solid credentials for their return to the marketplace.

Professor Carolyn R. Dexter

Q: How many members of the coalition forces does it take to screw in a lightbulb?
A: We are not prepared to comment on specific numbers at this time.

Wayne Saroyan

Q: What's the difference between American and Iraqi fighter pilots?
A: American fighter pilots break ground and fly into the wind.

Bob Ettinger

Kuwait is a banking system without a country, while America is a country without a banking system.

R. E. McMaster, Jr.

Sending women to fight for Saudi Arabia is like sending Blacks to fight for South Africa.

Barry Crimmins

Who can count the cost
Of a Young life
Lost?
The sharpest sorrow
Is for what might have been.

Kathy B.

THE TYRANT, SADDAM

You know, when he (Iraqi President Saddam Hussein) was born, they didn't give his mother a medical bill. They fined her for dumping toxic waste.

Ronald Reagan

Saddam Hussein is the father of the mother of all clichés.

Charles Osgood

The mother of all battles.

Saddam Hussein

After 22 years of living in obscurity, Saddam has activated the self-image he seeks of a latter-day Nasser—the hero of the radical Arabs standing up against the imperialist West. His rhetoric, his behavior, everything suggests that this is the major drama of his life—and it has gone beyond simply holding onto Kuwait.

Psychiatrist Jerrold Post

Saddam Hussein found it easier to wage war than to develop a sound economy. Rather than face widespread unemployment and unrest among young Iraqi men, he simply enlisted them and sent them to die.

Brad Edmondson

Saddam's motto is "Iran, Iraq, I Ruin."

Denella Drennan

1. By killing himself

*David Letterman
in his "Top Ten Ways Saddam Hussein Can Win
the Noble Peace Prize"*

Like every other government in the world, we foolishly did not realize that he was stupid.

*U.S. Ambassador to Iraq April Glaspie
explaining why she did not anticipate Hussein's invasion of Kuwait*

Saddam's huge underground bunker was built by Germany. They made him pay for it in advance, due to the bad experience they had in not getting Hitler's last payment.

Johnny Carson

Everyone thought either that Saddam's missles couldn't reach Israel or, if they did, they would miss. Well, they reached Israel, and they were accurate. This is the first time that an Arab leader has threatened to do something and really delivered.

Palestinian politician Assad Abdul-Rahman

Even if things get worse, we will never go back as long as Saddam is in power. Kurds have a saying: A serpent's head must be crushed, otherwise it will strike again.

Hazhar Abdullah
a Kurdish refugee

Did Same as Huns—Anagram for Saddam Hussein.

Reported in "Private Eye"

It is not that the Arab masses are so much in favor of Saddam as they are anti-Israel and, by extension, anti-U.S. Anybody who is willing to retaliate against Israel will become a hero to the Arabs—even a gangster like Saddam.

Mohammad al-Nashef

BUSINESS RESPONDS TO THE WAR

Patriot's Dream, seed combinations that grow red, white, and blue wild-flowers as "a living tribute to the troops."

Offered by **Clyde Robin Seed Co.**

The National Association of Hosiery Manufacturers has announced that its members are doing their part to help the troops by providing 412,000 knitted gun covers to protect weapons from sand and dust.

Leah Garchick

Heroes of Desert Storm $5 commemorative coin.

Produced by the **Republic of the Marshall Islands**
Coin Fulfillment Center

When they come home...let there be parades...Step forward, America, and shake their hands. Stand-up, America, and cheer them. Raise your voice, America and honor them.

From an ad placed by "Reader's Digest"

Condoms. Saddam Stealth Desert Shield for Piece in the East.

Marquee sign over a sex shop

A telephone in the shape of a Patriot missile.

Offered by LaJun Inc. of Newark, N.J.

Please tear this page into many small pieces and toss high into the air in celebration of peace.

*Moet & Chandon champagne
full-page newspaper ad*

The Foreign Relations Committee staff has reported that 132 companies from 14 Western nations have sold military-related goods to Iraq in recent years. Ten of the firms are from the United States, 68 from Germany.

Tampa Tribune

Anti-Hussein merchandise:

The "Beast of Baghdad, You Do Voodoo Doll," a Hussein doll pricked with pins, selling for $10.

The "Squash Saddam Doll," a squishable four-inch-high foam doll, selling for $7.

Twenty inch and 42 inch high punching bags, with an image of Hussein on the front and on the back a picture of his bare buttocks with an imprint of a soldier's boot, selling for $10 and $20.

The "Bully of Baghdad Golf Ball," featuring Hussein's head and shoulders with the words "Hit Me!" printed on it. Three balls selling for $6.95.

"Wipeout Hussein Toilet Tissue," selling for $5 a roll. The "Iraqi Wacker," a paddle with a drawing of a cross-eyed Hussein and a rubber ball on an elastic band, selling for $8.

Collected by Michael Quintanilla

The "Stars & Stripes" ensemble, which features bed, bath, and table linens with American flag motifs.

Offered by Kellwood Home Fashions

A $5 donation to the Red Cross each time a customer reserved a room.

Offered by Choice International Hotels

"Gulf Strike;" "A Line in the Sand"

Names of board games for adults

Free audiocassettes featuring 19 patriotic songs.

Mailed out by "Reader's Digest"

Whew! We all could use a little vacation now...Hope to see you soon. Love, Israel.

From an ad run by the Israel Government Tourist Office

Desert Storm Commemorative Sand

Orange County Register
from an ad

[Less than a year after the flag desecration hoopla] we are now treated to the sight of battalions of 'patriots' barreling around town sporting rain-drenched, wind-tattered and mud-spattered American flags of all sizes.

Mark Sloan

On the eve of what could be this country's first declaration of war since World War II, military personnel are finding their own ways to prepare for what may come ahead. Awaiting her call to duty in Saudi Arabia, military nurse Nancy Miller decided to have permanent makeup applied to her eyes and eyebrows.

From a press release from About Faces, which tattoos permanent eye makeup

In response to recent reports that Saddam has a profound fear of cockroaches, Orkin Pest Control is showing its stars and stripes by sending a shipment of "Bug the Thug" bumper stickers to the troops in the Middle East.

According to Judy Donner Orkin spokesperson

THE PRESS

It's odd being an American now. Most of us are peaceful, but here we are again, in our fifth major war of this century.

Columnist Pete Hamill

Clearly I've never been there, but it feels like we are in the center of hell.

CNN anchorman Bernard Shaw
reporting from Baghdad as bombs sounded around him

Only after the war was effectively over, did General Schwarzkopf explain that the press had been deliberately used to mislead the Iraqis.

Editor Debra Gersh
quoting a report submitted to Secretary of Defense Dick Cheney by
15 Washington Bureau Chiefs

If we let people see that kind of thing, there would never again be any war.

A senior Pentagon official
on why U.S. military censors refused to release video footage of
Iraqi soldiers being sliced in half by helicopter cannon fire

The number of Americans killed will exceed 10s of 1000s if a ground battle occurs with Iraqi forces...which are trained in defensive combat to an extent that no other force in the world has reached.

Baghdad Radio

If I could do what I really wanted to do, I'd be building tables and writing books.

Scud Stud Arthur Kent

If censorship protects only one life in the Gulf War, I can wait for the details, good and bad.

Hazel Reagan

There are 780 members of the press corp covering the Persian Gulf War. There were 2200 on hand at Superbowl V.

Merrell Noden

A journalist from Turkey told me that women in Turkey were naming their children after me. Even their girls.

Journalist Peter Arnett

If we've voted to send our young men into battle, we've got a duty to watch what they do. It ought to be almost compulsory to sit in front of the television set and have to view the horror that they're enduring. The military and the politicians don't like that kind of domestic exposure. But if we start seeing, live, on the air, people dying in combat, it's going to have one terrible effect.

Newsman Walter Cronkite

To suggest that the press not make its coverage too graphic so as to protect the public's sensitivity, is the ultimate obscenity. We need to see those lifeless bodies and weeping families to prevent us from denying the reality of what we are doing.

Claudia Caporale-Carabelli

The unnecessary bomb-by-bomb accounts and the constant whining by reporters that they are not getting all the facts, not only helps to make them look foolish but also erode their credibility as journalists...Allowing the enemy to put its finger directly, immediately and electronically on the pulse of American reaction and opinion, not to mention logistical information, could be a bad thing for our troops, our POWs in our country.

John Kushma

Those scuds over Tel Aviv and Riyadh are being knocked down by $600.00 toilet seats.

The Wall Street Journal *editorial*

THE GENERAL, NORMAN SCHWARZKOPF

Let me tell you why we succeeded. Superb equipment.

General Norman Schwarzkopf

He is neither a strategist, nor is he schooled in the operational art, nor is he a tactician, nor is he a general, nor is he a soldier. Other than that, he's a great military man.

General Norman Schwarzkopf
on Saddam Hussein

I admire General Schwarzkopf's qualifications, but with a sorrowful heart.

Chang-Chi Liu

I'm still the same person. Yes [the war] changed my life, but I hope it has not changed me.

General Norman Schwarzkopf

Old war horses like me look behind me and see the magnificent leaders ready to move up and take his place. He leaves thankful that he has had the honor and privilege of serving his country.

General Norman Schwarzkopf
as he relinquished command of the forces he led
to the Persian Gulf War

Norm would be the first to tell you that he isn't a hero, that it's everybody who was over there who are heros.

Brenda Schwarzkopf
wife of Norman

THE OBSERVERS

Kuwait is a banking system without a country, while America is a country without a banking system.

R.E. McMaster, Jr.

Sending women to fight for Saudi Arabia is like sending blacks to fight for South Africa.

Barry Crimmins

New world odor.

No blood for empire.

New world order, same old shit.

Signs at a protest rally

We want peace, but not with Saddam.

Sign at a protest rally

Short or long, the war is wrong.

Protester's sign

Vegetarians against carnage.

Protest Sign

Hey, Uncle Sam, we remember Vietnam!

Protest Sign

Beautify America. Send a protester to Iraq.

T-shirt

Heaping high praise on our politicians for ending the war is like cheering an arsonist for extinguishing a fire he started.

Arthur Katims

The parades were a clever public relations stunt to cap an almost year-long defense of an outrageously lopsided and massively destructive war that was begun to cover a serious lapse in diplomacy and the colossal misjudgment.

Harry T. Cook

By confronting aggression and stubbornness with threats and ultimatums, Bush has unwittingly been dragged down to Saddam's level of conflict resolution: Offensive warfare.

Mark Albrecht

The fighting has begun. Now comes the scramble for the high moral ground. Maybe we'll discover it has oil deposits.

Thomas Lee

Do you know what Iraq was called in biblical times? Mesopotamia. That's where algebra was invented—reason enough to blow it off the map.

Comedian Jay Leno

Read my lips, George: Why?

Columnist Herb Caen

The people are suffering, and the military industry is doing great business. Another war lost by mankind.

Frederico Saenz-Nagrate

Q: How many fools does it take to start a war?
A: Two.

Unknown

The treatment by the media and the nation of the "winning" of the Persian Gulf War struck me very much like a victorious football team returning from a game. The massive destruction of two nations, the deaths of 100,000 people, and the worst environmental damage in the history of warfare hardly deserves such elation.

Samuel Kjellman

Iraq's destruction—the suffering and death of thousands—in the end helped to make the U.S. government's deficit lighter...It also helped to give Americans a bit of trust in their capacity to kill and destroy after the trauma caused by the Vietnam War. This, in sum, was what people celebrated.

M. Dornbierer

There is tragic irony in the fact that American troops are not only putting their lives on the line but are also taking additional and unnecessary risks to defend some of the most undemocratic and intolerant regimes in the world.

Jerusalem Post

Some of our finest young men and women lost their lives on that battlefield. Was their blood shed so Republicans would have something to talk about in television political commericals?

Democratic Senator Albert Gore, Jr.

If we can create enormous military fire power, we also have the capacity to create peaceful solutions to conflicts.

Alexandra Tsounis

To those who advocate peace at any price: It's easy to appease the Tiger—just let him devour you.

Marie Ottiker

If you don't get your legs or your genitals blown off, battle can be very interesting and exciting.

Daniel Ellsberg
antiwar activist

The U.S. just needed some colonial-mined allies, a distracted rival like the U.S.S.R. and the colossal Third World fool like Saddam in order to put its boot on top of the Middle East's oil resources.

S. J. Rigby

Where the bare and insatiable aggressor is involved, peace is worse because it can lead to a bigger war.

Former President Richard Nixon

Bush said we were fighting the Iraqi leadership, not the Iraqi people. Well, we killed 100,000 of them and Bush has yet to offer one word of sympathy. I think that's awful.

Walter Cronkite

When we prohibited any sort of resolution of the issue in a peaceful fashion, then we made it inevitable that Saddam would not yield at all.

Former President Jimmy Carter

The war will not solve the problems of the Middle East, but it will give the kaleidoscope a shake.

British Foreign Minister Douglas Hurd

Kuwait, as such, is not worth dying for. However, as the object of the first truly international consensus to replace the fang and claw with law and equity, it is worth the ultimate sacrifice.

Bill McClellan

Bush has shown Iraq the meaning of wimp: War Is My Prerogative.

Joel Porter

Going to war is always a failure. It's a failure of diplomacy.

News correspondent Cokie Roberts

In some ways, the end of the Cold War has allowed for hot wars. We'd never have gone in with the bombs if the Soviet Union was around to retaliate. So what is this new world order? Will it require more use of force than in the past?

News correpsondent Cokie Roberts

Red, white and blue—these colors don't run.

T-Shirt

Let's free the people of China, the U.S.S.R., Syria, South Africa, the West Bank, Libya, Chile, and Cuba—and don't forget North Korea and Vietnam—instead of 363 oil wells in Kuwait.

Howell Harwood

There's nothing like contemplating the death of your son to make you focus your priorities.

War resister Alex Molnar

Now that the fighting is over, we should declare war on war and leave it where it belongs, in the Dark Ages.

Robert Dunlop

One of the first fruits of the new world order is the informal amendment of the Constitution so as to require the United States to act as the policeman of the new world order. Ever so gradually, our Congress is allowing U.N. dictates to supplant the U.S. Constitution.

Charles E. Rice

The Americans...no longer govern the world, but they preside over the global order of the moment. They are responsible for obtaining, by negotiation and patience or, if necessary, by force, the obedience of the most turbulent countries.

Bechir Ben Yahmed

The best way we can support the men and women who will be fighting is to continue to work for a peaceful solution.

Coretta Scott King (before the war)

If this were a prizefight, the referee would have stopped it long ago.

Columnist Mark Shields

We witness a war we are too confused to understand and watch our children fight an enemy we know nothing about. The enemy is created. We search for the enemy, and the enemy is us. Lord, have mercy on us.

Bishop Leontine Kelly

In the years to come, historians will trace the rebirth of modern America to the day Iraq was humbled. They will record that President Bush, his national-security advisers, Gen. Norman Schwarzkopf, and 500,000 soldiers, airmen and marines finally laid [to rest] the ghost of Vietnam in the sands of the Saudi desert.

The Age

It is our judgment that the primary reason for U.S. involvement in the Persian Gulf is to insure the flow of unlimited cheap oil, and not to protect Kuwait or Saudi Arabia from Iraqi aggression. We did not, for instance, mount a military response when Iraq invaded Iran or when the Soviet Union invaded Hungary.

From a public declaration by Pax Christi

Embargoes can postpone a tyrant's ability to realize his goals, but not his will to ultimately secure them.

Senator John Seymour

History shows that even brutal dictators have been toppled and defeated by sanctions. Sanctions are force. Sanctions are effective.

Rep. Richard Gephardt

At the beginning of Operation Desert Storm, the night of January 17, the Pentagon ordered 125 pizzas [from Pizza Hut]; the normal nightly order is three. And on the same night, for security reasons, the White House halted deliveries; the usual nightly take at 1600 Pennsylvania Avenue is five pies.

"U.S. News & World Report"

AND THE REST

From the list of songs the British Broadcasting Corporation suggested were inappropriate in light of the war: "Under Attack," "68 Guns," "We Gotta Get Out of This Place," "The Night They Drove Old Dixie Down," "Walk Like an Egyptian," "Love is a Battlefield," "View to a Kill," "Light My Fire," "Killing Me Softly," "Give Peace a Chance," "Saturday's Night Alright for Fighting," "Heaven Help Us All."

Song titles

The political and social events that occur during one's early adult years are the formative and binding events for each new generation. Today's teenagers will think of the Gulf War as a common memory that defines their generation, just as Vietnam defined the baby boom.

Sociologists Howard Shuman and Jacqueline Scott

American diplomacy...will now have to match the successes of the military by convincing wounded Arab pride that the new world order envisaged by Bush will be one founded on consensus, not coercion.

South China Morning Post

One out of every five children lives in poverty and hunger in America. This is an enemy that's even more dangerous than Saddam Hussein.

U.S. Representative Tony Hall

For Israel and the Western powers, victory and defeat are mentioned in terms of the concrete results achieved on the battlefield. For the Arabs...victory is measured in terms of an Arab leader's ability to challenge hostile powers and foil their plots against the Arab nation.

Mohammed Sid-Ahmed

It was like going to a movie: we paid our money, we went to the theater, we laughed, we cried, the movie ended and an hour later we had forgotten about it.

Saudi financier Adnan Khashoggi
on the return to business as usual after the Gulf War

How do we persuade Bush to bring as much intensity to bear on our massive domestic problems as he did on the war?

William R. Roof

The money spent by the U.S. each year on research and development on non-nuclear alternatives to oil is roughly equivalent to the amount spent on the Gulf War in one hour.

Professor Carl Sagan

War is always bad for the economy, but a short war is clearly better than a long war.

Thomas Thomson
of the Federal Reserve Bank of San Francisco

I think it was a time when Americans needed to believe in our country. I remember standing there and looking at all those people, and it was like I could see in their faces the hopes and prayers and fears of the entire country.

Singer Whitney Houston
on her stirring rendition of "The National Anthem"

When the Scuds were flying and the Patriots were knocking them down, Pat Benatar's "Hit Me With Your Best Shot" was a favorite and so was Queen's "Another One Bites The Dust." When the air war started, "Wind Beneath My Wings" by Bette Midler and "Somewhere Out There" by James Ingram were big requests.

Armed forces Deejay Sgt. Dee Peters

I thought a Sunni Muslim was what you got when you hung a Shiite out to dry.

Carlotta di Fasso-Nicholson

I'm gonna pop some popcorn and watch the war.

A University of Oklahoma student

How could the incumbent Palestinian leadership call for an end to the Israeli occupation of Arab lands and the right of self-determination for the Palestinians while supporting the principle of occupation through siding with Iraq in its invasion of Kuwait?

Al-Nadwa
a Saudi newspaper

Mother of all parades.

Headline for **USA Today**
story on the four-hour ticker tape parade in New York City

3

NATION

Happy Birthday, America! Another year older and deeper in debt!

From a Fourth of July cartoon titled
"Good News/Bad News"

If someone is invaded and they need help, we're the 911 of the world.

Karen Hall

On the whole, we get the leaders we deserve. We voted for Ronald Reagan because we wanted to believe that greed was good, that cutting taxes and disabling government would make us all richer. We cheered even as he did lasting damage to this country.

Columnist Anthony Lewis

Celebrity in American is extraordinary. It's like being in the royal family. It amazes me. They think you can cure cancer.

Comedian Tracey Ullman

Projected average speed of cars on California highways in the year 2010, in mph: 11.

Harper's Bazaar

It may make Western economists uneasy but history reveals that economically successful nations can have free markets without free people. Democratic reforms are not essential to explosive economic growth.

Michael Schrage

Since the birth of our nation, "We the People" has been the source of our strength. What government can do alone is limited, but the potential of the American people knows no limits.

President George Bush

Freedom and the power to choose should not be the privilege of wealth. They are the birthright of every American.

President George Bush

But what defines this nation? What makes us American is not our ties to a piece of territory or bonds of blood; what makes us American is our allegiance to an idea: that all people everywhere must be free.

President George Bush

Down through history, we've defined resources as soil and stones, land and the riches buried beneath. No more. Our greatest national resource lies within ourselves—our intelligence and ingenuity—the capacity of the human mind.

President George Bush

But you know and I know that all the drug prevention programs, all the pledges, all the preaching in the world won't pull you through that critical moment when someone offers drugs. At that moment, everything comes down to you. Yes or no: you've got to choose, and the answer will change your life. Your parents won't make the decision. Your teachers won't make the decision. Your friends won't make the decision. It's up to you.

President George Bush

1992 gives us a chance to reach back into history, to make this celebration a time of renewal. From Columbus' voyage to the settlers at Plymouth

Rock—to pilgrims bearing steamer trunks and filing through the portals at Ellis Island: America has always been the New World.

President George Bush

The postal service rates just went up 16% and they say they'll use the money to buy 100,000 new "Next Window, Please" signs.

Johnny Carson

The average income of the five wealthiest metropolitan areas:

1. Bridgeport-Stamford-Norwalk-Danbury, Connecticut—$82,479
2. Nassau-Suffolk, New York—$79,166
3. Middlesex-Somerset-Hunterton, New Jersey—$78,028
4. Bergen-Passaic, New Jersey—$75,185
5. Trenton, New Jersey—$73,089

According to "Sales and Marketing Management"

The essential U.S. policy is still: Keep our powder dry and have lots of powder. The "peace dividend" will be a little late, again.

Columnist George Will

The number of anti-Semitic incidents in the U.S. during 1990 climbed to 1,685 episodes, marking a fourth straight year of increases.

*According to a nationwide survey by the **Anti-Defamation League***

The country's five busiest airports:

1. Chicago (O'Hare)
2. Dallas / Ft. Worth
3. Atlanta
4. Los Angeles
5. San Francisco

*According to the **Federal Aviation Association***

Something will have gone out of us as a people if we ever let the remaining wilderness be destroyed; if we permit the last virgin forest to be turned into comic books and plastic cigarette cases; if we drive the few remaining members of the wild species into zoos or to extinction; if we pollute the last clear air and dirty the last clean streams and push our paved roads through the last of the silence, so that never again will Americans be free in their own country from the noise, the exhausts, the stinks of human and automotive wastes.

Novelist Wallace Stegner

To be white and conservative is to be part of the American mainstream. To be black and conservative is to be part of the lunatic fringe.

Stephen L. Carter

Currently, a rancher in Texas gets 53 cents a pound for his lambs, while we pay $6.99 a pound for leg of lamb at the grocery store.

Senator Lloyd Bentsen

Almost half of all Americans believe that there are fewer than 500,000 abortions annually, while the actual number is more than 1.6 million annually or about 4,400 a day.

According to a survey by the Wirthlin Group

Many current speed limits are set too low to be reasonable for the vast majority of drivers, who tend to travel faster than posted limits but still travel at safe speeds.

According to a preliminary report by the Federal Highway Administration

The civil rights establishment has, in many respects, made itself irrelevant because it is fighting battles which have already been won, and refuses to confront the real dilemmas of the present time.

Allan C. Brownfield

Today, five airlines—American, United, Delta, Northwest, and USAir— dominate air travel in the United States, handling 71 percent of all the traffic and controlling 21 of the nation's 29 hub airports.

Louis Uchitelle

The United States ranks 13th in a list of the world's freest countries, as ranked by the U. N. Development Program. The human freedom index covers such things as freedom to travel abroad, freedom of religion, the right to assemble, freedom from child labor, trade union rights, homosexual rights, absence of the death penalty, a free press and sexual equality. No. 1 was Sweden, followed closely by Denmark, the Netherlands, Finland and Canada and Switzerland.

Reporter Edward Epstein

Pizza Hut wants to be able to sell pepperoni pizzas to school lunch programs around the country. The Agriculture Department says they can do that only if they put no more than 20 slices of pepperoni on each one.

Malcolm Gladwell

Winning is better than losing.

John F. Kennedy, Jr.

The average monthly cost of downtown parking:

1. Manhattan	$339.00
2. Boston	$212.00
3. Los Angeles	$129.00
4. Philadelphia	$144.00
5. Washington, D.C.	$144.00

According to "Consumer's Digest"

No weight is added to a position because someone is black. One has to evaluate an argument on its own merits, not on the race of the person making it.

Stephen L. Carter

Graham Green predicted that long after the war was over, Americans would be paying a high price for the Vietnam adventure. He was right. They are now paying $100.00 a ticket for "Miss Saigon" at the Broadway Theater.

Critic Stefan Kanfer

We have a school in East St. Louis named for Dr. King. The school is full of sewer water and the doors are locked with chains. Every student in that school is black. It's like a terrible joke in history.

A 14-year-old girl

The five most populous states:
1. California
2. New York
3. Texas
4. Florida
5. Pennsylvania

*According to the **Bureau of the Census***

Americans cannot be expected to slay all the dragons in the world at once...It is not required that we slay these dragons; we just need to stop feeding them.

Fred Clark

The cost of a pregnancy test at Planned Parenthood is roughly three and a half times more expensive when the government pays the bill: $16.36 average cost for cash customers, versus an outrageous $57.51 average cost when Joe Taxpayer picks up the tab.

Robert Ruff

Housing is becoming an endangered part of the American dream.

Jack Kemp
Secretary of Housing and Urban Development

Top U.S. places to visit:
1. San Francisco
2. New Orleans
3. Boston
4. Maui
5. Washington, D.C.

*According to the readers of "**Conde Nast Traveler**"*

If we have learned nothing else from the experience of losing the ERA and almost losing the right to reproductive choice, we have learned that not appealing to most middle-and-working class women can be deadly to our efforts.

Felicia Kornbouh

Washington, a city of frequent comings and goings and many short leases, is so busy trying to divine the future it has little energy left over for learning about its past.

George F. Will

One of the things that really bothers me is that Americans don't have any sense of history. The majority of Americans don't have any idea of where we've come from, so they naturally succumb to the kind of cliché version that Ronald Reagan represented.

Robert Massie
Pulitizer Prize-winning historian

Number of tax returns filed electronically: 7.2 million.

According to "Computer World"

Safest U.S. Cities:
1. Pittsburgh, PA
2. Nassau/Suffolk, NY
3. Bergen/Passaic, NJ
4. Cleveland, OH
5. Philadelphia, PA

According to FBI Statistics

I don't believe racism is as powerful a force today as what it's left in its wake—the cycle of cultural poverty that gets perpetuated.

Shelby Steele

The Statue of Liberty is becoming one big blob of chewing gum. It is disgraceful. The statue needs some help.

M. Ann Belkov

The best history is based on the premise that the dangers of arbitrary power are vastly greater than the disadvantages of shared power. If we give up this premise, we must become a very different country, with a very different constitutional foundation.

Theodore Draper
in A Very Thin Line: The Iran-Contra Affairs

A South Dakota grandmother is carrying her daughter and son-in-law's baby....I know grandparents are supposed to babysit, but this is ridiculous!

Johnny Carson

Non-Hispanic whites are now a minority of New York City residents, at 43%. Hispanics are 24%, blacks are 25%, and Asians are 7%.

Judith Waldrop

When someone whose movie did $30 million gets coverage while the leader of an embattled nation is ignored, things have gotten a little bizarre. That's when you've just gotta suck back and worry about your kids and your car and your laundry.

Actor Michael J. Fox

The Supreme Court, which last term ruled that flag-burning is protected "free speech" under the First Amendment, this year will decide whether nude dancing is also a protected right.

David Kupelian

It amazes me how much of the media...considers the Supreme Court's move to the right to be a step backward. Decades of steady liberal "progress" have seen the loss of school prayer, the replacement of victims' rights with criminals' rights, and reverse discrimination in the guise of affirmative action. After these devastating wrong turns, a step backward is a step in the right direction.

Patrick J. Gravitt

We can't afford to put a person on the nation's highest court unless we know where he stands on our constitutional freedoms.

Robert Maddox

Each day, the average American throws away four pounds of garbage.

According to the **Business Recycling Manual**

You don't become a world-class pole vaulter by lowering the bar. The bar is being raised and a large majority of our population is not good enough.

South Carolina Governor Carroll Campbell
on new national educational goals

CRIME

The age-old complaint, "Where is a cop when you need one?" is answered when you learn that two dozen were in pursuit of a single speeding motorist.

Jim Blewer
on the King case

If a jailed rapist is going to strike again, it usually happens within 90 days of release.

Judson Ray
of the FBI Behavioral Science Unit

In at least 20 criminal trials, murder defendants have attempted a "Prozac defense" gambit in which lawyers said their clients were not responsible for their actions because they were on the drug at the time of the killings.

Charles Petit

Our country has a $10 billion drug budget, but the proportions are absolutely backward. Seventy percent is directed toward interdiction and enforcement, and 30% for prevention, treatment, and research. It should be about the same proportion in the other direction.

Avram Goldstein

Sexual assualt is the sexual expression of aggression, not the aggressive expression of sexuality.

Dr. A. Nicholas Groth

There are 1.7 million hard-core cocaine abusers.

*According to the **Drug Control Policy Office***

Incarceration rates per 100,000 people:

1. United States   426
2. South Africa   333
3. Soviet Union   268
4. Hungary   196
5. Malaysia   126

*According to the **Sentencing Project and
Penal Reform International***

We are not here to search for the roots of crime, or to discuss sociological theory. The American people demand action to stop criminal violence, whatever its causes.

Attorney General Dick Thornburgh

Americans spent somewhere between $40 billion and $50 billion on illegal drugs in 1990.

Linda Atkins

The chances of an American being murdered are 1 in 10,504.

*According to **USA Today***

An almost erotic affection for guns inherited from pioneers, is responsible for the highest murder rate in all of the industrial countries.

Warner Meyer-Larsen
on gun control in the U.S.

The United States will set a new record of murders this year if present trends continue, with an estimated 23,700 people losing their lives to violence.

Senate committee

What the Los Angeles thrashing shattered was not the reality of the daily war in American cities but the myth that the policeman is still, in the age of crack, machine guns, gangs, and racial tensions, the good-natured Big Brother who helps old women across the street and lost kids find their way home.

Vittorio Zucconi
on the beating of Rodney King

We are devastated by this. We are devastated because this is a good department. It's a fine department.

Los Angeles Police Chief Daryl Gates

I do not condone police brutality, but if one knew, even vaguely, the stress that police officers endure each day, one would marvel at their restraint.

Naomi W. Higginbotham

First Policeman: Is he armed and dangerous? Second Policeman: Yes. He's got a camcorder.

From a cartoon in the **Summers-Orlando Sentinel**

The Los Angeles police promised "to Serve and Protect." After watching the latest display of brutality, I think their motto could be "To Harm and Enjoy."

Eduardo M. Tinoco

You know you're in a bad neighborhood when you see nine police cars in one block and there's no doughnut shop.

Buddy Baron

How could the beating of Rodney King be an isolated event? The odds against capturing it on videotape are enormous unless such occurrences are more common than we thought.

Rob Adelman

The gun-control lobby may laugh when its opponents point to China and the Baltics as examples of how government officials can oppress unarmed citizens...The brutal beating of a defenseless black man by L.A. police is evidence that it can happen here. It is perhaps no coincidence that Chief Darryl Gates is a proponent of gun control, and yet his police department is a leader in brutality and corporation.

Larry Pratt
Executive Director of Gun Owners of America

We must punish the criminal that preys upon others and reform the criminal justice system that allows them to do so. "Swift and certain punishment" is a foreign concept in America. The average stay in death row for a convicted murderer is eight years due to a system that allows frivolous appeals. The reform of habeas corpus is absolutely essential to bring sanity to the criminal justice system.

Congressman Jim Ramstad

In 1991, one out of every three preborn babies will be brutally killed. It's more dangerous to be in the womb than on the front lines of battle.

Sheryl Chandler

State prison construction budgets are up 73% since fiscal year 1987. 44 states are building new prisons or expanding existing ones.

According to "Corrections Compendium"

Crime hit 23.7 percent of America's households [in 1990], the lowest level in 16 years.

According to a Justice Department report

When we as a society refuse to talk openly about rape, I think we weaken our ability to deal with it.

Newspaper editor Geneva Overholser
about rape victims speaking out

That crime problem in New York is getting really serious. The other day the Statue of Liberty had both hands up.

Comedian Jay Leno

Enough automobiles will be stolen in the U.S. during 1991 to fill the parking spaces at more than 170 major shopping centers. Up to 15% of all auto insurance claims turn out to be fradulent.

According to **Aetna Life & Casualty**

Of the approximately 23,000 murders in the United States last year, about 25 percent are unsolved.

Susan Okie

There are approximately 168,000 rapes annually in the U.S. Of that number, 13,000 involve male victims.

U.S. Bureau of Justice's National Crime Survey

I would hear a buzz saw running in the early evening. I thought he was building something.

Pamela Bass
who lived across the hall from serial killer Jeffrey Dahmer

Indeed, publishing the man's name and photograph forces him to prove his innocence. Even if he succeeeds in court, realistically he will never manage to do so for many in the commuinity. The solution is simple enough: Identify both parties prior to judgment, or, far better, identify neither.

William Ratliff
on sexual harrassment

One in five persons arrested and charged with a felony was released from custody and rearrested for a similar felony.

According to **"The Daily News Digest"**

A university is not a drug-use safe house. Compliance with the law of the land isn't too stringent a requirement for American students.

Bob Martinez
U.S. drug czar

Six million individuals per year are raped, robbed, beaten, or murdered—it is deeply disturbing that the likelihood of becoming a victim of violent crime is now greater than that of being injured in an automobile accident.

Senator Strom Thurmond

President Reagan probably doesn't fully understand the Brady bill or he would not approve it.

Representative Harold Volkmer
Brady bill opponent, on Reagan's endorsement of the measure

TAXES, RECESSION, ETC.

Keep the bad news in perspective. Recessions are not economic calamities. Most people don't lose their jobs, and many unemployed find new work relatively quickly.

Columnist Robert J. Samuelson

The recent performance of the U.S. economy, although improved significantly from the 1970s, has not matched the growth of the 1950s and 1960s. Most economists, including the major macroeconomic forecasting firms, believe that the near future will be very much more like the recent than the distant past.

Frank Levy and Richard C. Michel

I think that I shall never see
A tax form plain enough for me
A form that I can understand
Without a lawyer close at hand
To guide this poor belabored me
So I won't owe a penalty.

Formulated by an anonymous taxpayer

In 1950, the average family of four paid 2% of its earnings to federal taxes. Today it pays 24%.

William R. Mattox, Jr.

President Bush sent to Congress yesterday a 1992 budget request of $1.45 trillion that admittedly understates the cost of the Persian Gulf war, offers no measures to combat the recession and seeks to redistribute some federal subsidies that now go to the most affluent.

Reporter Robert Pear

With war and recession staring us in the face, I would characterize this as a "cross-your-fingers, close-your-eyes and hope-for-the-best budget"—hope that the recession is shallow and that the deficits don't spin completely out of control.

Senator James Sasser

PRESIDENT BUSH'S $1.45 TRILLION BUDGET

I am not naive. We're going to have to fight together to get this through Congress.

President Bush
on his budget proposal

The deficit is an inside-the-(Washington, D.C.)-beltway fight. The only deficit the rest of the country worries about is Visa and Mastercard.

Prof. Stephen J. Wayne

If you started a business when Christ was born and lost $1 million a day, it would still take another 700 years before you lost $1 trillion.

Rep. Phil Crane
on the $3 trillion national debt

My message...is: Recessions do end, markets find a bottom, and recovery does occur.

Alan Tubbs
the incoming president of the American Bankers Association

POLITICS

Our country is in peril if individuals, in order to conduct themselves in a just and moral manner, must have a law to cover every action. Is there no end to the devious lengths to which some politicians will go to extract money from the tax-paying public?

Elsie Simon

There is no more powerful combination in American politics than deeds of war and the common touch. It will be very difficult for anyone to mount an effective challenge to the President in 1992, even though he still has no real domestic program.

Peter Stothard

Thirty-four percent of Americans now call themselves democrats and 31 percent call themselves Republicans.

According to **The New York Times** *and CBS News Poll*

Domestic issues are important, but playing prince of peace is pretty important too. Bush wants to be remembered as a president who made the new world order a more peaceable world order.

Stephen Wayne

The nation's elected representatives...maintain the status quo by making the marginal changes required by external forces, rather than grappling directly with worsening problems.

Kenneth Hunter

You can't run for political office today without having a gag writer on your staff.

Comedy expert Mel Helitzer

At least 250 current or former members of the House owed more than $300,000 for meals and catering services from Capitol restaurants. More than $47,000 of the bills dated back as far as 1986, and more than 50 congressmen owed $1,000 or more.

"Newsweek"

The General Accounting Office, which just audited the House bank, says there are two dozen members of Congress who bounce big checks at the House bank—upward of $1,000—month after month and never pay a penalty.

Christopher Matthews

Congressmen who bounce checks should be bounced. If they can't handle their own personal affairs and finances, it proves they can't handle our national budget deficit, either.

Ernest Faisz

I believe a more correct term for what many of these congressmen are doing is "kiting" checks, which means they are writing checks for money they know they do not have.

Cannon Alsobrook

The veto strategy as a weapon for battle between a Republican president and the Democratic Congress has become one of the standard tools. It's now what a six-shooter was to a cowboy—it's part of your politcal clothing.

Michael S. Johnson

The social programs that the Democrats are likely to enact are going to cost me tax money, and they probably aren't going to be directed at me. I vote for what I think is the best for most people.

Faye Boom

When Republicans are in office, it's hard to get any type of training. The Republicans sacrifice education whenever they are trying to fix the economy.

George Prappas

The Democrats have Tsongas, Wilder, Harkin, and Jerry Brown. All they need now is a little dog named Toto and an oil can.

Johnny Carson

As long as everybody is claiming to be a political outsider, there might as well be a political outsider in the field.

Actor Tom ["Billy Jack"] Laughlin
declaring himself a Democratic presidential candidate

They say that if no one announces their candidacy, Ted Kennedy could have the nomination in his pocket. Now if only he could find his pants.

Comedian Jay Leno

There are those who say that we're a long shot, that we can't win. I'm here to tell you that George Herbert Walker Bush has feet of clay and I intend to take a hammer to them.

Senator Harkin
joining the presidential race

I want to lead because I believe almost everyone but our present leadership knows what we must do. I believe Americans know deep in their bones that something is terribly wrong and that business as usual—the prescription of the '80s—will not work for the future.

Nebraska Senator Bob Kerrey

To forcibly remove a politician from public office, one has to meet a much higher standard of dishonesty.

Attorney Michael Cooney

Biosphere II: A small group of people on a two-year journey inside a self-sustaining environment sealed off from the rest of the world.

Roger Harvell
in a cartoon featuring the U.S. Congress as Biosphere II

Average presidential vetos per year:

1. George Bush, 8
2. Ronald Reagan, 10
3. Jimmy Carter, 8
4. Gerald Ford, 26
5. Richard Nixon, 8

According to the **White House**

If the Democrats were an Olympic entry, they would be the Jamaican bobsled team.

The Washington Post *columnist Mark Shields*

The insatiable appetite for campaign dollars virtually has turned the government into a stop-and-shop for every greed and special interest in the country.

Presidential hopeful Jerry Brown

The idea of political leadership means inspiring people, persuading people, saying, "Look, listen to me, I've got the right idea. Come with me and we can do this." And that's performance.

Actor Charlton Heston

The Black community is not monolithic and need not be held captive by the liberal plantation. The days of blacks being politically aligned to the liberal [Democratic] party are about to be ended.

Claudia A. Butts

[Democrats] go more for vegetarian pizza, [Republicans] go more for meat—pepperoni, ground beef, sausage.

Ron Newmyer
president of Armand's Chicago Pizza in Washingon, D.C.

The present mood of American voters would seem to be that of consumers out to protect their own interest...and attentive to neither general nor particular issues that do not appear to have an immediate effect on their own lives.

Sociologist Robert Bellah
and his associates

Those damned drums are keeping me up all night.

George Bush
on the drumbeat kept up by antiwar activists
across from the White House

Voters believe that among politicians, women are more honest than men. But since politics is a dirty game, those same voters worry, female candidates may not be able to get things done in all that mud.

Reporter Peter A. Brown

The nation could benefit by closing a base the size of Carswell. I'm just not sure it ought to be Carswell.

Rep. Richard Armey
author of law creating the base-closing commission,
defending a base in his district

POVERTY

The poor stayed poor. The middle class got poorer. The rich got richer.

Andrea Stone
reporting on Census Bureau income figures

We have to find ways in our communities, and with help from all levels of government, to blunt the effects of poverty on children and families so that families can become educationally sound institutions that serve youth well.

Harold Howe II

Those dominated by full-time family farms were better off than those with high concentrations of large-scale corporate farms or small part-time ones. Family-farm areas had lower unemployment and poverty rates, higher family income, less income inequality, and lower infant mortality....

Linda Lobao
assistant professor of agricultural economics and rural sociology,
Ohio State University

Among (those surveyed) industrialized countries, the United States has the highest incidence of poverty among the nonelderly and the widest distribution of poverty across all age and family groups....It is also the country in which the poor experience the longest spells of poverty and the only Western democracy that has failed to give a significant proportion of its poor a measure of income security.

*According to a report by the **Joint Center for Political***
and Economic Studies

For the first time in the nation's history, a larger fraction of Hispanic men than black males are poor.

*According to **"The Emerging Hispanic Underclass"***

The unspoken assumption in this country is that being white is enough [to be successful], but there are poor whites, drunks, bums; whites living on the margin. They're hurting in Gary and Pittsburgh and Appalachia because of the decline of the steel industry and petered-out coal mines.

Columnist William Raspberry

In its annual study of poverty and income, the Commerce Department reported that 33.6 million Americans were officially poor, an increase of nearly 2.1 million over 1989.

Ramon G. McLeod

YOUTH

Black teenage girls from low-income households are significantly less likely to get pregnant if they are employed.

According to research from Ohio State University

The states with the highest scores on measures of child well-being:

1. Vermont
2. Utah
3. Massachusetts
4. Minnesota
5. New Hampshire

The states with the lowest scores:

1. Washington, D.C.
2. Georgia
3. Lousiana
4. South Carolina
5. Mississippi

According to the 1991 **Kids Count Data Book**

National infant mortality rates and death rates for children ages 1-4 and high school graduation rates have improved; teenage violent deaths, teenage out-of-wedlock birth, juvenile incarceration, the number of children in poverty have gotten worse.

According to the 1991 **Kids Count Data Book**

Trial use of marijuana by 13-year-olds has declined 52% since 1987, while 69% fewer are trying cocaine.

According to a survey by the **Partnership for a Drug-Free America**

Almost two-thirds of all births to teenagers—about 1 million annually—are to unmarried girls; the number of Black males age 15 to 19 who were killed by gunfire tripled in the past four years; a total of 3.2 million 12-17-year-olds live in poverty; and more than 30 percent of high school seniors are binge drinkers (imbibe more than five drinks in a row).

According to a study by the **Children's Defense Fund**

One in five high school students—and nearly one in three boys—sometimes carries a gun, a knife, or some other weapon with the intention of using it if necessary.

Associated Press

Dropouts are five times more likely to have repeated a grade than are high school graduates. Students who repeat two grades have a probability of dropping out of nearly 100 percent.

According to the **Harvard Education Letter**

56 children are born to teenagers every hour.

According to the **National Center for Health Statistics**

The proportion of students who are top performers peaks in fourth grade and then declines through 12th grade. It should be the other way around.

Educational Testing Services president Gregory Anrig

THE NOMINATION OF CLARENCE THOMAS

We're not going to discriminate against [him because] he's Black. [I've] kept my word to the American people by picking the best man for the job on the merits.

President George Bush
nominating Clarence Thomas

But for the efforts of so many others who have gone before me, I would not be here today...Only by standing on their shoulders could I be here.

Supreme Court Nominee Clarence Thomas

A judge must not bring to his job, to the court, the baggage of preconceived notions, of ideology, and certainly not an agenda, and the judge must get the decision right.

Supreme Court Nominee Clarence Thomas

The Supreme Court, of course, in the case of "Roe vs. Wade" has found an interest in the woman's right—as a fundamental interest—the woman's right to terminate a pregnancy. I do not think at this time that I could maintain my impartiality as a member of the judiciary and comment on that specific case.

Supreme Court Nominee Clarence Thomas

I have no reason or agenda to prejudge the issue...or a predilection to rule one way or another on the issue of abortion.

Supreme Court Nominee Clarence Thomas

There is nothing natural about natural law. It's as subject to redefinition as food labeled natural. And so also is Clarence Thomas subject to redefinition, and that is our only hope for the next 30 or 40 years.

Rob Morse

Clarence Thomas is the best only at his ability to bootlick for Ronald Reagan and George Bush.

Columnist Carl Rowen

If confirmed, Judge Thomas would indeed vote...to take this nation back to the days when women had no alternative but the back alleys for health care.

Kate Michelman
National Abortion Rights Action League Director

[Judge Thomas is] a man with a singular disrespect for the rule of law, and apparent indifference to fundamental civil liberties...and a painfully cramped view of the government's role in repairing the damage of discrimination.

Author J. Cropp
President of People for the American Way

He was poor. He was a zero. Clarence Thomas is the best argument against affirmative action.

Skip Enlow

What you have is a nominee who wants to destroy the bridge that brought him over troubled waters.

Rep. John Lewis
on Clarence Thomas

Thomas made himself vulnerable to the kind of attack under which he now reels. Asking to be judged by his background rather than his convictions, he made the vague question of "character" everything, which made anything relevant.

Columnist George Will

George Bush's only question, yet again, was how to avoid another Robert Bork. For Republican senators and conservatives, the question was how to market Clarence Thomas' character instead of his judicial ideology; for Democrats and liberal groups, it was how to assualt that character—while staying out of trouble with their Black constituencies.

Donald Baer

I oppose the Thomas nomination because his legal decisions will help create and reinforce a world based on individualism and competitiveness—a world that has led to the disintegration of families, friendships, and solidarity among peoples and is filled with isolation and political paralysis.

Editor Michael Lerner

His marrying of a white woman is a sign of his rejection of the Black community. Great justices have had community roots that served as a basis for understanding the Constitution. Clarence's lack of a sense of community makes his nomination troubling.

Professor Russell Adams

This week, we have Robert Gates up for CIA director and Clarence Thomas for the Supreme Court. Why not a switch? Since Thomas makes such a secret of everything, send him to the CIA.

Comedian Mark Russell

If Thomas were white, he would not have been nominated...[Bush's] meritocratic language is fatuous unless one takes both color and ideology into account in deciding what it means to be the best qualified.

Thomas is likely to spend the next 40 years on the highest court in the land. We need to focus on his qualifications and record, not his family, his poor beginnings, or his race. By focusing on substance rather than image, we just might realize that he's no more than a relatively inexperienced, mediocre judge and that there are African-Americans who are far more qualified.

Eric D. Ort

He is the Black Horatio Alger for our time. A man who lifted himself up and out from Southern poverty to the peaks of power.

According to "Newsweek"

None of us has gotten where we are solely by pulling ourselves up from our own bootstraps. We got here because somebody—a parent, a teacher, an Ivy League crony or a few nuns—bent down and helped us pick up our boots.

Retired Supreme Court Justice Thurgood Marshall

How ironic to spend a lifetime opening doors for Blacks and to see a successor coming through those doors who disagrees with much that you hold dear. How ironic that your seat may be taken by a man who profited from remedies that you support and that he opposes.

Columnist Ellen Goodman
on how Justice Thrugood Marshall might feel about the nomination
of Clarence Thomas to the Supreme Court

He wants to show his people...that you can make it. You don't have to just say, "OK, I'm poor, I'm nobody." Just because you're poor, that doesn't mean you're nobody. You're always somebody.

Leona Williams
mother of Clarence Thomas

This guy is not qualified to shine Justice Marshall's shoes, much less fill them.

Jon Bradley

DAN QUAYLE

I think Quayle will be on the ticket in '92 because he serves the purpose of making Bush look good.

Humorist Roy Blount, Jr.

You know why Dan Qualye told the ABA there are too many lawyers? Because he thought he was addressing the AMA.

Jim Nirenstein

My suggestion that we have a constitutional amendment making a C average a requirement for the presidency brought me mail from [Dan Quayle's] supporters. The letters are quite stirring. They say things like, "He's probably not as dumb as all that."

Columnist Calvin Trillin

I'd like to have a little of the money that they've made off of me. I think they ought to share.

Vice President Dan Quayle
on comedians Jay Leno and Johnny Carson

I love California. I grew up in Phoenix.

Vice President Dan Quayle
according to "Newsweek"

Number 1: Phony steering wheel so Quayle can pretend he's flying plane.

David Letterman
"Top 10 new features on Air Force One"

4

WORLD

Middle East peace is important to our own well-being....The U.S. has a tangle of specific strategic, political, and economic interests in the region that ought to make Americans care about achieving peace—and its corollary, stability.

Columnist Jill Smolowe

The fact that the parties to the [Middle East] conflict are meeting in one room changes the agenda in the Middle East. It means de facto recognition of one another and acknowledging that they must find some form of coexistence.

Political analyst Judith Kipper

There will be enduring difficulties, occasional disruptions, some dramatic abortions, but in the end I think there will be a peace treaty.

Former National Security Advisor Zbigniew Brzezinski

All the players [in the Madrid Middle East Conference] invested a lot of political capital in going to the conference, and they didn't do that because of war or because of United States pressure....Rather, they believe the world has changed and they realize they'd better change with it.

Political analyst Robert Oakley

You do not reform a world by ignoring it.

President George Bush

It is wrong to isolate China if we hope to influence China.

President George Bush

When today's newborns are 70 years old (in 2060) there will be almost 11 billion people in the world.

According to the Population Reference Bureau

Turkish health authorities are warning citizens to be more careful, because during the summer months about one dozen people a year are killed and many more injured when they fall asleep after making love and roll off the roof.

Mark Lundgren

Annual divorces per 1,000 existing marriages:

1.	U.S.A.	21.2 divorces
2.	United Kingdom	12.9 divorces
3.	Canada	12.9 divorces
4.	Sweden	11.7 divorces
5.	France	8.5 divorces

According to the House Select Committe on Children, Youth, and Families

The aid package will kill the democratic process. By providing the Communist establishment with monetary salvation, all incentive for real reform will be lost.

Moscow Mayor Gavril Popov

Economic development is not about getting foreign governments or agencies to build new bridges for Third World nations; it is about helping unleash the individual in these societies so that he may build these bridges himself.

Michael Johns

Gorbachev set in motion purges that he did not understand or control, whose consequences he could not predict. He changed the world more than any other member of his generation, but if he had known six years ago how it would all turn out, he certainly would have done something else—and probably something less hopeful.

Newsweek

In 16 industrial countries surveyed, the average death rate for unmarried men was twice as high as for married males; for unmarried women, it was 1 1/2 times that for married females.

*According to a study by **Professors Yuanreng Hu and Noreen Goldman***

It can take 30 years to get a telephone from the government in Ghana. And while it takes only eight years to get a phone in Indonesia, only 1 in 3 local calls ever gets through.

According to **The Wall Street Journal**

The cold war is over and Japan won.

Candidate Paul Tsongas

As long as the U.S. strives to fulfill the role of a superpower, it must have the last word with regard to insuring the supply of oil at a price that Western economies can pay.

Avraham Schweitzer

The world has been made "safer" for local or regional conflicts...With the nuclear threat effectively gone, would-be antagonists feel less inhibited.

Author Marvin Setron

Here at the ministry we have other, more urgent situations to deal with.

Peruvian Labor Ministry official Jorge Luna
on reports that jungle gold miners have enslaved thousands
of children

The world's most widely spoken languages:

1. Chinese	1.12 billion speakers
2. English	360 million speakers
3. Spanish	240 million speakers
4. Hindi	230 million speakers
5. Turkish	164 million speakers

As reported by the **United Nations**

The new Europe...is not only a continent where wars have lost meaning, where there will be many fewer soldiers and weapons than the "norm"; it is the continent where people will be able to live the way rational creatures are supposed to, according to the laws of reason.

Aleksandr Bovin

In Germany, long known for its smug sense of carmaking superiority, drivers are forsaking BMWs and Mercedes for the likes of Chrysler LeBarons, Buick Park Avenues and Jeep Cherokees. Germans who once thought of American cars as "flashy" now see them as offering more luxury for their money.

Auto analyst Paul Warren-Smith

The Japanese Finance Minister confessing lax surveillance over brokerage firms' activities...publicly fell on his wallet by slashing his salary by $1000.00 per month for three months—something like committing hari-kari with a thumbtack.

Commentator John Rutledge

During the 1990's Japan is fated to remain America's number one illuminator of shortcomings in United States' economic policies and business practices, and the principal source of frustration to American trade policy makers.

Professor Stephen D. Cohen

Because of the world's skewed growth patterns, the balance of numbers will shift radically. In 1950, Europe and North America constituted 22% of the world's population. In 2025, they will make up less than nine percent. Africa, only nine percent of the world population in 1950, will account for just under a fifth of the 2025 total. India will overtake China as the world's most populous country by the year 2030.

Nafis Sadik

We have many questions right now and only a few answers. We are checking the whole world for some of the answers.

Boris Kirt,
Vice chairman of the Committee of the
National Economy of Estonia

The Japanese are now among the richest people on earth...The average person's material lot has visibly improved, but the quality of life remains less than satisfactory because of...the poor housing situation, long work hours, the high cost of living, and astronomical land prices.

Professor Robert S. Ozaki

The most important challenges facing humanity are population growth, war threats/defense costs, and environmental degradation, the need for arms control/disarmament, development of a world federation or world government, hunger in the Third World, and the need for education.

According to a poll of 36 Nobel laureates by
Professor Howard F. Didsbury Jr.

What is important is that our two cultures are coming closer. The United States is spending huge amounts trying to create a cultural presence in Latin America. But we are doing it an easier way. Little by little, with 30 million Latin Americans already here, we are taking over this country.

Nobel Prize-winning novelist Gabriel Garcia Marquez

By January [1992], the amount of pollution from Kuwait's oil-well fires will equal the quantity of poisonous emissions from all the world's automobiles—and it has already doubled the level of global carbon-gas pollution...The fires are causing higher-than-normal temperatures not only in the Middle East but also in China.

"Al Watan al Arabi"

The ending of apartheid and the repeal of the last remaining discriminatory laws will bring us to the end of an era.

South African President F.W. de Klerk
announcing the repeal of all major apartheid laws

De Klerk is a traitor to his own people. He is trying to kill the Afrikaner nation...I really hope we don't have to resort to violence, but I can't rule that out.

Conservative member Koos van der Merwe

Despite continued U.S. pressure to isolate him, Fidel Castro now boasts of having diplomatic relations with 120 nations, twice the number Fulgencio Baptista had in 1958.

Saul Landau

Nations with highest percent of women in legislature:

1. Sweden	38.1
2. Norway	35.8
3. Cuba	33.9
4. Finland	31.5
5. Denmark	30.7

(United States 5.8)

Columnists David Wallechinsky and Amy Wallace

The market economy, though still an infant, is already making small miracles here.

Polish politician Wojciech Beblo

Only the British left, cowed and unforgiving, disputes that Margaret Thatcher has been the greatest British Prime Minister of her century.

Johannesburg Sunday Times

I can offer no panacea for the problems of developing countries, but certainly trade is the best form of aid...Free trade brings in needed capital equipment and also disciplines the inefficient producer.

Sir John Whitehead
British ambassador to Japan

The current collapse of industrial society may well be the planet's way of avoiding a larger death.

Morris Berman

One-third of French foreign legion recruits are now from Central and Eastern Europe...The men are escaping "unwanted freedom" in their home countries...Due to their familiarity with authoritarian rule, they tend to be well-disciplined.

Frankfurter Rundschau

The great majority of Africans have never seen a lion. They're not allowed in their own parks, and they get no advantages from the wildlife or the tourist's income.

Peter Matthiessen

Perhaps the lasting symbol of the Thatcher years will be that of the "homeless and hungry" teenagers picketing in the streets of London's financial district, where fortunes were being made by others just out of school.

David Brindle

Rural Japanese are beginning to protest the proliferation of golf courses...The country now has 1,700 courses, with 300 more under construction.

Mainichi Shimbun

We recognize that some obstacles in the way of democracy have been removed and some pillars of apartheid have gone. But political apartheid still exists.

Robert Mugabe
President of Zimbabwe on South Africa

THE SOVIET UNION

A new Soviet revolution has begun—a revolution marked by the emergence of many voices, inside and outside government, in the proliferation of political parties, here in Moscow, and across every part of the vast reaches of this great and wonderful land.

President George Bush

Whenever our devotion to principle wanes, we will think of this place [Babi Yar]. We will remember that evil flourishes when good men and women refuse to defend virtue.

President George Bush

The joke in Moscow is that President Mikhail Gorbachev has succeeded in eliminating the lines outside the food shops—by eliminating the food.

Financial Post

They've got horse racing in Russia? He'll introduce it. He'd rather bet on a horse than eat.

Duke Zeibert
on newly appointed ambassador to Russia, Robert Strauss

If Gorbachev plays poker within about three months, Strauss will own the Ukraine, the Baltic States, and all of the Volga boatmen.

Jack Valenti

The Soviet Communist Party will soon end up like the American Communist Party, where members have to meet in their leader's kitchen.

Vladimir Yakovlev

First, is it now arguable that Russia's largest city is more civilized than America's largest. Sure, Moscow is beset by scarcities of most essentials. But it is much safer than New York, where stray—think about that—bullets kill people.

Columnist George F. Will

Thanks to Gorbachev's "new thinking," we have been allowed to move from a world dominated by the stark calculus of the arms race and the nuclear first strike, to one concerned primarily with the economics of world trade and competition, and to the issues of human poverty, global warming, the quality of life, and the care of the environment.

Hedrick Smith
former Moscow correspondent for The New York Times

In the absence of radical reform, the Soviet Union will become an irrelevant and crippled empire—a nuclear superpower with a Third World economy, unable to play a major role on the world stage.

Richard Nixon

As concerns the republics...secession will have to occur....We cannot prohibit them or refuse them...but let it be done constitutionally.

Former Soviet President Mikhail Gorbachev

Yeltsin wrote himself two glorious firsts by becoming the first elected president of Russia and second by being willing to put his life down to defend that process. But he cannot rule the country, and Gorbachev cannot rule the country. They need each other.

Princeton Sovietologist Stephen Cohen

More than a quarter of their grain is wasted, and more than half of their fruit and potatoes rot before getting to consumers. Their railroads are breaking down. They don't have much of a real trucking industry. And they never had a modern storage system.

A senior U.S. Treasury official

The deepest corruption of the Stalinist system was in removing man as much from the center of society's goals, and in replacing him with a state as a machine which magnified one man only.

Dmitri Volkogonov

You're all worse than the Fascists. At least Hitler gave us bread.

Alexandra Dubevich
an elderly woman, demonstrating against communist rule in Minsk

Having less people than needed leads to a greater load on those who are in the army, which is against the principles of social justice.

Soviet Defense Ministry
on ordering the Red Army into secessionist republics
to enforce the draft

We will never be like America. There's a big lag between our countries. Only hard labor and iron discipline will help here. It's too early for democracy. We don't even have coats and boots. How can democracy flouish under these circumstances.

Fydor Trusov

It will be a healthy society with healthy youth. We will smoke marijuana, make money. We'll have hippies and Yuppies—just like in the rest of the world.

Ilya Reznikov
student council president at the Russian State University

It is obvious that this nation in the world is having a difficult time right now as the Soviet Union goes through the process they're hopefully going through—that of reform of the system. It's a critical time, no: just for the Soviet Union but the world.

Robert Strauss
American Ambassador to the U.S.S.R.

We are pro-Gorby. He is a man with a terrible problem. He is trying to make history when events are out of control. That is one hell of a business.

Avril Connard

THE ABORTED SOVIET COUP

Vice President Gennady Yanayev has taken over the duties of president of the U.S.S.R., in keeping with Article 127, Clause 7 of the Soviet Constitution due to Mikhail Gorbachev's inability to perform his duties for health reasons.

Tass

Mikhail Gorbachev is now on vacation; he's undergoing treatment in the south of our country. He is very tired after these many years and he will need some time to get better.

Genady Yanayev
coup leader

You are all going to meet defeat.

Mikhail Gorbachev
to coup leaders

We found some type of old receivers in the maintenance rooms, and we fixed the antennae...and we began to get whatever we could from there. We got the BBC best of all...(Radio) Liberty, and then the Voice of America came on.

Former Soviet President Mikhail Gorbachev
on how he got news during his isolation

Whatever Gorbachev was, he was legally elected by the Congress of People's Deputies, and only the Congress has the right to depose him.

Olga Balankova

Many comrades are asking how I could appoint people who then betrayed me...That is the hardest question for me to answer...The only thing I can say is what I said before. We have to ensure that these very serious personnel mistakes not be repeated.

Former Soviet President Mikhail Gorbachev

We are sorry for any temporary inconvenience.

A sign posted by Ukraine officials on a statue of Lenin
that has not yet been demolished

We spent a whole week of not knowing whose finger was on the Soviet nuclear button. And we still can't say for certain whose finger will be on it next month—Yeltsin, Gorbachev, or the head of the K.G.B.

Senator Bob Dole

The empire has struck back. Across the United States, people huddle in fear. Your fear should be nothing new. Your distrust should have remained constant throughout...Just look at the eyebrows on those people.

Rush Limbaugh
Conservative radio commentator

They're strong with their guns, but I'm strong in my soul. I have nothing to gain but I'll still go out there to face them.

Viktor Shudin
on the military showdown in Moscow

The New Communists couldn't do anything right—joke sweeping Moscow about the failed coup.

According to Bill Keller
of The New York Times

You can build a throne out of bayonets, but you can't sit on them long.

Boris Yeltsin
on the Soviet coup

That's not the way to do a coup. You remember how it was in Chile: fast and energetic. Ours was a thick porridge, a Russian idiocy.

Muscovite Andrei Alepin
on the coup

In 1945 Soviet soldiers marched through Red Square to mark the final victory over fascist totalitarian Germany. We have now returned. Now is the beginning of the victory against our own totalitarianism.

Soviet writer Ales Adamovich
on overthrowing the coup

[Radio Liberty's] broadcasts in Russian and 11 other Soviet languages became Mr. Yeltsin's foremost means of getting his message to the population with the media tightly controlled by the coup leaders. His vibrant call on Monday for a general strike against coup leaders was broadcast within minutes by Radio Liberty to the furthest reaches of the nation.

Leslie Colitt

They're just boys. They don't even have ammunition in their guns. What's to be afraid of?

Moscovite
on occupying Soviet soldiers

Who could not be moved by seeing thousands of unarmed Russians facing down tanks? They put their lives on the line for freedom, and few of them paid the ultimate price. Those poor, tired Russians we saw in the streets face a winter short of food, clothing, and medicine. Why don't we support some real freedom fighters for a change?

Douglas Spaulding

From August 19 to 21, Pizza Hut delivered 260 pies to Boris Yeltsin and his party at the Russian Parliament during the Soviet coup.

According to "U.S. News & World Report"

The Soviet people's dramatic defeat of the coup demonstrates once again the great power inherent in nonviolent struggle. Clearly, nonviolent struggle has the power to prevent coups, overthrow dictatorships, and bring about freedom and democracy.

Roger S. Powers

5

BUSINESS

Anybody who can look at the business world today and give me a logical explanation for what's going on out there clearly isn't informed.

Charles Garfield

Upjohn Co., which makes Halcion, the most widely prescribed sleeping pill in America, has confirmed that it submitted incomplete data on the side effects of the controversial drug to the Food and Drug Administration when it sought approval to sell the drug here.

According to **The Washington Post**

If there was any justice in this world, oil company executive bathrooms would smell like the ones in their gas stations.

Johnny Carson

The reliance on electronic monitoring is almost forcing managers to manage poorly in terms of human relations.

Michael Smith

Economists talk about the profit motive, but nothing motivates modern man more than the chance to avoid taxes!

Peter F. Drucker

Apple® [computers] has been hurt in the market place, so they're becoming more combative in the courtroom.

Jim Poyner and William K. Woodruff
on Apple's plan to broaden its suit against Microsoft®

Pelt-ranch mink from Harold Rubin in Manhattan only costs $5,500 this year, down from $8,000 last year.

According to "Forbes"

They can cut as many people as they want, but it won't do any good if people aren't buying their systems. And they aren't; that's the problem.

Kevin Cuskley
on IBM®'s financial outlook

One of the most surprising findings of the survey was the number of executives who are dissatisfied with their management of environmental risk and opportunity. They realize they must do things better, differently, and soon—but are unsure how.

According to a survey conducted by Booz, Allen & Hamilton

The nation's top department stores:

1. J.C. Penney
2. Mervyn's
3. Dillard's
4. Macy's Northeast
5. Nordstrom

According to "Stores"

Even a whiner can help you be a winner.

Mark Berey

In the infancy of the auto age, some retailers experimented with gasoline wagons that delivered fuel from house to house. That idea never caught on, partly because of the frequency with which the wagons tended to explode.

Daniel Yergin

My social life is very low at this point. I call it SSC rule for entrepreuners—sex, sleep, and cash flow. One out of three is all you can expect when you're starting a company. If you get two out of three, you're doing pretty good. Three out of three—you're a mature company.

Alan Robbins

I don't know anything about business. I'm proud of that. Fear those who do. They're the dangerous ones.

Anita Roddick
founder of the The Body Shop International

Wall Street is stress, highly emotional, and loaded with rejection. You have to be able to survive that. That's perhaps why women haven't achieved the record that they have in other areas.

Financier James E. Cayne

Women tend to go into the market with clearer objectives and to see money for what it is—a tool. They understand that money buys things and security, whereas men tend to have an ambiguous view of money. They know it's a tool, but it's also an extension of their masculinity, a measure of how they're doing vis-a-vis other men.

Louis Rukeyser

Buy the business, not the stock...Stock prices are subject to emotional cycles of excitement and depression and can be affected by rumor and speculation, while the business itself remains solid.

Charles Brandes

[The market] is about the sum total of capitalist commercial activity. By such criteria, the world is only at the beginning of a great boom. That boom, in this half-century, has been fueled by surging technology. That surge continues.

Ben Wattenberg

As major league batting averages go up, stock market averages go down. As the color yellow becomes more popular, stocks go up. As men's ties get wider, stocks go down. As women's hemlines rise, stocks go up.

Columnist L.M. Boyd

Educate yourself about the business. If you have the opportunity, go to college and become knowledgeable about the capitalist system, because economics is the key to maintaining financial stability. Once you make some money in the business, stay creatively original.

Rapper Kool Moe Dee
to youngsters who want to pursue a career in the music industry

I'm deleveraging. That's a positive thing.

Donald Trump
on his general financial status

If all the pages faxed in 1990 were strung together, they would stretch from the Earth to the moon nine times.

According to Sharp Electronics

The top five U.S. companies:

1. General Electric
2. Exxon
3. IBM
4. Phillip Morris Cos
5. American Tel & Tel

According to "Forbes"

When big business meets technology, the result is a blunting of the cutting edge.

Laura Cohen

The top five corporate money earners:

1. Steven J. Ross, Time Warner	$78.1 million
2. Stephen M. Wolf, United Airlines	$18.3 million
3. John Sculley, Apple Computer	$16.7 million
4. Paul B. Fireman, Reebok	$14.8 million
5. Dean L. Bentrock, Waste Management	$12.5 million

According to "Forbes"

ADVERTISING

All We Are Saying Is Give Peas A Chance.

From an ad for U.S.A. Dry Pea And Lentil Council

We could tell you all the ways Federal agents use Skypagers but then we'd have to kill you.

From an ad for Skypager

Homeowners' Insurance.

From an ad for washable Crayola crayons

Our sun isn't half as hot as our market.

From an advertisement for The Miami Herald

Two years in a row parents have chosen Chevy Lumina as "Family Circle's" domestic car of the year.

From an ad for Chevy Lumina

And to my favorite grandchild, I leave my Viking with the stipulation that she must do the same.

From an ad for Viking Stoves

We build cars as though we were buying them, not selling them.

From an ad for Saab

How can a person who puts high technology on her feet, put no technology in her mouth?

From an ad for Interplak electric toothbrush

If you are better at making money than saving or investing it, the journey toward the things you want most in life never seems to get any shorter.

From an ad for Chase Lincoln First Bank

Mother asked why I charged Jack's ticket to my credit card. And I told her it's a Private Issue. She said, "I understand completely, but don't tell your father."

*From an ad for **Discover's Private Issue credit card***

Television advertisement expenditures:

1. General Motors $1 billion
2. Procter & Gamble $973 million
3. Philip Morris $755 million
4. Toyota $401 million
5. Kellog $391 million

*According to the **Television Advertising Bureau***

The More You Buy—The More You Save!

*From an ad for **Montgomery Ward***

Half of all the money I spent on advertising is wasted. The problem is, I don't know which half.

Paul B. Brown

The most support you can get for any woman's movement.

*From an ad from **Lily of France sport bras***

Some people don't care who in the entertainment world goes out with whom. Who was seen at what party. Wearing what. Saying what. To whom. For them, there's "Smithsonian."

*From an ad for **"US"***

The first computer to understand you don't just have a job. You have a life.

*From an ad for **IBM PS/1 computers***

We didn't design [it] to be like apple pie. Jalapenos were what we had in mind.

*From an ad for **Mazda's MX-3***

Give Eggs a Break.

From an ad for the **California Egg Commission**

Our new stretch jeans solve two major problems. Inhaling and exhaling.

From an ad for **Lee Jeans**

Organic denim.

From an ad for denim cloth by **Burlington Industries**

Last year AT&T spent half a billion dollars advertising reliability. We spent that much delivering it.

From an ad for **Sprint**

The worst secrets are the ones you keep from yourself.

From an ad for **Menninger of Mills-Peninsula Hospitals**

Now, what can you really put into a Porsche—besides too much money?

From a **GMC ad**

A new mint so cool your mouth may need mittens.

From an advertisement for new **Blizzard Mints**

The theory has it that sunlight reduces depression. Consider us your therapist.

From an ad for **Pella Windows and Doors**

It's everything uptown isn't.

Line from an ad for **Downtown Girl Perfume**

As the day wore on, my face wore off.

Line from an ad for **Maybeline**

People believe ads, health warnings, and other persuasive messages for a longer time if they are urged to pass them on.

According to an **Ohio State University study**

Five years ago, we dined on wedding cake. This anniversary, let's feast on carats.

From an ad for **Ben Bridge Jewelers**

This is not a pizza...At Iris, we give your eyes more than an hour.

From an ad for **Iris Optometrist's Shop**

Many are picked, few are chosen.

From an add for **C&W frozen peas**

If we all aged half as well, the world would be a much more civilized place.

From an ad for **Ballantine's scotch whisky**

Today's group of star baseball players seems to lack the all-American, squeaky-clean image that football and basketball players seem to have in abundance. Baseball players may be making a lot of money but not as endorsers [of products].

Bob Dorfman
of Foot, Cone & Belding

BANKS

As a society, the U.S. is in big trouble, and Saddam Hussein does not have a thing to do with it. But we cannot go to war against the Keating Five, can we?

Donald Brennan

Customer: Is my account safe?
Banker: Of course—we're federally insured.
Customer: So if you go bust, I still get my money back?
Banker: Sure—we just take it out of your taxes.

From a cartoon by **Wasserman**

As many as one in four homeowners with adjustable rate mortgages are receiving incorrect monthly bills. Some people are paying too much due to lender's miscalculations.

According to the **General Accounting Office**

What is really scandalous is that for all appearances, the Bank of Credit and Commerce International was able to operate for more than a decade as a kind of world government on the sidelines....and, the U.S. Central Intelligence Agency was one of the bank's big customers.

Bernard Wittkowski

This is so goddammed unfair. Robert [Altman] and [Clark] Clifford would have been the first to run to the Feds if they suspected something was wrong. They were duped. Everyone was duped.

Actress Lynda Carter
on the involvement of her husband Robert Altman in the discredited
Bank of Credit and Commerce International

The top five American banks:

1. CitiBank
2. Bank of America
3. Chase Manhattan
4. Morgan Guaranty
5. Manufacturers Hanover

According to **U.S.A. Today**

A few years ago, the government bailed out Chrysler. Recently, the entire auto industry has been looking for a bailout. Airlines had bail-outs and, of course, the S&L is the biggest catastrophe. Now, they're talking about bailing out the banks...Give me a break! I am a small businessman. If I have financial difficulties, no taxpayer comes to my aid.

Larry Giles

Drexel Burnham Lambert Inc., in a maneuver resembling a final betrayal, yesterday blamed its demise on Michael Milken and sought billions of dollars in back pay, legal fees, and damages from the junk-bond pioneer.

According to the **Associated Press**

When this deal is completed, gentlemen, we'll never have to worry about money again. Instead, we'll probably have to worry about going to jail.

From a cartoon in **"Punch"**

While the S&L bailout has hung a $300 billion albatross around the taxpayer's neck, we in the insurance industry bury our dead. Insurance companies pick up the tab when one of their own fails.

American Express Chairman James D. Robinson III

There are three reasons why so many banks are in trouble: Greed, greed, greed. It seems that banking directors and managers sold out for profits...rather than looking to the long-term interests of their own home town.

Jonathan Edwards

The-blame-it-all-on-Milken scapegoating has become a perceived path of riches for law firms and an attempt to deflect blame from those who are responsible.

Milken
complaining about law suit against him

It was very easy. And there was a certain euphoria, a certain high...I was out of control. I craved it.

Convicted former Wall Streeter, Dennis Levine
on insider trading

The banks really aren't at fault. The system wrote laws that told them they could write any kind of loan and the government would bail them out. They took advantage of a free lunch. Immoral? Yes, but not illegal.

K. Z. Don Dooven

FOR AND ABOUT THE CONSUMER

Samples of national brands that have changed the contents of products without changing packages and prices to match:

Knorr Leek Soup—reduced from four 8-ounce servings to three
Starkist Tuna—reduced from 6 1/2 to 6 1/8 ounces
Brim Decaffeinated Coffee—reduced from 12 ounces to 11 1/2 ounces
Lipton Instant Lemon Flavored Tea—reduced from 4 to 3.7 ounces

As reported by Associated Press

13,244 consumer products—such as toilet paper, yogurt, catfood, insect spray and so forth—were introduced in 1990.

According to **New Product News**

The common element to the baby-boomers right now is that they've got kids. If you want to reach that group, probably the most efficient way to reach it is through family.

Marketing expert Jake Winebaum

Prices are not as important as they once were. Many consumers today are more constrained by time than they are by money.

Peter Dickson

The average grocery store carries 17,901 items.

According to **Progressive Grocer**

The number of adults who frequently shop at malls declined from 42 percent in 1987 to just 36 percent in 1991, while the number who never shop at malls rose from 12 percent to 18 percent.

According to **The Roper Organization**

JAPAN

Rumors of a buyout of the entire U.S. economy by the Japanese sent the stock market soaring.

From a cartoon by **Schwadron**

The Japanese are much more familiar with the preferences and needs of customers in our country than we are of the Japanese.

Former President Jimmy Carter

Japan is transplanting a modern manufacturing infrastructure into America's industrial heartland, right beside the factories abandoned by U.S. companies. The Japanese investment punctures the myth that overpaid workers and a poor investment climate have ruined U.S. manufacturing.

"Technology Review"

Britain is half the size of Japan and invests twice as much, yet no one mentions them. Foreigners other than Japanese own A&P, Howard Johnson's, and Burger King and nobody kicks about that.

Bernard Gordon

Whatever the rationale for Japan-bashing, it has little to do with the facts about foreign investment. The Japanese are given no credit for the much greater share they spend than our other allies on new plants and plant expansions.

Edward John Ray

The purpose of [Japanese] capitalism seems less diluted in contrast with ours. Ours is to make money; theirs is to make products of excellence, which if they do well, will also, they are sure, make them money.

David Halberstam

MARKETING

In the 1990s, cars and light trucks will explore an ever-widening range of colors, from ruby reds to bright teals to pastel purples. Because more and more Americans are viewing cars as a statement of lifestyle, the wider range of colors will let car buyers more easily express who they are or who they'd like to be.

Robert S. Daily

California sets the cultural agenda for the world.

Peter Sealey
Coke's senior vice president and director of global marketing

In the 1960s and 1970s, the big focus for marketers was young people because that's where all the action was. In the future, people in their 50s and 60s will be the bull's eye.

Greg Gable

Nothing is less productive than to make more efficient what should not be done at all.

Management consultant Peter Druker

Perfumeries are turning to film and video to lure customers. Estee Lauder has produced a 2 1/2-minute videocassette to promote its new Spellbound perfume (...$200 an ounce), mailing 250,000 copies to consumers and packaging another 14,000 with newsstand copies of the September "Elle" magazine.

Alan Mirabella

A brand is like a reputation. If you have a good reputation, you can ride it to death. But once it turns on you, it's really hard to bring it back.

Professor David Aaker
in "Managing Brand Equity: Capitalizing on the Value of a Brand Name"

Paula Mochel is back from the U.S.S.R., where she bought one of those Gorbachev "nesting" dolls for $7; she found the same item at Pat Montandon's Perestroika shop at Pier 39 (in San Francisco) for $107, which should teach Gorby yet another lesson about capitalism.

Herb Caen

The "fat-free" label isn't misleading! The fat is free! We're only charging for the other ingredients.

Food industry spokesperson
according to a cartoon by Mike Luckovich

Among supermarkets with sales of $4,000,000 annually, 86% now sell fast-food items, with salad and soup bars being particularly common. Delicatessen sections are the most prevalent.

According to "Nielsen Marketing Research"

THE RECESSION

The time to start a business is when things are a bit depressed, because that's when people are looking for a little light, a little newness, a breath of fresh air.

Randolph Duke

What effect has the recession had on me? I sleep like a baby—every three hours I wake up and cry.

George Gendron

In a sign that the recession may be lifting on Seventh Avenue, Calvin Klein has taken 116 pages of advertising space in a single issue of "Vanity Fair" magazine.

Woody Hockswender

Just as we slid into this recession rather slowly over a long period of time, we're just going to slowly scratch our way out.

Jeff K. Thredgold

6

HEALTH

Models not only drink Evian but spray it on their faces to keep their skin moist. America has gone insane on the subject of health.

Model agency director Eileen Ford

A national health care system? Wouldn't work, too expensive, an abridgment of freedom. Never mind the evidence of countries that stay healthier than we do and spend a good deal less at it. Let's protect the freedom of doctors and hospitals to bleed us from the wallet.

Andrew B. Schmookler

The fact that some people want to live to 100 does not mean that we are obliged to shape public policy to help them obtain that goal.

Moralist Daniel Callahan

The average cost of developing a presciption drug: Financing, $231 million. Time, 12 years.

According to "Science"

Leading U.S. prescription drugs:

1. Zantac, for ulcers
2. Cardizem, for hypertension
3. Procardia, for angina

4. Prozac, for depression

5. Mevacor, for high cholesterol

According to "Medical Advertising News"

Expenditures for prescription drugs have become the second-highest out-of-pocket cost for older Americans.

*According to a survey by the **American Association
of Retired Persons***

Prescription-drug prices have outpaced inflation in the past decade and in the first half of this year. If that trend continues, a prescription that cost $20 in 1980 will cost more than $120 by the end of the decade; at the general-inflation rate it would cost less than $50.

*According to a **Senate Aging Committee** report*

This prescription has one-side effect: Poverty.

*From a cartoon by **Glasbergeno***

Best suited for minor life adjustment issues, [therapy-by-mail] allows clients to sit down when they are most comfortable and spend as much time as they want writing about what concerns them.

*Psychotherapist **Brad Whetstone***

Drink water, eat an umeboshi plum to restore alkalinity to the digestive tract; take vitamin C to detoxify the blood; take a B supplement to replenish the B vitamins destroyed by alcohol; try evening primrose oil to stimulate prostaglandin activity; drink a glass of barley juice concentrate for a general detox and a quick energy boost.

*Prescription for a hangover, received by author **John Berendt**
from a health food store clerk*

The cigarette industry came before the Supreme Court yesterday, seeking protection against lawsuits by smokers who assert that the manufacturers induced them to smoke through fraudulent advertising and by failing to warn of the dangers of cigarettes.

The New York Times

Fetuses may trigger their own births by sending a "Go!" order to the mother from deep within their brains, suggests a study that might help lead to better prevention of premature births.

Associated Press

There's a real problem in the house of medicine and the AMA wants to solve it by just taking out ads saying, "Everything's OK, let's go back to the good old days when ignorance is [was] bliss."

Dr. Sidney Wolfe
on the American Medical Association's plans to spend $1.75 million
on ads to try to spruce up the tarnished image of doctors

A woman died and went to heaven. Her husband followed shortly. "Really beautiful here," she said. "Yeah," he said "and if it weren't for you and your damned oat bran, we'd have been here five years earlier."

Unknown

Crying is really a physiological response to intense emotions and no more than that. But in many ways in our society, crying has become related to negative emotion, fear, or pain.

Psychiatrist George Woods

Researchers for the first time say that they have discovered that tiny areas inside the human brain appear to differ strikingly between homosexual and heterosexual men—findings that could confirm a biological basis for homosexuality and profoundly affect the way society views the gay world.

David Perlman

If used ethically, [it] can shed light on human sexuality and prove what we've always believed—being a gay or lesbian is not a matter of choice. Used unethically, the data could reinforce the political agenda of antigay groups that advocate "curing" or "repairing" homosexuals—the notion that gay people could be made straight by tweaking a chromosome here or readjusting a cell there.

Robert Bray

Pregnancy is the No. 1 reason females aged 15 through 20 go to doctors. Reason No. 2 [is] pimples.

Columnist L.M. Boyd

Gerber's top five baby foods:

1. Bananas
2. Applesauce
3. Pears
4. Peaches
5. Sweet potatoes

As reported in "Health"

An additional $500 million a year is added to hospital bills around the nation for the care of infants who were exposed to crack while still in utero.

According to a study reported in the "Journal of the American Medical Association"

Heterosexism and homophobia as socially transmitted mental health diseases.

Title of a workshop at the National Lesbian and Gay Health Conference

Any man who is young enough to be a lover is not too old to need a vasectomy.

Abigail Van Buren

One Martian to another, talking about recently arrived American astronauts: Well it's going fine at the moment, but if they ever find out we're chocolate coated with a minty center, we can be in big trouble.

From a cartoon in "Punch"

The booming trade in human body parts is threatening to make India the great organ bazaar of the world...In five years, the trade in kidneys has boomed so rapidly that 2000 or more kidneys change bodies annually.

Prakash Chandra

In a practice called cost shifting, hospitals are transferring most overhead costs to items less flashy than the cost of a room, resulting in $9 Tylenol tablets and $455 nursing bras.

Douglas Frantz

We are not a drugstore. We provide these items as part of the entirety of our patient care and, for better or for worse, we price them and charge for them only as an integral component of the total cost of patient care.

Humana Hospitals chairman David A. Jones

All these adult children just nauseates me.

Dr. James Mason
a behaviorist

Reaching the ripe age of 100 is no longer the rare achievement it once was. No fewer than 37,000 Americans are now centenarians—and by the year 2000, this, the country's most rapidly growing age group, will probably number 100,000 members.

Degen Pener

High doses of calcium may help alleviate the mood swings and physical discomfort many women experience before and during menstruation.

According to psychologist James G. Penland

AIDS

Physicians who are HIV positive...have a right to continue their career in medicine in the capacity that poses no identifiable risk to their patients.

From an American Medical Association
statement on HIV-infected physicians

Do I blame myself? I sure don't. I never used IV drugs, never slept with anyone and never had a blood transfusion. I blame Dr. Acer and every single one of you bastards. Anyone that knew Dr. Acer was infected and had full-blown AIDS and stood by not doing a damn thing about it. You are just as guilty as he was.

From a letter by **Kimberly Bergalis**
the first known patient to contract AIDS from her dentist,
to Florida health officials

Although the possibility of transmitting AIDS in a dental office is very remote, wouldn't it be reassuring to know that your dentist has tested negative? If you would like that peace of mind Dr. Voyne ad Dr. Walker have tested negative to the AIDS virus.

From an ad by the dentists named

Black women of childbearing age in California are 14 times as likely as whites to carry the AIDS virus.

According to a survey by the **California Department**
of Health Sevices

Mother's milk was the root of HIV transmission for nine infants who became seropositive 16 months after birth. The mothers were seropositive.

According to the **"New England Journal of Medicine"**

I'm not asking that we be able to live in a risk-free world. I want people to be able to choose their risks. I didn't have a choice to walk out of the office and seek another dentist.

Kimberly Bergalisa

[AIDS was] an illness in stages, a very long flight of steps that led assuredly to death. But whose every step represented a unique apprenticeship.

Herve Guibert
describing the illness in a recent novel

It is much more likely that a dentist will contract AIDS from a patient than the other way around, since it is the patient's blood and saliva being sprayed around. Yet, we are required by law to see AIDS patients or else be accused of discrimination.

John E. Lorincz

FOOD AND DIET

Remember the commerical featuring sprightly yogurt-eating Soviet Georgians who lived well past 100?...To avoid conscription into military service during World War II, these young men assumed the identities of their fathers, who in turn took the names of their fathers. This way, most everyone was too old to be drafted.

From "Health After 50"

Being too thin is linked with...greater risk of early death in both men and women. Recent research suggests that people can be a little heavier as they grow older without added risk to health.

According to "Dietary Guidelines for Americans"

Playing a video game while standing for thirty minutes burns as much energy as walking about two miles an hour.

According to a study by Karen Segal

The best "headache diet" includes freshly prepared foods and excludes aged, fermented, pickled, or marinated foods.

According to Dr. Seymour Diamond

There is no doubt that the life span of animals can be extended by more than fifty percent by restricting their calories.

Ray Walford
author of "The 120 Year Diet: How to Double Your Vital Years"

Good health is more than just exercise and diet. It's really a point of view and a mental attitude. You can have the strongest body, but it's not good unless the person inside you has strength and optimism.

Actress Angela Lansbury

Our results indicate that some coffee drinkers exhibit common signs of drug dependence, i.e., they self-administer coffee for the effects of caffeine, have withdrawal symptoms on cessation of caffeine and experience adverse effects from caffeine intake.

According to research reported in "Archives of General Psychiatry"

Each American consumes an average of 20.7 pounds of candy per year.

According to the National Candy Wholesalers'
Assocation

Californians are health conscious. They think it's bad luck to spill salt substitute.

Johnny Carson

Studies are coming out showing that dieters who successfully keep their weight off are the ones who take part in a consistent, sustained exercise program.

Dr. Adam Drewnowsk.

Keeping to a reduced-fat diet over a lifetime will increase average life expectancy by only three to four months, and then only if all Americans follow official recommendations.

According to a study in the "Journal of the American
Medical Association"

The McLean Deluxe low-fat burger contains 10 grams of fat. That compares with almost 37 grams of fat in McDonald's McDLT.

According to the "Mayo Clinic Health Letter"

Southern California restaurants, hoping to lure dedicated dieters, are now featuring Ultra Slim-Fast on their menus...Selling at $3 a pop, [La Petit Four] gets 15–18 orders a week.

"Newsweek"

Ounce for ounce, raw green peppers have 2 1/2 times as much vitamir C as oranges, and red peppers nearly 4 times as much.

"University of California at Berkeley Wellness Letter"

Research supports a basic message about diet and cancer. People who eat large amounts of vegetables, and to a lesser extent, fruits, have a lower risk of cancer. It's not very original—but it's very sound.

Dr. Lee W. Wattenberg

It's alright letting yourself go, as long as you can let yourself back.

Rock Singer Mick Jagger
on dieting

Sexual activity expends around 6.4 calories per minute during the highest pre-orgasmic stage and the stage immediately after orgasm. If you're seriously overweight, it's probably faster to lose weight by eating a well-balanced low-fat diet and doing regular aerobic exercise.

Dr. June M. Renisch

America is the fattest nation on Earth, and we're getting fatter. We consume more calories than people in other countries, more snacks between meals, and more sugar-rich sodas. Fat makes up almost 40 percent of all the calories we consume.

Humphrey Taylor

The best current estimates are that 95% of all dieters regain all or most of their lost weight within five years.

Professor Dean Krahn

Low-intensity exercise—five 30-minute sessions a week of moderate exertion on stationary bicycles or treadmills—is just as good for improving fitness in sedentary older adults as high-intensity exercise.

According to a study by Stanford University researchers

Today's Special: 1 lb.—$1.98

Sign on a weight reducing salon in a cartoon by Lepper

ENVIRONMENT

Do-it-yourselfers dump about 240 million gallons of used oil into the environment each year—the equivalent of five oil tankers spilling their entire load.

According to the Automotive Information Council

Everyone has gone back to a place that they remember from childhood and seen an apartment complex or a K-mart. When I was growing up, we were on the edge of the Everglades. Now we're in the middle of mall hell.

Carl Hiaasen

The nation's wealthy are out of touch with the environmental problems that we face, probably because they're the cause of them. The Earth is not dying, its being killed, and the people who are killing it have names and addresses.

Darryl Cherney
a member of Earth First

Five percent of the people in the world consume one-third of the planet's resources...Those people are us.

From a public service announcement by the Vancouver
(Canada) Media Foundation

With increasing population, environmental changes, urbanization, and travel, we will experience increasing numbers of different diseases caused by new or emerging viruses as well as other agents.

Llewellyn J. Legters

ANIMALS AND THEIR RIGHTS

From civil rights to women's rights, the history of the past two decades has been highlighted with dramatic and meaningful advances in the direction of a better and more equitable world. Rights and protection for animals is the final link without which our dream of a more decent and human world cannot be completed.

Annette T. Lantos

Most [pet owners] are unaware that advances in biomedical sciences have made a major difference in the health of their pet. Diseases that were rampant among dogs and cats are now readily treated or prevented by agents that were developed through animal research.

Bernard D. Goldstein

Minks are mean little critters. Vicious, horrible little animals who eat their own. They're not beavers. I wouldn't wear beavers. I'd rather have a mink coat made of mean little critters that are killed in a very nice way and treated nicely for their short mean lives, so that I could be kept warm.

Actress Valerie Perrine

Why am I being called upon to respect animal rights when animals don't?

Anonymous

Tiny Game Hunting

A new paperback detailing environmentally safe ways to trap and kill pests in the home and garden.

Milwaukee...July 1991. They were drugged and dragged across the room...Their legs and feet were bound together...Their struggles and cries went unanswered...Then they were slaughtered and their heads sawn off...Their body parts were refrigerated to be eaten later...It's still going on. If this leaves a bad taste in your mouth, become a vegetarian.

*From an ad by **People for the Ethical Treatment of Animals***

The human race deserves itself, but the other species of the planet should not have to endure our follies.

R. Packard Martin

A Chicken McNugget doesn't die any easier than baby fur seals, and the fact that somebody could be so insipid to think that the chicken has less rights than the baby fur seal because it's not as cute can kiss my ass.

Ted Nugent

Food prices would rise less than 1% if alternative test-control practices replaced half of the chemical pesticides now used in U.S. agriculture.

*According to a study by **David Pimental***

HEALTH HELPS

One of the surprises in our research is that niacin, the oldest and least-used treatment, is perhaps the cheapest way to lower cholesterol significantly.

Dr. Terry Jacobson

A new study of 333 men indicates that alternate-day low-dose aspirin can greatly reduce the risk of a first heart attack in men who have chronic stable angina, but no previous history of heart attack or stroke.

According to a study by P. M. Ridker, et al.

If you help people find a better way to live, they also do better physically.

Dr. Bernie Siegel

Improving your mood may be as simple as breathing through your nose...like mood-altering medications, nosebreathing may change the body's level of neurotransmitters—chemicals that produce feelings of anxiety, excitement, and relaxation.

According to Professor Robert Zajonc

It is my observation that a more likely explanation (of absence of breast cancer) is that the Navajos never eat rare meat—thus avoiding the consumption of oncologic bovine viruses, papilloma, and leukemia viruses.

Dr. Lamar Gibbons
explaining the rarity of breast cancer in Navajo Indians

According to two new studies, the men who took their pills regularly— regardless of whether those pills were the actual medication or the placebos—had one-half the number of deaths than the men who didn't take their pills as prescribed.

According to "Men's Health"

The additions to the presidential budget request, which are expected to yield an extra $70 million or so for women's health projects by the time the 1992 budget is finalized, will allow a start to be made on the much-publicized Women's Health Initiative of the National Institute of Health.

Peter Aldhous

Persons under general anesthesia can hear what is being said in the operating room, and saying the right thing can reduce postoperative pain.

According to the "British Medical Journal"

The consumption of green tea cut the lung cancer rate by 45 percent in mice exposed to one of the most potent cancer-causing agents in cigarette smoke. Other studies in animals suggested that drinking green tea could cut the rates of stomach and liver cancer.

Allan Conney
director of the Laboratory for Cancer Research
at Rutgers University in New Jersey

About a quarter of Americans take daily vitamin and mineral supplements. Multivitamins are the most popular supplement followed by vitamin C and calcium.

National Institutes of Health

Chew sugarless gum for 10 minutes after eating sweets and starch-laden foods and you'll lessen your chances of tooth decay.

According to Dr. John Brown

Lung cancer and leukemia have been treated effectively in initial human trials with a new class of drugs that make cancer cells "grow up" and act more normally.

According to Ronald Breslow
of Columbia University

Good sleep habits are learned.

American Medical Association

There is a protective factor against cancer in fruits and vegetables, and Vitamin C is the most consistent factor. The strongest evidence for Vitamin C is with stomach cancer, than colon, breast, and cervical.

Dr. Geoffrey Howe

Sucking on zinc-filled lozenges may shorten the misery of a cold by several days, a study of coughing, sneezing college students has found.

Doctors at Dartmouth College's Health Service

The doctors in New Jersey asked my mother three times if they could disconnect the life support system. The first time, she told them no. The second time, she told them no. The third time, she told them to sign my release. And she brought me here.

Denise Johnson
who was in a coma after being hit by a drunken driver
and recovered at the Kentfield Rehabilitation Hospital

Women who take regular doses of estrogen after menopause have a significantly lower death rate—particularly from heart and blood vessel diseases—than postmenopausal women who have never used the hormone replacement therapy.

*Reported by researchers **Brian E. Henderson, Annlia Paganini-Hill** *
*and **Ronald K. Ross** *

Birth defects such as Down's syndrome have for the first time been diagnosed with just a prenatal blood test of the mother.

Mike Snider

Patients with cervical or prostate cancer who have radiation treatment alone often have as good a chance at recovery as those who go in for surgery, two recent studies show.

Karen Cacero

New health guidelines released by the U.S. Departments of Agriculture and Health and Human Services:

1. Eat a variety of foods.
2. Maintain healthy weight.

3. Choose a diet low in fat, saturated fat and cholesterol.
4. Choose a diet with plenty of vegetables, fruits, and grain products.
5. Use sugars only in moderation.
6. Use salt and sodium in moderation.
7. If you drink alcoholic beverages, do so in moderation.

HEALTH HAZARDS

People who reported high levels of psychological stress were twice as likely to develop a cold as those reporting low stress levels.

According to researchers at **Carnegie Mellon University**

Repeated experiments in England indicate that people shivering outdoors are no more likely to catch a cold than those who stay warm indoors.

Rick Hampson

Since the early 1970s...the incidence of breast cancer has increased about one percent a year...The number of deaths rose from 30,000 in 1970 to 44,000 in 1990.

Marian Segal

People whose weight fluctuates dramatically from year to year appear to be at greater risk of coronary heart disease and fat-related cancers than those who maintain a steady weight.

According to a report in the "New England Journal of Medicine"

Uninsured hospital patients have a higher in-hospital death rate than patients covered by private insurance.

According to a study by **Prof. Jack Hadley**

The failure rate for contraceptives:

The pill	6 percent
Condom	14 percent
Diaphragm	16 percent
Spermicides	26 percent

Rhythm	16 percent
Sponge	18-20 percent

*According to the **Alan Guttmacher Institute***

Substance abuse and alcoholism are three times more prevalent among gay men and women than in the general population.

*According to a study by the **National Lesbian and Gay Help Foundation***

In Bhopal, India, health problems from exposure to the methyl isocyanate spewed by the Union Carbide chemical plant six years ago appear to be growing. Indian researchers cite increased reports of birth defects, miscarriages, cataracts, and respiratory ailments.

The Economic Times

The leading causes of death in the United States:
1. Heart disease
2. Cancer
3. Stroke
4. Accidents
5. Chronic obstructive lung disease

*According to the **National Center for Health Statistics***

The top 10 causes of death and disability in our society are conditions which are heavily influenced by personal behavior.

Louis Sullivan
Health and Human Services Secretary

If you look at the top 10 or 12 causes of death, every one kills more men.

*Epidemiologist **Deborah Wingard***

In the Soviet Union, 40 years of nuclear-weapons testing in Kazakhstan are causing leukemia deaths today at a rate 3 times higher than the national average...The rate of children born with physical defects is also 3 times greater, and the number who developed problems in infancy is 5 times the national average.

"Die Tageszeitung"

Patient to doctor: "But if I'm a hypochrondiac, how will I know when I really do get sick?"

*From a cartoon by **McCotic***

This study points to a relationship between mouthwash and mouth and throat cancer, but it doesn't prove a specific risk.

Phillip J. Sheridan

By binding to sperm, cocaine may be carried directly to an egg during fertilization and cause birth defects among male users' offspring.

*According to a study reported in the **"Journal of the American Medical Association"***

Lung cancer has now surpassed breast cancer as a primary killer of women.

*According to **Professor John R. Benfield***

70 percent of all new cigarette smokers start the habit by buying Marlboro brand cigarettes.

*According to **"Business Week"***

A study of 34 adult male cigarette smokers and 61 adults who had never smoked shows that smokers have more cavities than nonsmokers. In part, the increased decay rate in smokers may be due to their poor oral hygiene.

*According to a study published in **"General Dentistry"***

Warning: When Used As Directed, Cigarettes Kill.

*From an Ad by the **California Department of Health Services***

Smoking before becoming pregnant is directly linked to a rise in the number of ectopic pregnancies.

*According to **Dr. Joel Coste***

Fathers who smoke have an increased risk of having children with brain cancer and leukemia.

*According to a study by the **National Institute of Environmental Health Sciences***

A research team has placed the costs of hospital care for cocaine-exposed newborns at more than $500 million a year because so many of them are born prematurely with health problems that need costly specialized care.

David Perlman

Substance abuse and alcoholism are three times more prevalent among gay men and women than in the general population.

According to a study by the National Lesbian and Gay Help Foundation

Many diseases are created and recreated by society. The organisms that biologists and medical scientists implicate in infectious diseases have their terrible effects as a result not only of biological mechanisms, but of social organization in human behavior.

Daniel M. Fox
summarizing a statement made by Stephen S. Morse

Sufficient information exists to warrant further studies of the potential toxicity of aluminum, but it is not yet time to throw out the aluminum cookware.

According to an article in "The New England Journal of Medicine"

The Sun Also Fries Us.

Newsletter headline

Fetal alcohol syndrome is now recognized as the leading known cause of mental retardation in the United States, surpassing Down's syndrome and spina bifida.

According to "Health Line"

Halcion has the advantage of not leaving patients sedated the morning after, but it is more likely to cause agitation and memory impairment.

Dr. Rodney Burbach

One in nine American women can now expect to develop breast cancer at some time in their lives.

*According to the **American Cancer Society***

After four months, wine that sat in crystal decanters had absorbed up to 200 times the level of lead that the Environmental Protection Agency deems hazardous in water.

*According to a study by researchers at **Columbia University***

Allergic reactions to latex may be as mild as a runny nose or a rash, but contact with latex during dental work, surgery or barium enemas can cause life-threatening anaphylactic shock.

*According to a study by **G. L. Sussman, et al.***

Despite the belief that handwashing is the most important measure to prevent the spread of infection in hospitals, less than one third of physicians wash their hands between patients.

*According to a study by the **American Hospital Association***

Physicians and nurses should not ask a patient to make a fist when blood is being drawn. Clenching of the fist can alter serum potassium levels considerably.

*According to researchers at **San Francisco General Hospital***

Some individuals are suicidal but so depressed that they don't have the energy to commit suicide. However, as the antidepressant begins to work, there can be a short period when they are still suicidal but their depression has improved enough that they now have sufficient motivation to carry out their plan.

Dr. David E. Comings

Mothers whose daughters had eating disorders were more likely to be dissatified with their families, to have an eating disorder themselves and to put direct pressure on their daughters to be thin.

*According to a study by **K. M. Pike and J. Rodin***

Women with more upperbody fat may be 15 times more likely to develop cancer of the uterus lining.

According to a study by **David V. Schapira**

Every year some 30,000 amputations are performed on Americans with diabetes, and half of the patients who lose one leg will lose the second within five years.

As reported in **"The Science Teacher"**

Each year there are approximately 205,000 residential fires of electrical origin causing 1,100 deaths, 16,300 injuries, and $950 million in damage.

According to the **American Society of Safety Engineers**

It's the real thing. We know that, throughout the general population, moods vary on a seasonal basis. Typically, people feel more depressed as fall and winter approach and more hopeful with the coming of spring.

Dr. Karl Doghramji

Studies have shown that fluorescent lights are more harmful, in terms of stimulus, than incandescent [ones], which are the regular old-fashioned light bulbs. For a person who is easily stimulated or hyperactive, modern-day intense lighting can cause a problem.

Sharon Nelson

7

THE WRITTEN WORD

The only thing that keeps us from floating off with the wind is our stories. They give us a name and put us in a place, allow us to keep on touching.

Tom Spanbauer

On any given day, 71 percent of Americans read a newspaper, 36 percent read a magazine, 38 percent read a book for work or school and 33 percent read a book for pleasure.

*According to a **Gallup Poll survey***

Sometimes you just want to read something where you don't have to think when you read it.

Newly crowned Miss America Carolyn Suzanne Sapp *on why she likes her 132 "Archie" comic books*

The Waldorf-Astoria...buys about 200 used books a year. The hotel puts these on shelves in the rooms and along the hallways so wealthy guests can steal them.

John Maxwell Hamilton

If one reads [the classics] with concentration...the effort gives us possession of a vast store of vicarious experience...Through this experience, we escape from the prison cell, professional or business or suburban. It is like gaining a second life.

Jaques Barzun

Due to a typing error, Gov. Dukakis was incorrectly identified in the third paragraph as Mike Tyson.

From a correction in a Massachusetts newspaper

The 90s are definitely the decade of men. Presses are gobbling up manuscripts.

Chris Harding
editor of the men's journal "Wingspan"

Not all smut is equally newsworthy.

Journalist Jonathan Alter

Television can stir emotion, [but] doesn't invite reflection as much as the printed page.

TV commentator Bill Moyers

During the summer heat I eat, with pleasure, roots and kraut, also butter and radishes, making excellent wind, which cools me off.

Wolfgang Mozart
in one of his recently discovered, unpublished,
scatological canon texts

In some sense, Freud has to be seen as a prose version of Shakespeare the Freudian map of the mind being in fact Shakespearean...What we think of as Freudian psychology is really a Shakesperean invention, and, for the most part, Freud is merely codifying it.

Harold Bloom

The great thing about selling a book to the movies is that nobody blames the author.

Author Tom Wolfe

Mystery and crime fiction...is virtually the last literary frontier of the American hero. It's a rough genre, this field that includes police procedurals and private-eye novels along with the more genteel amateur-detective story of ratiocination, so its male and female heroes are not always as shiny as their mythic models.

Marilyn Stasio

It used to be difficult to get approval to publish books by Blacks on a variety of subjects. Publishers would say there's no audience for such books because Black people are not buying them and others are not reading them. It was a convenient myth.

Marie Brown

There is no single, infallible form of knowledge, forming a standard against which all others must be measured and by whose help they will all finally be made impregnable. Instead, there are many different ways of knowing, each with their own standards and their own suitable kinds of evidence.

Mary Midgley

Cities with the highest bookstore spending per household:

1. Austin, Texas
2. Madison, Wisconsin
3. San Jose, California
4. Boston, Massachusetts
5. San Francisco, California

*According to the **American Booksellers' Association***

A Japanese company now provides a diary service for people who just can't find the time every day to write down their entries. They can phone the company to tape record their day's activities and at the end of the month receive a nicely bounded transcription of their musings.

Harriet Blodgett

The stories are false. The names are real to stimulate sales.

*From a cartoon by **M. Twohy***

BOOKS

Yes, the maestro of the macabre, the czar of the zany, the sultan of shock, the liege of loathsomeness, is back with another of his gruesome novels...As in most of Mr. King's work, the premise here is that if one scratches just below the surface of normality in small-town America, one will unearth terrifying gushers of weirdness and depravity.

Joe Queenan
reviewing Needful Things *by Stephen King*

When a life ends badly, the great temptation is to construe it as a long, inevitable journal to ruin. But the death is not the life. Ms. Middlebrook gives us a living Sexton [in her biography], a gifted, vivid woman who strove, even at her worst for health, clarity, and human connection.

Katha Pollitt

Exposing Myself

Title of Geraldo Rivera's
autobiography

Generally speaking, men who talk about their sexual conquests aren't all that fond of women because it really is hurtful. Men who really love women are close-mouthed about their relationships.

Dr. Joyce Brothers
talking about Geraldo Rivera's new tell-all biography,
Exposing Myself

He's obviously a scumbag, because he started making love to other people and betraying my daughter and her innocnece from the very beginning. If I see Gerry [Rivera] again, I'll spit in his face...The boy obviously has a screw loose.

Kurt Vonnegut

Reagan's book [*An American Life*] is so clogged with patently untrue fantasies that some reviewers have suggested as a more appropriate title, *An American Lie.*

Columnist Calvin Trillin

Mailer here [in his novel *Harlot's Ghost*] espouses just about all known and several unknown forms of fiction....He comes closest to another highly gifted, overexuberant ex-Harvard man, Thomas Wolfe, whose voluminousness he certainly has. What he lacks is his editor.

John Simon

[Simon is] a man whose brain is being demented by the bile rising from his bowels. I don't want to be reviewed by Dracula.

Normal Mailer

Too much research is deadly to a novel. Mailer hasn't written this one from what he knows, but from what he's learned; it doesn't spring from his hormones, or his pulse, but from his file cards. And a dry and dusty thing it is for nearly all its incredibly long way.

Peter S. Prescott
reviewing Harlot's Ghost

Famous rejections:

You have buried your novel underneath a heap of details which are well done but utterly superfluous.

"Madame Bovary" by Gustave Flaubert (1856)

The girl doesn't, it seems to me, have a special feeling or perception that would lift the book above the "curiosity level."

"The Diary of Anne Frank" by Anne Frank (1952)

We do not think it would be at all suitable for the juvenile market in this country [England].

"Moby Dick" by Herman Melville (1851)

An autobiography can distort, facts can be realigned. But fiction never lies. It reveals the writer totally.

V. S. Naipaul

Books were my pass to personal freedom. I learned to read at age three, and soon discovered there was a whole world to conquer that went beyond our farm in Mississippi.

Oprah Winfrey

I thought it [*The Crisis Years*] would take three years, since I was writing about a three-year period. Three years of history, three years of writing. I often say it was a good thing I wasn't writing about the Hundred Year's War.

Michael R. Beschloss
whose book took six years to write

How To Toilet Train Your Cat: 21 Days to a Litter-Free Home

A new book by **Paul Kunkel**

Why doesn't anybody talk of it as a nightmare? It's a psychotic nightmare. There's no reality to it at all. I mean, you can't decapitate a woman and have it stink up the apartment without the landlord getting concerned about it.

Editor George Plimpton
on the controversial novel, American Psycho

Books have become products like cereal or perfume or deodorant.

Alexandra Ripley
author of Scarlett—The Sequel to Margaret Mitchell's
'Gone With the Wind'

The reason for my book is to cope with terminal illness. If someone misuses it for something else, that's sad.

Derek Humphry
on his book, Final Exit

We have to take history as it is dealt. I brought him [Rabbit] to the end of the Reagan years and the end of the Cold War. It is a good place for him to end. The postwar world he grew up in is over.

John Updike
on the end of his Rabbit *series*

Do It! Let's Get Off Our Buts

Title of a book by **John-Roger**
and Peter McWilliams

He should stick to songwriting—he does it better.

Cher
on Sonny Bono's biography, And the Beat Goes On

Many of the self-centered, egotistical, and arrogant involved in politics will think this book is about them. It is not. The characters in this novel are fictional.

Author Linda Proaps
about her novel, Capitol Punishment

A lavishly illustrated book on the restored Sistine Chapel ceiling is on sale at the suggested retail price of $1,000, the most expensive general trade book in publishing history.

Associated Press

Books hold different meanings for the authors who write them, the editors who acquire them, the critics who judge them and the readers who take them home. It falls to scholars to recover all of these meanings.

Marc Aronson

Ulysses seemed to be deliberately mystifying and mainly puerile, and I have never been able to get over a suspicion that Joyce concocted it as a vengeful hoax.

H.L. Mencken
from his recently opened seven unpublished volumes of work

People who are offended by my book have to...have me banned from restaurants because they are afraid they are going to run into me and don't know how they're going to deal with it...These are people who wake up in the morning, look in the mirror and say, "Are they going to find out I'm a fraud today?"

Julia Philips
on reactions to her book You'll Never Eat Lunch in This Town

A book like this can provide information, particularly to the young, where there has not been an adequate exploration of the emotional problems underlying the suicidal thinking. We know that over 90 percent of those who end their lives are suffering from a mental illness, which in many cases is very treatable.

Susan J. Blumenthal
on Final Exit

The Kathryn Hepburn that emerges here [in her autobiography *Me*] is unsaintly, an archetypal American actor: narcissistic, ambitious, sometimes ruthless, and rarely concerned about people other than herself or ideas other than those of practical use in her advancement.

Frank Rich

JOURNALISM

We have one square inch of principle and we're standing on it.

Washington Post *editor Ben Bradlee*
on his decision not to print the name of the woman who says she
was raped by William Smith

The guys who did serve in Vietnam, mostly officer rank...say "Duty, honor, hate the media."

Tom Brokaw

There's always been a touch of anit-Semitism at the News. There's no editors there who have been properly circumcised, so there are things to do.

Robert Maxwell
on the New York Daily News

New York Panel Backs School for Minority Men.

The New York Times
January 10

South Africa Moves to Integrate Schools

The New York Times
January 10

Sportswriting is a dying art, a victim of antagonistic players, constricting deadlines, debilitating travel and salaries so modest that sportswriters now work on their as-told-to books before games instead of their reporting.

Alan Richman

I'd go to Hell itself for a story if someone important down there wanted to be interviewed.

CNN's Peter Arnett

We [tell our readers] about the socioeconomic implications of a debate in Botswana; what they really want to know is what the guy next door sold his house for. If we feed them quiche and Evian water, they want hamburgers and a Coke.

Retiring editor Frank McCulloch

When the flow of information to the public is totally controlled by the government, then the division of civilian control of the military is flouted, when the Pentagon tries to shoulder a political as well as a military role, then a democratic society is in power.

Paul McMasters
USA Today *associate editor*

You say what you think needs to be said...If it needs to be said, there are going to be a lot of people who will disagree with it or it wouldn't need to be said.

Cartoon journalist Herb Lock

There is in the democratic impulse a need to record reality without restraint. Such a record assures not that wars won't be undertaken again, but that they won't be undertaken in ignorance.

Paul McMasters

It's not the world that's gotten so much worse, but the news coverage that's got so much better.

Columnist Abigail Van Buren
quoting G.K. Chesterton

I know that the most effective means of insuring the government's accountability to the people is an aggressive, free, challenging, untrusting press.

General Colin Powell

Newspaper writers are supposed to report the news. They aren't supposed to make it. And when they vote for awards, they're helping to make the news.

Ira Berkow
The New York Times *columnist*

Not every column has to have a solution, but if I can't nudge a reader a little in the direction of a solution or at least a better analysis of a problem, I shouldn't write that column.

Columnist William Raspberry

If truth in packaging were applicable to the media, their product would not be permitted to enter the marketplace.

Frank A. Fusco

POETRY

Poetry is threatened when poets take too lively a theoretical interest in language and make it into a constant subject of meditation...Dante was obsessed by what he had to say, not by the saying of it.

E. M. Cioran

Poetry is an orphan of silence. The words never quite equal the experience behind them.

Charles Simic

We suppose that every poet, in order to be recognized...has to have an individual style and tone and personality...He is a poet when he can write as no one else can write. This is peculiar, because in the past you were recognized as a poet only when you could write just the same as everyone else, and with no lapses from the common standard.

Peter Levi

The impulse to write a poem is based on a need to fix something...to find a solution for some kind of eternal problem.

Carol Snow

Poetry is language at its most beguiling and seductive while it is, at the same time, elusive, seeking to mock one's desire for reduction, for plain and available order.

Mark Strand

As you get older, the subject of a poem is astonishment at what is before you. It's almost a religious experience, one of standing apart and seeing yourself in awe before the world.

Charles Simic

Poetry is the art of using words charged to their greatest intensity.

Poet Dana Gioia

WRITERS

I have already written an account of myself in 20 or more volumes, most of them called novels.

Kingsley Amis
in his Memoirs

Gordimer writes with intense immediacy about the extremely complicated personal and social relationships in her environment. At the same time as she feels a political involvement—and takes action on that basis—she does not permit this to encroach on her writings.

The Swedish Academy
on awarding the Nobel Prize to Nadine Gordimer

As a guest, Auden was totally dominating. Breakfast had to be at 8 on the nose, then he expected to be helped with the *Times* crossword puzzle...and at 11 he wanted the light snack that the English call elevenses. He always wanted to get back to "mother and home and tea at exactly 4:30." At 6 precisely, he wanted martinis, and if dinner wasn't at 7:30 on the dot, he got very drunk and blamed you for it.

Poet Stephen Spender
on poet W. H. Auden

It'll be nice to go back to being a writer instead of an author.

Curt Gentry
exhausted from radio-TV interviews and book signings for his new
best seller on J. Edgar Hoover

I want people to feel good about life. I hate to walk away from a book or a movie feeling that life isn't worth a damn. People don't need that. I think, maybe most of all, they get hope from my books. The characters are in a difficult situation, and they don't get off scot-free, but they prevail.

Danielle Steel

I can't look forward to going out and getting drunk on a given night anymore, which I used to love. That was the way to get back to oneself, and I can't do it. Because I wake up in the morning and I can't get out of bed.

Norman Mailer

I'm the world's greatest writer in basic English and that's all I know.

Author Harold Robbins

A lot of romance novelists are Catholic, but it's not the religion. It's the discipline—the sense that if you're not being productive, you're heading into sin.

Vera Roberts

One connection I see between novelists and terrorists is that we both attempt to alter consciousness.

Don DeLillo

The great paradox about W. H. Auden is this: How can the writer of the sanest, most liberal and chaste poetry in English of the 20th century also be the crotchety, opinionated old fossicker of the *Table Talk?*

Peter Forbes
in a review of The Table Talk of W. H. Auden

I'd rather have written *Cheers* than anything I've written.

Novelist Kurt Vonnegut

Ken Follett has moved to Dell Publishing with a $12.3 million deal for two books in six years.

USA **Today**

Royalties from U.S. sales of [Tom Clancy's] 5 million hardcover books and nearly 20 million paperbacks plus foreign rights, book club, and movie sales, add up to probably $45 million.

Fleming Meeks

We should see him...not as a "repressed homosexual"...but as a man caught between his habitual, torturing detachment, and his passionate longing for attachment...He certainly experienced homoerotic feelings...It was men with whom he could—just occasionally in reality, but mostly in imagination—be physically close and uncomplicatedly happy.

*Biographer John Worthen
on D. H. Lawrence*

[Sidney] Sheldon is a graduate of "The Terrible Secret" School of Fiction Writing, in which most of his characters hide huge chunks of their past from each other so we'll keep the pages turning. Protagonists also spend endless hours harboring a horrible legacy or painful lie, only to find that personal catastrophe may often lead to romance, riches, and the possibility of a sequel.

Patricia Holt

Favorite authors of Americans:

1. Stephen King
2. Danielle Steel
3. Louis L'Amour, Sidney Sheldon
4. James Michener, V.C. Andrews
5. Charles Dickens, Mark Twain, Ernest Hemingway, John Steinbeck, William Shakespeare, Tom Clancy.

According to a **Gallup Poll**

I have only one reader: me. I'm the average reader. If I like it, that's all I worry about.

Author Judith Krantz

The suggestion that if a writer is gay he must write about gay subjects, that he has a responsibility to write about gay subjects—I find that preposterous. That lets heteros off the hook by letting them assume that if something is the work of a "gay writer," then it has nothing to do with them.

Playwright Edward Albee

I much prefer working away modestly and gloomily—the more I can feel like a monk on retreat, the better it is. I like working in a mild depression, never thinking of anything larger.

Norman Mailer

Each time I go up to bat I try to write at the peak of my ability. Each successful writer has certain talents. Scott Turow can't write *Dazzle* and I can't write *Presumed Innocent*. I put so much into a book. I do my homework.

Judith Krantz

I'm a storyteller. I never write long descriptions; it'll stop the story. That's why my novels are so easy to translate.

Sidney Sheldon

I'm so busy with my writing. I'm on my 544th book. No, wait it's my 543rd.

Romance novelist Barbara Cartland

My principal mission is to tell an entertaining story, and if people want to learn from it, so much the better. I'm an author, not a prophet.

Tom Clancy

It is my intention as an author to try and do some good. I have a core of social concern, and if that can get transmitted and things can get done differently, I will be happy. For me, this isn't just storytelling.

Avery Corman

Shakespearean characters are not so much remarkable for their subtlety as for their size. For subtlety he could not hold a candle to Henry

James, for instance, or George Meredith, but in the weight and force of passion he is like no one else.

Robertson Davies

I've spread my legs in the back seat in a creative sense quite a few times.

Stephen King
best selling horror novelist, on the issue of compromising
artistic integrity

Many write but few are paid.

Randi Hacker and Jackie Kaufman

If my hands tremble with desire, they tremble likewise when I reach for the chalice on Sunday, and if lust makes me run and caper it is no stronger a force than that which brings me to my knees to say thanksgivings and litanies. What can this capacious skin be but a blessing.

John Cheever

Scarlett is functionally illiterate and as selfish as a pig. It was hard getting inside her head because the furniture there is so different from my own. But I imagined what it felt like to think you've lost every one you love. Then I could write about her with real feeling instead of clenched teeth.

Alexandra Ripley

THE TABLOIDS

Our job is to try and come up, as best we can, with what people want to read. We don't report on all of the murders and recessions and crimes like other papers do. What we do, instead, is present stories that you're curious about, or stories that can just plain help you.

Iain Calder
National Enquirer *editor*

It's like rough sex. You've got to know when to hold back.

Jerry Nachman
The New York Post *editor, on tabloid journalism*

We want the best and we pay for it. We have reporters making more than $90,000 a year and editors in the six figures, but we just don't give the money away. We work our writers very hard, and we expect results.

Iain Calder
National Enquirer editor

Bigfoot Escapes—Kills Two!

Weekly World News

World's First Potty-Trained Frog!

Weekly World News

Barbara Eden's golden rule: Never compare husbands.

Star

Hero chimp lands plane after pilot passes out!

Weekly World News

Woman grows diamond toenails: Mom trims them with industrial cutters and sells them for big buck$.

Weekly World News

Arizona man marries 3,000-year-old mummy! "She's the woman of my dreams," says happy groom!

Weekly World News

Computer talks with the dead! Special code enables machine to make contacts beyond the grave!

Weekly World News

Gun Crazy Delta [Burke] and Gerald [McRaney] keep secret arsenal of assault weapons.

Star

Crashed UFO Found On Mt. Everest.

Sun

Sizzling shocker!: Bathing Beauty Baked Alive At Beach.

Sun

Man kills self after reading his own obituary.

Sun

Doctors remove dead fetus after 10 yrs: "It was hard as a stone statue."

Sun

You gotta hand it to him! Doctors transplant cadaver's limb onto accident victim.

Sun

Nervous man proposes on roll of toilet paper.

Sun

Doctors Remove Alien Implant From Man's Body.

National Examiner

Liz [Taylor] Shuns Old Pals For Gays & Larry's Louts: Beer-swilling kinfolk topped the guest list and the best man's date was his hunky boyfriend.

Globe

My Neighbor's An Animal—He Killed My Dog & Ate It!

Globe

Love Addict Ed McMahon Goes To Shrink For Cure.

National Enquirer

Madonna's night of terror—bound and beaten by Sean Penn.

National Enquirer

Towering teen is 7-foot-3 and still growing: He eats 10 burgers at a time—and has to drive his car from the backseat.

National Enquirer

Sexpot Madonna Is So Lonesome She Picks Up Latin Boys Off Street
Corners....And makes love to them in her limo.

Globe

Prince Edward dates Norwegian Princess—but has gay affair with her
fiance.

News Extra

Liberace is alive! He's been spotted in New York.

Sun

Grieving Hubby: I Ate Shark That Ate My Wife.

Sun

Our Government Has Secret Treaty With Space Aliens...former U.S.
intelligence agent reveals.

Sun

Jim Bakker. His Gay Lover Tells All: Jim Blackmailed Me Into Having
Sex.

National Enquirer

King of the Worm Eaters: Yuk! World champ ate 315 of the slimy
critters in 24 minutes!

Weekly World News

Liz Taylor's Bridegroom Invites A Killer And A Robber To their Wedding.

Star

Beatty dumps pregnant "Bugsy" co-star because she won't abort his
love child. Enraged Annette Bening: He's a selfish slimeball!

News Extra

Ready-to-Pop Tanya Tucker Splits from Baby's Dad.

Star

Princess Stephanie Caught Smooching Her Married Bodyguard.

Star

Danny Kaye Had Wild Gay Affair with Olivier, Claims Shocking New Book.

Star

Sex-mad [John] Lennon wanted to torture his lovers.

Star

Trump Splits with Marla After New Book Reveals He Cheated with Robin Givens.

Star

Holy mutt-rimony—Bride's dogs have their day as ring bearer and flower girls!

National Enquirer

He has world's best part-time job—getting women pregnant...and it was his wife's idea!

National Enquirer

Mystery disease turns girls into boys!

Weekly World News

Macho trucker shifts gears...and Becomes A Gal!

Weekly World News

Fan kills himself because he can't afford a nose like Michael Jackson's!

Weekly World News

WRITING

It's like striking a match. Sometimes it lights. I started "Lost in Yonkers" maybe two years ago. I had an idea about a boy who was left with his grandmother and he had an Aunt Bella. That was all.

Neil Simon

If an author alters a speaker's words but effects no material change in meaning, including any meaning conveyed by the manner or fact of expression, the speaker suffers no injury to reputation that is compensable as a defamation.

Recent Supreme Court ruling

Who knows where inspiration comes from? Perhaps it arises from desperation. Perhaps it comes from the flukes of the universe, the kindness of muses.

Novelist Amy Tan

It usually takes me about 30 years to write a book—29 to think about it and a year to write it down.

Charles McCarry

A great novel is fueled by its writer's obsessions, not by his or her obligations—and if that obsession is of a world the way the writer would like it to be, rather than the world as it is, then that is the world the novelist must describe.

Boman Desai

I take the last line and I throw it as far as I can. And then I walk to it. It's as simple as that.

Mark Helprin
on writing fiction

Place conspires with the artist. We are surrounded by our own story, we live and move in it. It is through place that we put out roots.

Eudora Welty

Everything used in this book is from public sources. The stuff that's available publicly is far more frightening than a lot of people realize.

Tom Clancy

The sexual matter must be integral to the action and characters and only as explicit as is appropriate to the story, not just stuck in by the author because of a mistaken belief that every book has to be jazzed up with a "hot" scene or two.

Ruth B. Cavin

The travel writer's task has become harder—to find the choice and the special out there amidst the treating quotidian and the shrinking alien, and to keep on finding it for two or three hundred pages.

Robert Eisner

You never know what you will learn till you start writing. Then you discover truths you didn't know existed.

Anita Brookner

Plots, somewhat like themes, develop of themselves if the writer has a story clearly in mind.

A. B. Guthrie, Jr.

If the stuff you're writing is not for yourself, it won't work.

Stephen King

Don't confuse "care" with "like." It isn't necessary for the reader to like the main characters in your novel; you might want the reader actually to dislike them. But you do want the reader to care.

Novelist Jill M. Morgan

When I sit down to write a story, I'm not saying to myself I'm going to write a Jewish story. Just like when a Frenchman builds a house in France, he doesn't say he's going to build a French house. He's going to build a house for his wife and children, a convenient house. Since it's built in France, it comes out French.

Isaac Bashevis Singer

Nothing is more depressingly snobbish than the idea that good writing can't be popular; but high sales are not necessarily a proof of literary excellence.

John Mortimer

When I write a story for children...I'm seeking to tell a story from my heart...with the hope that it will speak to another heart.

Katherine Paterson

You don't create something so that people can draw conclusions, but to enlarge them, just as you have been enlarged by the experience of making it up.

Novelist Jim Harrison

A brilliant idea may come to mind, but then you find yourself writing garbage, and you don't know how to get past it. Well, you do it by writing and writing, but the process seems so defeating: Everything you write looks like more garbage. For me, slowly it got better.

Poet Stephen Dobyns

When you have a reasonable success, I think what some writers do is try to produce something they think will please people again. Not just for financial reasons, but because they feel this obligation to their publisher and readers. I think you've got to try and rest that and remember that the only obligation is to your imagination.

Charles Palliser
author of Quincunx

When I write, I consider my life to be at stake; the values that help me to measure it, and the moments, memories, and emotions of it that I cherish—the people, therefore, whose presence in it makes me want to keep experiencing my life—all are at risk when I work.

Novelist Frederick Busch

I think it's dangerous to be a serious writer. Not in the sense that you are tempted to take chemicals or cut off your ears, but that as a serious writer, you drive yourself. You go to dark places so that you can get there, steal the trophy, and get out.

Frederick Busch

Wide reading and a good mind will take an author far. But passion has to kick in somewhere.

Laura Shapiro

The best characters in fiction reveal themselves slowly, taking on a life so real they begin to live beyond their novels.

Gail Caldwell

Some novels are still whodunits, but most of us write whydunits: What drives a person to kill someone else?

Robert Richardson
British crime fiction writer

One cannot make up stories; one can only retell in new ways the stories one has already heard.

Carolyn G. Heilbrun

I don't know all the certain words to word it.

Rapper Vanilla Ice
on why he used a collaborator to write his autobiography

Part of the challenge of what I write is...in demonstrating that even the quietest lives can be as complex and rich, as joyous, conflicted and anguished, as other, seemingly more dramatic lives.

Richard Nicholls

8

SPORTS

I'd have scored higher on SAT but I was on steroids and kept breaking my pencil.

From a cartoon by **Cochran**

I can deal with the losses. It's the losing I can't handle.

Expos manager Tom Runnels

You never see anybody yelling at the horse.

Jockey Eddie Delahoussaye
objecting to the abuse that fans heap on members
of his profession

The responsibility to bring athletics into a sincere relationship to the intellectual life of the college rests squarely on the shoulders of the president and faculty.

One conclusion of an 18 month, $2 million study by the
Knight Commission

"Fame is fleeting, respect is everlasting." If you work hard and trade your values on and off the ice, you earn people's respect.

Former Toronto Mapleleaf Lanny Arnold

I don't believe women belong where men are dressing and I don't believe that men belong where women are dressing.

Yankee pitcher Scott Sanderson
on his refusal to give interviews in the locker room
if female reporters are present

A National Collegiate Atheletic Association survey found that white student-athletes are twice as likely as their Black counterparts to graduate from college within five years.

Reporter Mark Rogowsky

The 1993 Florida Marlins are going to smell worse fresh than other fish do after a week.

Palm Beach Post Columnist Dave George

There's no mystique there. They should burn it down.

Tigers manager Sparky Anderson
on Boston's Fenway Park

I'd like to blow up Tiger Stadium. That cat box around home plate is six inches deep in kitty litter. That Velcro grass in the infield is six inches deep. They doctor their field. It's idiotic for him to complain about ball parks.

Red Sox third baseman Wade Boggs
responding to Anderson's comments

May is National Physical Fitness and Sports Month, as well as National Arthritis Month, Mental Health Month, National High Blood Pressure Month, and Older Americans Month.

According to the National Exercise for Life Institute

Play golf with Toby.

A golf instruction book for kids

College athletic programs should offer financial help to high schools. High school athletics are on the decline because of severe budget cuts. In many school districts across the country, students must pay to play sports.

Richard McHugh

Giamatti didn't go through half the stress that I went through, may God rest his soul. I liked him. We both cared about the game, loved the game, and worried about it.

Pete Rose
on baseball Commissioner Bart Giamatti

The National Center for Catastrophic Sports Injury Research, which has been monitoring the frequency and severity of football injuries on sandlots and in schools, colleges, and professional leagues since 1965, announced for the first time in 60 years, no player died from a football-related injury last season.

According to "Sports Illustrated"

When Lyle Alzado was using steroids 20 years ago, like he says, there was no information about the dangers and side effects. But people who do it now, it is not tragic. It's dumb.

Joe Greene
former defensive tackle

You have to watch your language. You have to turn your four letter words into five letters.

Glenn Wilson
Commentator, and former outfielder

What today means is that I've made the cut, I'm on the team. Now I have the honor of playing alongside the greatest heroes to ever play the game.

John Hannah
on his induction into the Pro Football Hall of Fame

Most skiers who break a leg in France break a left leg while most who break a leg while skiing in this country break a right leg.

L. M. Boyd

The inflatable AirFLEX mitt—a new baseball glove that features a tiny air pump that molds the mitt to the wearer's hand.

*Developed by **Spalding***

Baseball is the belly button of society. Straighten out baseball and you'll straighten out the rest of the world.

Former pitcher Bill (Spaceman) Lee

One has to know more than sports to be successful and live in society...It's not about winning games—it's about winning the game of life.

Former football player Jim Hester

Play bald!

Yanks KO mane man

Doo or Die

Titles from articles on Don Mattingly's resistance to getting a haircut

One reason professional tennis players can outlast other people on the court is their blood. Each player has as much as 2 liters more blood...which carry oxygen and nutrients to the athlete's muscles and dispel excess heat.

*According to **Dr. Ethan Nadel***

Lose the wet look. In L.A. slick hair means culture. In New York, it means your late uncle is buried under Giant's Stadium.

Journalist Rick Bonnell
to new New York Knick's coach Pat Riley

About 20 million Americans participate in some form of hiking, camping, backpacking, mountain biking, or related activity.

According to "Outdoor Retailing"

THE BUSINESS OF SPORTS

There's going to come a time where I think the greed of athletes is going to destroy all sports.

Kansas City Royals star George Brett
who makes an estimated 2 million dollars a year

You have a far greater chance of success if you spend money than if you don't. But it is not guaranteed.

Oakland A's general manager Sandy Alderson
on big player salaries

Money is the driving force in sports. If NBC tells Notre Dame to kick off at 3, all they ask is, "a.m. or p.m.?"

ESPN commentator Beano Cook

There is only one winner in professional boxing. I have never known a promoter suffering from punch-drunkenness or brain-damage.

James Callaghan

Being No.1 only means something when the alumni write the checks.

Keith Jackson

Average salary for NFL starters:

1. Quarterback	$1.25 million
2. Running back	$666,000
3. Wide receiver	$494,000
4. Linebacker	$494,000
5. Defensive line	$444,000

According to the NFL Players Association

Talking about baseball, there is one thing I want to complain about. I think they have nearly destroyed the game by putting those goddamn big television screens out in the center field....I'm sure it must affect the players, too.

Dr. James M. Buchanan
winner in 1986 of the Nobel Prize in Economics, in Spy

Magic Johnson competing in the MBA finals was asked by Pepsi to do the "Pepsi Summer Chill Out" hand gesture after any dunks that he might perform.

According to USA Today

Roger "Rocket" Clemens became the highest-paid baseball player ever by signing a four-year contract for $21.5 million with the Boston Red Sox. Assuming the Rocket stays healthy for the duration of his contract, he will receive in excess of $1,000 per pitch, including foul balls.

Kevin Kerr

The all-time largest signing bonuses offered for baseball players:

1. Brien Taylor, New York Yankees $1.6 million
2. Shawn Green, Toronto Blue Jays $700,000
3. Mike Kelly, Atlanta Braves $575,000

According to "Baseball America"

Congratulations, Denver. With the addition of major-league baseball, you now have three of the most worthless franchises in all of professional sports.

Denver Post *columnist Woody Paige*

It's a cold business—a cold, cold business. And its even colder in New England.

Dallas Cowboy Eugene Lockhart
on being traded to the New England Patriots

Communist East Germany fed steroids to virtually all its Olympic track and field stars throughout the 1980s, at a time when it dominated many events, according to confidential government documents.

Marc Fisher

When you don't fit into the computer on things like size, speed, and vertical jump, you are basically a reject. You are a possession receiver. A possession receiver is a polite term for slow.

Tom Waddle
Bears wide receiver

NFL owners should quit worrying about silly things like players celebrating in the end zone. They should give them something to really celebrate. Get rid of those artificial surfaces.

O. J. Simpson

Top baseball salaries:

Roger Clemens, Red Sox	$5,380,250
Jose Canseco, Oakland As	$4,700,000
Tony Gwynn, Padres	$4,083,333
Darryl Strawberry, Dodgers	$4,050,000
Don Mattingly, Yankees	$3,860,000

Associated Press

Oldtimer: The trouble with you younger players is the game is just another day at the office to you.

From a cartoon by **Cochran**

If you're a pro coach, NFL stands for "Not For Long."

Jerry Glanville
Atlanta Falcon coach

Being an umpire is like being a king. It prepares you for nothing.

Ron Luciano
Retired American League umpire

Lou Gehrig's 1938 New York Yankees flannel road jersey fetched a record $220,000 at the Treasures of the Diamond auction.

Michael McCabe

A multicolored baseball card depicting Honus Wagner, the great shortstop for the Pittsburgh Pirates, was sold for $451,000 to Wayne Gretzsky, the Los Angeles King's hockey great and Bruce McNall, the club's owner.

Reported in **The New York Times**

New baseball slogans:

We're a Major League Good Time—Cleveland Indians
You Gotta Be There—Milwaukee Brewers
Let Yourself Go—Houston Astros
Dancing in the Seats—St. Louis Cardinals
Sounds Like a Good Time—San Diego Padres

As reported by **The Sporting News**

I think we've been overstaffed for years. You see more guys on the bench with suits and ties than players.

Coach Dale Brown
on the size of coaching staffs in the NCAA

Everyone has different tastes in cars, women and food, and it's the same with players.

Willis Reed
New Jersey Mets Vice President

In the never-ending quest to produce something that somebody somewhere will find collectible, NFL Properties has produced a series on current and former players and their wives. That is, their current wives.

Columnist Tom FitzGerald

Somehow, I don't mind being such a bad golfer when I'm at Pebble Beach. Because when I send a ball flying into a sand trap there, at least I know it's going first class.

Comedian Flip Wilson

The NFL realizes it's in the entertainment business, not the military. You'll no longer see 5-yard penalties for high-fives and throwing footballs in the stands.

Lesley Visser

Since 1919, no one has ever had to pay a Chicago baseball team to lose.

Scott Simon

It's obvious that teams are preparing for free agency. They want longer contracts with their better players, even if it costs more money. They know that soon they won't be able to keep good players against their will.

East Bay lawyer/agent John Maloney

Back then, if you had a sore arm, the only people concerned were you and your wife. Now it's you, your wife, your agent, your investment counselor, your stockbroker, and your publisher.

Jim Bouton
on how baseball has changed

He has a contractural and constitutional right to fight. If we were to postpone the fight, he'd be punished without due process.

Boxing promotor Lou Duva
on the Mike Tyson-Evander Holyfield fight

THE GAME

Football is so barbaric. Sometimes I wonder what I was thinking by playing it. I feel almost like I escaped from boot camp...With Seattle, I had my shoulder operated on and I was back out there the next week.

Brian Bozworth
Former Seattle SeaHawk linebacker

For years, [the Bengals] drafted kids that looked like Tarzan and played like Jane.

Former Bengal Cris Collinsworth

Most teams are copying the Giants' smash-mouth football. Scoring is lower, but they're getting back to the way football use to be played.

Terry Bradshaw

In a way, you have something to look forward to only if you lose. After we won the Super Bowl, I looked over at Charlie Waters and whispered, "But who do we play next?" When you win the Super Bowl—I hesitate to say it—you're depressed.

Ex-Dallas Cowboy Cliff Harris

The record says we're mediocre. We were mediocre the year before, and the year before that. We've only been able to be competitive with mediocre football teams. I'm not saying that, the record is saying that.

Pittsburgh Steeler's coach Mean Joe Greene

They call us predictable and conservative, but I know one thing. Power wins football games. It's not always the fanciest way but it can win games.

Bill Parcells
Superbowl winning coach of the New York Giants

[Football is] the greatest game that's ever been and ever will be, as long as people who were trying to sell it as a business don't destroy it. It's getting close.

John Hannah
Former New England Patriots offensive lineman

The NFL has done a lot of dumb things, but nothing dumber than fining players who celebrate when they score a touchdown.

Larry King

It's like golf. The five-yard line is the green, and the end zone is the trap.

Philadelphia punter Jeff Feagles

If I can get away with it, I'll try to do something to make an opposing player mad. I might hit 'em, say something to 'em out of the way. It's all in the game. If you can't take it, you don't need to play.

Clemson defensive tackle Brentson Buckner

I think one of the greatest events in sports would be a college football play-off. It would dwarf the Super Bowl. No doubt in my mind.

Jim Valvano
North California State basketball coach

Sometimes quarterbacks get hit. But that's the price you pay for getting your name in the paper and having all the pretty girls hanging around you.

Florida coach Steve Spurrier

I'll take my job over [my wife's] job [of raising our children] because hers is tougher.

Quarterback Joe Montana

Football isn't a game of numbers. It's a game of heart, of playing your butt off and having your teammates play their butts off.

Cal quarterback Mike Pawlawski

The Patriots are sending their game films to "America's Funniest Home Videos."

Announcer Dave Coombs
on the New England Patriots' 1-15 season

They have a good defense but we made it look awesome. They played well but I haven't figured out if they played that good or we played that bad.

Pat Ryan

A back-up quarterback can't take a team to the Super Bowl, but I don't know that I don't believe he couldn't do it.

Sportscaster John Madden
on New York Giants' substitute quarterback Jeff Hostetler

The problem you have sometimes is you don't have an opportunity to miss tackles. We had the opportunity. We just flat missed them. But we can fix that.

Tampa Bay coach Richard Williamson

The greens are so long that you have to take into consideration the curvature of the earth when making a putt.

English golfer David Feherty
at the Ryder Cup

I used to play golf with a guy who cheated so badly that he once had a hole-in-one and wrote down 0 on the score card.

PGA golfer Bob Brue

Fifty percent of the fairways we play on today are better than 90 percent of the greens we played 30 years ago.

Senior golfer Jim Ferree

I was three over—one over a house, one over a patio, and one over a swimming pool.

George Brett
on his performance in the Bob Hope Classic

Condolences to Beth Daniel, who pulled out of the LPGA duMaurier Classic because her dog died. I know. I couldn't believe it, either.

Dan McGrath

When a pro hits [the ball] left to right, it's called a fade. When an amateur hits it left to right, it is called a slice.

Professional golfer Peter Jacobsen

Sixty-two percent of golfers who hit the green an average of two times a week have sustained some type of injury from the game. The most common cause of injury is excessive play.

According to "The Johns Hopkins Medical Letter"

Anyone who likes golf on television would enjoy watching the grass grow on the greens.

Andy Rooney

If you see an alligator basking on the edge of a water hazard and you are a club's length from him, the best thing to do is to take the penalty stroke.

Dennis David
of the Florida game commission

Our pitching could be better than I think it will be.

Detroit Tiger manager Sparky Anderson
on his team's 1991 prospects

It was voodoo coaching. The Giants employed sophisticated computer readouts which covered every conceivable aspect of a player's performance, and then diluted it with quack psychology—like Reagan and astrology.

Baseball player Warren Cromartie
on playing for the Tokyo Giants

The Mets are so mismanaged these days, that you can't be sure which Harrelson is in charge, Buddy or Woody.

Columnist Tom Verducci

If it had been raining soup, we'd have had forks.

Tom Watt
Toronto Maple Leaf's coach, on their dismal season

They remind me of a National League team.

Tommy Hutton
on the Toronto Blue Jays

The chances of pitching a no-hitter are 1 in 676 games; the chances of a rookie pitching a no-hitter are 1 in 7,455 games.

Elias Sports Bureau

In 1971, I had 17 saves and got a raise. In 1985, I had 17 saves and got released.

Relief pitcher Rollie Fingers
on the evolution of the relief pitcher's role

Coaching that team is like having a window seat on the Hindenberg.

Bob Plager
on the Toronto Maple Leafs

I laid it in there, hoping he'd hit it hard at someone. He did, but the someone he hit it hard at was sitting in the seats.

Pitcher Bob Walk

The beautiful thing about this is everybody contributed.

Steve Smith
manager of the Peninsula Pilots baseball team, after the team's record 20th straight loss

It's not a matter of life and death. It's more important than that.

Lou Duva
trainer of Evander Holyfield, on upcoming fight against Mike Tyson

The point is not to get in the ring and beat the crap out of someone. For women, boxing teaches coordination, balance, hand-eye reflexes, endurance, and to be aware of your body and your space.

Lynn Snowden
on women's growing interest in boxing for fitness

You can sum up this sport in two words: You never know.

Trainer Lou Duva
on boxing

NBL finals have become so big and overblown with all the hype that sometimes you wish you could just go to a gym somewhere with no refs, no TV and no crowds and just play and have a good time.

Earvin "Magic" Johnson

In good light and in fair weather, when it comes up and takes the dry fly, the trout is a wonderful thing. But it is not enough...There are springs to see, and the shadows of small wild trout flicking across the bed of a side creek...Every year, fishing takes me farther from the river.

M. R. Montgomery

In a final at Wimbledon, tactics are not that important; it's who has the stronger mind, and it was [Michael Stich] day. It hit me during the match that if he is not going to make big mistakes, I'm not going to win.

Boris Becker
who lost the Wimbledon title to Michael Stich

If you see European hockey, there are no fights, and it's boring.

Ed Johnston
Hartford Whalers general manager, in defense of NHL brawls

The top amateur sports:

1. Aerobics
2. Backpacking
3. Baseball

4. Basketball

5. Bike riding

According to the National Sporting Goods Association

The number of Americans throwing darts has grown 73.4 percent since 1985.

According to the National Sporting Goods Association

THE PLAYERS

At the top of the runway, I went over the jump in my mind. I tried to be oblivious to the crowd. I told myself I wasn't as fast as Carl [Lewis] so I had to feel not just fast but springy. When I land, I let out a yell. I'm not sure why. Then when I landed, I still had that aggression, so I let out another yell.

Broad jumper Mike Powell
breaking the longest-standing and most venerated record in track
and field, Bob Beamon's 1986 29 feet, 2 1/2 inches jump

My feeling is I still have some golf left in me. And when I spend time working at it, I have gotten results. My biggest problem is I don't have time to work at it.

Golfer Jack Nicklaus

She should have known that to a tennis star, love means nothing.

Stephen J. Lee
on the palimony suit between Judy Nelson
and Martina Navratilova

Probably 80 to 90 percent of athletes don't rest enough. They tend to overtrain and get the injuries that end their careers. I take lots of naps, and I dedicate at least two days a week to sleeping late. Sometimes I take two naps a day.

Olympic hurdler Edwin Moses

Roger Maris finally got baseball's single-season home run record to himself. An eight-man committee on statistical accuracy voted unanimously to drop the mythical "asterisk" associated with Maris' 61 home runs, formally eliminating Babe Ruth's 60 homers from the record books.

Associated Press

The wait had a lot to do with his career. He gives his all to basketball, and he finds it hard to share himself. But he's reached a point in his career that he can share of himself, and give time to marriage and a family.

Cookie Kelly
who recently married Magic Johnson, on their long courtship

I don't have one bad memory from my 13 seasons. I don't have a memory at all for that matter.

Retiring defensive end Al (Bubba) Parker

I feel like when I'm on the court, that's my court. Especially at home. I feel like I can do no wrong. Even when I'm away, I feel like it's my court. Like if I want to slide from halfcourt to the base line, I could do it. That's how I feel. Like I'm bulletproof.

Tim Hardaway
of the Golden State Warriors

Boz makes Arnold Schwarzennegger look like Laurence Olivier, and Sylvester Stallone is Rex Harrison by comparison.

Steve Kelley
on Brian Bosworth's acting debut

If you can miss getting up in the morning and running into a wall, I miss playing football.

Former linebacker Brian Bosworth

Boz hasn't lived long enough to write a book. At least I'm 54 years old. He's too young. I tell people, hell, he hasn't been masturbating five years.

Former football coach Barry Switzer
on Brian Bosworth's foray into writing

You don't hesitate with Michael or you'll end up on some poster in a gift shop someplace.

Felton Spencer
on defending against Michael Jordan

[Michael Jordan] goes up, stops for a cup of coffee, looks over the scenery, then follows through with a tomahawk jam.

Basketball great Bob Cousy
commenting on Michael Jordan's extraordinary "hang time"

Today, the biggest decisions I make aren't related to the heavyweight title. They are whether I visit McDonald's, Burger King, Wendy's, or Jack-in-the-Box.

Prizefighter George Foreman

He's not all that bad. If you dig deep, dig real deep, dig, dig, dig, dig deep, deep, go all the way to China, I'm sure you'll find there's a nice guy there.

George Foreman
on fellow heavyweight Mike Tyson

Good thing Mike Tyson didn't have a network kiddie show, or he'd never work again.

Bernie Lincicome

If television ever deserved live access to a trial it will be when and if that model of grace and charm Mike Tyson ever comes before the bar of justice. Bet Don King is thinking pay-per-view this very instant.

Phil Jackman
of the Baltimore Evening Sun

I don't try to intimidate anybody before a fight. That's nonsense. I intimidate people by hitting them.

Boxer Mike Tyson

There's nothing on the planet that can stop me from confronting the world, or stop me from living my life. I train hard, then I go out and have fun and party. I am not going to stay in the house because of a [legal] situation.

Boxer Mike Tyson

I know you're really a transvestite and really like me...I'm gonna make you my girlfriend.

Mike Tyson
to Razor Ruddock during a press conference announcing
their rematch

But when I make a big hit, the world around me goes silent. I don't hear a thing. My eyes close, roll back into my head and begin to tear. Oftentimes snot sprays out of my nostrils, covering my mouth and cheeks—and squirting on anybody nearby—and my chin strap lodges under my nose. My ears slowly begin to ring, and my brain goes blank. The wind gets knocked out of my lungs and I gasp for air.

Former 49ers star Ronnie Lott

I think they didn't vote for me [to the All-Star team] because I make so much money and they didn't think I performed up to [their standards]. It is sad the fans are caught up in that. That's why I get booed at home.

Oakland A's Jose Canseco

I am being treated better by the fans on the road than I am by the fans at home. I have asked my agent to...explore (my) playing elsewhere.

Oakland A's star Jose Canseco

Are you kidding? You hear the way they boo me here. They'd be throwing grenades at me there.

Oakland Athletics' outfielder Jose Canseco
on the possibility of playing for the new National League
franchise in Miami

For a bunch of guys who would rather pass kidney stones than a basketball, it was pretty amazing.

Atlanta Hawks coach Bob Weiss
after a game in which his own players worked well as a team

I don't know if we'll ever see his full potential, what he could've been. But you need to recognize that even an 80 percent Bo Jackson is still above the rest of the field.

Reggie Jackson

No, but they gave me one, anyway.

Los Angeles Laker Elden Campbell
when asked if he had earned his degree from Clemson

[Pete] Rose was such a model prisoner that they're thinking of retiring his number.

Columnist Allan Malamud

I had a coarse personality at times when I played. I may need some time to show that I've matured.

Reggie Jackson

The last legacy of the 1991 [Daytona 500] race may be the fact that Richard By-Gosh Petty, Loving Legend, competed while wearing a helmet-cam.

Larry Guest

They call me the Hawk because [my opponents] are chicken and are running from me.

Boxer Julian Jackson

Lou Gehrig represents many things that are good in our society. He was famous for his unfortunate demise, for the way he faced his disease.

Michael McCabe

Average major-league baseball player's salary: 1. 1990 $580,000 2. 1991 $890,844.

L. Boyd

The truth is, on the bench, he is not the big loudmouth we see in public. He's intense and shrewd, and his approach is kind of delightful. So many managers live with computers and statistics and have reduced

baseball to a parade of numbers. [Tommy] Lasorda doesn't know from
any of that. He still manages by the seat of his pants.

Lowell Cohn

[Forty Niners defensive lineman Kevin Fagan] is the only guy in the
National Football League who does not wear a jockstrap. He just wears
his regular underwear. Fagan claims that if you wear a jockstrap it
will cut the natural flow of testosterone into your system and therefore
you will be weaker.

Frank Cooney

If I had to choose between my wife and my putter, well, I'd miss her.

Gary Player

Many times Billy and I would just hang around the clubhouse...Billy
and I kept water pistols in our locker, and some nights Billy would
fill his pistol and begin squirting water at me. Then I would get my
pistol and fill it with water and I'd start shooting at him. This would
go on for hours.

Baseball great Mickey Mantle
on his relationship with Billy Martin

[Jackie Slater] is living proof that they played football in prehistoric
days. I've even seen the calluses on his feet where he use to stop his
car like Fred Flintstone.

Jim Everett
L.A. Rams' quarterback, on the Rams' 37-year-old offensive tackle

He'd knock a guy down at second base and pick him up and say, "I
love you."

Baseball player Brett Butler
about the kind of baseball player Jesus Christ would be

He looks like Rocket, he talks like Rocket, he's even got some of the
same facial expressions. He's slightly faster than Rocket and more experienced coming in at wide receiver. But I do not expect him to be
another Rocket.

Lou Holtz
on recruit Mike Miller

It was a very interesting weekend.

Jim Ryun
commenting on the race 25 years ago (July 17, 1966) in which he
was the first person to break the four minute mile

A pitcher is the only man in baseball who can probably look on the ball as being his instrument, his accomplice. He is the only player who is granted the privilege of making offensive plans.

Roger Angell

If all I'm remembered for is being a good basketball player, then I've done a bad job with the rest of my life.

Isiah Thomas

My sister beat me, my wife beat me in a race, I just hope my daughter doesn't grow up to beat her dad, too.

Triple jump star Al Joyner

Believe me, if a chemist announces this afternoon that there is a magic ingredient in leather that will enable you to run one tenth of a second faster in the 40, this evening, 1,000 athletes will be hunkered down in their closets, munching on Italian shoes.

Tony Kornheiser
of The Washington Post

Writers like to say they've seen a lot of players come and go. I've seen a lot of writers come and go.

Twenty-five season veteran Nolan Ryan

Nolan Ryan is the all-time major league strike-out leader, with 5,474 strike-outs. He's also the leader in walks with 2,680.

According to USA **Today**

I love it when I hear the media describe someone 44 years of age as mature and well-seasoned.

Vice President Dan Quayle
on Nolan Ryan

Three things [make pitcher Nolan Ryan's longevity possible]. First, genetics. Second, work ethic. I'm told most athletes get 70 to 90 percent of their potential. He gets close to 100 percent. Third, mechanics. He's as close to mechanically efficient as you can get.

Dr. Gene Coleman
Fitness expert

I think genetics play the biggest role.

Nolan Ryan

Bo Jackson, asked when he might be ready to play baseball: "Bo don't know everything."

Tom Fitzgerald

If my doctor says I can play, believe me, you'll see me out there getting the [guts] kicked out of me, or me kicking the [guts] out of somebody else.

Bo Jackson
being quoted by USA Today

I'm running and jumping in dirt. When you break it down, who really cares about that?

Mike Powell
on why success won't change him after breaking
the long jump world record

I'm between the twilight and the no-light of my career.

32-year-old pole vaulter Billy Olsen

[Lyle Alzado] thought by taking steroids, he would have an advantage over his opponents, and so be able to beat them. That isn't winning, it's cheating.

John Paul White

I'm going to show the whole world that age 40 is not a death sentence. People are putting me down, not because I can't punch but because of my age. Well, there's going to be an overhaul in this country.

Boxer George Foreman
before his comeback fight with Evander Holyfield

I'm going to eat him like he's a porkchop sandwich.

Boxer George Foreman
before his comeback fight with Evander Holyfield

The top five highest-paid athletes in the world:

1. Boxer Evander Holyfield   Total income $60.5 million
2. Boxer Mike Tyson   Total income $31.5 million
3. Basketball player Michael Jordan Total Income $16.0 million
4. Boxer George Foreman   Total Income $14.5 million
5. Auto racer Ayrton Senna   Total Income $13.0 million

According to "Forbes"

I think a 45-year-old man doing underwear commercials is even more amazing.

Bob Matthews
on pitcher Jim Palmer's comeback attempt

If I've lost a step, it's a step a lot of other guys never had.

Indianapolis Colts Eric Dickerson
on his apparently fading ability

I'm just glad to get off 399. It sounds like something you'd purchase in a discount store.

Dave Winfield of the Angels
on hitting the 400th home run of his career

The only thing I'm doing different is I'm not doing anything different.

Tony Glynn

Football gives me the spotlight to tell people that Indians are not Hollywood stereotypes, circling the wagons and killing people. I want to enlighten the white population about Native Americans and help some of my own people at the same time.

Offensive tackle Jim Warner

Dad taught me everything I know. Unfortunately he didn't teach me everything he knows.

Al Unser, Jr.

I don't think because I can dunk a basketball, they should want me to be a role model. I know drug dealers who can dunk the basketball.

Philadelphia 76ers' Charles Barkley

I'm not hanging it up. I still feel I have some really good tennis in me. I just don't know how much of the heart is left.

Martina Navratilova
after her Wimbledon loss to teenager Jennifer Capriati

I deserved every hit...Of course, there were some close ones, but that happens. Sure, there was pressure near the end, but other things had to be overcome. Remember, we were winning in Yankee Stadium, and that meant so often I only had eight innings a game.

Joe DiMaggio
on the fifthieth anniversary (July 17, 1991) of his
56-game hitting streak

I just go out and do the best that I can do.

Rookie pitcher Wilson Alvarez
on throwing a no-hitter in his second major league start

Maybe I have lost a step, but I had a few to lose.

Roy Green
veteran wide receiver of the Cleveland Browns

Hell, I make 10 times more money now than I ever did as a player, but it's not so much fun. In fact, I'd go back to making $100,000 a year in a second if I could just play ball again.

Yankee legend Mickie Mantle

You know that old saying, "No man is an island?" Stanley comes close.

Orlando Magic general manager Pat Williams
on 7-foot, 300-pound draft choice Stanley Roberts

Everybody knows you're a recovering alcoholic—how did it feel when your teammates poured all that beer over you?

Question posed by a local sportscaster
to Montreal's Dennis Martinez after he pitched a perfect game

This is a guy who likes to complain a lot about not playing, but that's what he does best—not play.

Blue Jays general manager Pat Gillick
on California Angels' Mike Marshall

He had terrible mechanics as a hitter.

New Hall of Famer Rod Carew
on Babe Ruth

The only thing I know for sure about Joe Montana's condition is that he's not suffering from Pee-wee Herman Elbow.

Mike Cannon

It was the best he's ever made me look bad.

Lonnie Smith
on his 0-4-4 performance against pitcher Bruce Hurst

Three things happened over time. I think people began to look at me with different eyes. I was bad out there. It would be stupid to deny that. But people began to get a sense that that helped me play better tennis, give them a better show. I got married and became a father and that changed me to a certain point. And McEnroe came along. After that, just about anything I did was going to be OK.

Tennis star Jim Connors

The atmosphere was great. The fans helped me. They gave me power. I felt very fast and very strong.

Sergei Bubka
on breaking the 20-foot pole vault mark

I never perceived myself to be the big star. I'm only one of nine guys. I think it is good to think that way.

Baseball great Cal Ripken, Jr.

Fueled by my own anger, which I seemed to draw from an inexhaustible source, I watched almost as a spectator as my body operated beyond

my control. I wasn't just aching for a fist fight, I was begging for it.
I longed for the release.

> *Bodybuilder Samuel Fussell*
> *describing steroid rage*

To tell you the truth, there was a second when I didn't know if it
was me down there. Did I do it or not? It was like I was dreaming.

> *Montreal Expo pitcher Dennis Martinez*
> *after he became the 15th pitcher in major-league history to throw*
> *a perfect game retiring 27 consecutive hitters*

At 30, the sentence is the same for all athletes: "You are finished."
But I am not dead! It's the beginning of my life.

> *Tennis ace Yannick Noah*

We've got guys that don't hear as well. They don't listen. Kenny's
attentive; he's real smart.

> *Broncos defensive coordinator Wade Phillips*
> *talking about deaf rookie Kenny Walker*

There's adjustments that I have to make, but there's nothing out there
that I don't want to do.

> *Former Giants pitcher Dave Dravecky*
> *recuperating from having his cancerous throwing arm*
> *and shoulder amputated*

9

ENTERTAINMENT

At Walt Disney World on an average day: 148 pairs of sunglasses are turned into the lost and found; 1,013 Mouse Ear hats are sold; 1,000 bandaids are dispensed; 43,836 packages of ketchup are used.

According to **Walt Disney World**

Amenities that are necessities in celebrity homes: Electric gates, his-and-hers bathrooms (with bidet, sunken tub, Jacuzzi, stall shower, sauna and working fireplace), tennis courts, swimming pool, gym, walk-in closets and housekeeping quarters with Jacuzzi in maid's room.

Elaine Young
Beverly Hills real estate agent

Pending a public hearing and final approval from the judge, each of the 7 million U.S. consumers who bought the album will be entitled to cash rebates of $3 per CD, $2 per tape or LP, or $1 per single. Anyone who attended a Milli Vanilli concert (and can provide proof) will be entitled to 5 percent of the ticket price, and those who bought T-shirts or other merchandise will be listed as contributors to BMG's promised $250,000 donation to various charities.

The judgment on the Milli Vanilli fraud

One umbrella is not art. What is art is 3,100 umbrellas in two countries.

Artist Christo Javacheff
on his "Umbrellas" art project

If it wasn't on the specific day the wedding was canceled, it was mutual shortly thereafer. There was a mutual appreciation for the fact that it didn't happen.

Actor Kiefer Sutherland
on the cancellation of his wedding to actress Julia Roberts

In 1990, the average VCR household spent $102.33 on videocassette rentals and $66.67 on purchasing tapes.

According to Veronis, Suhler & Associates

Art is moral passion married to entertainment. Moral passion without entertainment is propaganda, and entertainment without moral passion is television.

Rita Mae Brown

Favorite animated character among adults:

1. Bugs Bunny
2. Mickey Mouse
3. Roadrunner
4. Donald Duck
5. Garfield the Cat

According to a Gallup Poll

You can [sleep around] one million times and it's never going to alter your psyche in a significant way unless it's a spiritual thing.

Actor Woody Harrelson

Last year, I was thinking about becoming a nun. It came at a moment when men really pissed me off, and living away from the world in a convent seemed simpler. But it was a brief thought.

Actress Laura Dern

COUNTRY MUSIC

It's easy to see why America loves country music. Country music loves America.

George Bush

You say it best when you say nothing at all.

Line from a country music song

(For Every Inch I've Laughed) I've Cried a Mile.

Song title

I'm not sure anybody under 29 understands a country lyric. You need to have been knocked around.

Lon Helton

Two of a Kind Workin' on a Full House.

Song title

She was All Over Him (I Guess She's All Over Me).

Song Title

Came Home at Two with a Ten and Woke up at Ten with a Two.

Line from a country song

You Done Me Wrong (And That Ain't Right)

Song title

All I Can Be (Is a Sweet Memory).

Song title

Her Thinkin' I'm Doing Her Wrong (Ain't Doin' Me Right)

Song Title

What do you get when you play country music backwards. You get your girl back, your dog back, your pick-up back, and you stop drinking.

Louis E. Saaberdra

ENTERTAINERS ON ENTERAINING

The good old days were pretty damn good. I was short and fat with red hair and freckles, yet I took my entire high school cheerleading squad to the senior prom. By the time I was 15, I had raised millions of dollars for charity, hung out with movie stars, had my own table at my favorite restaurants, met the President, and most significant, seen Bianca Jagger's breasts. What kid could ask for more.

Danny Bonaduce
Former child star of "The Partridge Family

For years, Blacks had no choice but to watch Shakespeare or Beaver Cleaver and see the universal humanity in those white faces. There's no reason white audiences can't make the same imaginative leap today.

George Wolfe

[The fans] that scare me and my wife aren't the lookers in half T-shirts and nice ringers who come to the bus askin' where you're goin' later. It's the ones that know all the lyrics, who tell you how your music changed their life, how they played "The Dance" at their husband's funeral. You almost fall in love because of how they feel, but, as a married man, you move on.

Country singer Garth Brooks

I believe that our purpose is to inspire and, in some way, guide and heal the human race, of which we are all equal members.

Singer Sinead O'Connor

The only time she was a problem was when she gave me a big hug and kiss at the end of a workday—and that problem went away in about half an hour.

Director Blake Edwards
on actress Kim Basinger

Comedy is the blues for people who can't sing. You get on stage and fall down...people laugh. Pain's funny.

Chris Rock

What's the big deal about Jim Morrison, for instance? Why did they make a movie about him? Why is he is a rock martyr? The idiot drowned in a bathtub. Is that cool? I don't think so. It's a lot harder to stay alive and deal with it. And he couldn't even sing for shit. He OD'd—anybody can do that. That's pitiful.

Guitarist Joe Walsh

An article appeared in the July 2, 1991, edition of the *Globe* concerning, among others, Tom Selleck. By publishing the article, the *Globe* did not intend to express or imply that Tom Selleck is or ever was a homosexual, and the *Globe* apologizes to the extent that any statements made by any *Globe* editors concerning the article were construed to express or imply that Tom Selleck is or was a homosexual.

Globe
clarification of the Selleck article

Those people and organizations who insult me and hurt my family with these malicious lies will only serve to trivialize, defame, and ultimately bankrupt that which is noble in the gay movement...I am as proud of my sexual preference as those who happen to be gay are of theirs.

Actor Tom Selleck
in response to allegations made about his sexual preference
in the supermarket tabloid, Globe

It seems like some rite of passage for every actor to play a cop with a big gun. But I would be wary that I finally became a man by playing a cop. Actually, I'd rather play a Nazi transsexual in a buddy film.

John Cusack

The first "Terminator" was a very big stepping stone for me. It was then that Hollywood realized, "I think this guy can also be sold to the public with his clothes on."

Actor Arnold Schwarzenegger

Now I can pay for the house, but I don't ever get to see it.

Vince Gill

We'll go out on tour when the [new] album's hot, and it'll be our triumphant return. And if the album isn't hot, we can always pretend it's our triumphant return.

Singer Huey Lewis

Part of the reason is that most men who say that [I'm gay] want to jump into my pants. So they just think, "Well, she's gay. She don't want to be bothered. So she must be gay." It's something that happens to people in my position. I don't know why. You're either gay or on drugs.

Singer Whitney Houston

I think the pictures are nice. There's nothing lewd about them. They're like artsy-fartsy, topless, sort of T-shirt stuff. There's nothing that suggests "crotch anything," if you know what I mean.

Actress Linda Blair
about pictures of her in   Qui

I've been underexposed so long, I don't think I'm going to suffer from overexposure.

M.C. Hammer

I wouldn't do nudity in films. For me, personally...to act with my clothes on is a performance; to act with my clothes off is a documentary.

Actress Julia Roberts

The whole business has really gone right over and is going over a precipice and down, as far as doing good, tight material...[You] have to blow up heads and bodies and all sorts of other crap.

Jack Lemmon

THE MOVIES

Movie houses used to be called pleasure palaces, now they're more like combat zones.

Ruth Liney

Cannes is everything you hate about show biz packed into one small piece of time and real estate—the hustling, the lying, arrogance.

Judd Rose

Today, you couldn't get "2001" made, you couldn't get "Taxi Driver" made. It doesn't have enough violence.

Critic Roger Ebert

Seven bucks to see this movie? I saw "The Doors" live and it only cost me two!

Tom Henry

It's difficult being homosexual in life, but in cinema it's almost impossible. Heterosexuals have hogged the screen so much we've barely got space for a kiss left.

Director Derek Jarman

The kind of random violence...in films like "Total Recall"...confuses me and perplexes me. I really don't understand it. Violence in films today is so abstract. Horror films and the disemboweling of people. Maybe that satisfies a need in human beings that was satisfied by real blood just 2,000 years ago. I don't know what's happened to our society. I don't know why we have to see our entrails being dragged out. I don't get it.

Director Martin Scorsese

Subtlety doesn't play in some overseas markets. There's no language barrier in action-adventure because there's rarely any talking. You don't see many women in these films because women are verbal and subtle.

Movie executive on action films

In spite of what people may think, Black directors don't all have barbecues together on the weekends....We're as different as Scorsese and David Lynch and Rob Reiner, and nobody expects them to all know one another.

Filmmaker Mario Van Peebles

"Boyz N the Hood," the new movie about young black life in south central Los Angeles, has an antiviolence theme, but gang-related shootings at more than a dozen theaters around the nation have overshadowed its debut....Following the "Boyz N the Hood" premiere across the nation, one moviegoer had been killed and 31 wounded.

Charles C. Hardy

It wasn't the film [that caused violence]. It was the fact that a whole generation [of Black men] doesn't respect themselves, which makes it easier for them to shoot each other.

John Singleton
director of "Boyz N the Hood"

When I came up with the idea of "City Slickers," I was watching a television show, and I went, "Boink, cattle drive." I mean, I pretty much wrote the whole idea for the movie in about 35, 40 seconds.

Billy Crystal

By the end of 1991 there will have been more Black commercial films made than in the entire eighties decade.

Armond Waite

It started with the love affair with movies we all have, but gradually I became fascinated with the extraordinary effect movies can have, how they touch us at the deepest level, beyond consciousness; how they can be brilliant yet demonic, full of greatness and corruption at the same time.

Social critic Theodore Roszak

We are only usually allowed to see a certain type of Black woman depicted on screen. The hooker or the drug abuser....How can we keep telling the rest of America that we should be respected if we are portrayed like this.

Robin Givens

Black cinema is making well-made movies. The reason the public is coming to see Black cinema isn't because they're saying, "Hey, here's a Black movie." They're generating revenues because they're new and innovative movies.

Cuba Gooding, Jr.

Basically action and violence are the same thing. The question is a matter of style, a matter of degree, a matter of the kind of moral stance taken by the film, the contextualization of the violence....I think of "Terminator 2" as a violent movie about peace.

Director James Cameron

Chevy Chase continues his string of starring roles in bad movies. His latest is "Nothing But Trouble," which...must go down as one of the strangest pieces of junk ever turned out in Hollywood's heap of dud comedies—where a lot of other Chevy Chase movies also reside.

Reviewer Peter Stack

Movies released at year's end have a better shot at an Oscar than films released before September.

According to researchers from Eckerd College

MUSIC

Rock 'n' roll music is three chords, no matter what anybody says.

Harry Connick, Jr.

This whole urban rap thing needs to be pulled back some. The ghetto is being glorified, and there's nothing good about the ghetto except getting out of one.

Franklyn Ajaye

There is no question that heavy metal and rap lyrics can have a bad influence on children...They don't see any satire or irony in destructive lyrics. By itself, the music can't do anything. But if you throw in a lack of education, no sense of right or wrong, a negative self-image, and drug and alcohol abuse, you have the potential for danger.

Psychiatrist Robert B. Millman

Rap singer M.C. Hammer's new video, "Here Comes the Hammer," is hyped as the most expensive music video ever made. Production costs reportedly topped $1.4 million.

News correspondent Thomas D. Elias

The all-time record for gold albums by a male soloist:

1. Elvis Presley   32
2. Elton John   24
3. Neil Diamond   21

4. Bob Dylan   21
5. Kenny Rogers   20

*According to the **Recording Industry Association of America***

Soul is honesty. I sing to people about what matters....I express problems, there are tears when it's sad and smiles when it's happy.

Aretha Franklin

Efil4zaggin

Title of album (read it backwards) by N.W.A.

The reason this music came back is that you can't keep a good idea down for too long. If people stopped cooking food next year, how long would it be before someone said, "Wait a minute, didn't there use to be cuisine?"

*Jazz trumpeter Wynton Marsalis
on the resurgence of jazz*

The central message of most of these music videos is clear: Human happiness and fulfillment are experienced by becoming a sociopath and rejecting all responsibility.

Senator Robert Byrd

A Rembrandt rarely becomes available. When it does, there are many people who are determined to get it. I was determined.

*Virgin Records Chairman Richard Branson
on signing singer Janet Jackson for $32 million*

Back then, you couldn't even get signed if you sounded like someone else. Now, you can hardly get signed if you don't.

Veteran jazz pianist Joe Sample

Using dirty words to make hit records is not helping our youth. They hear garbage on the streets and at school, but they don't need to listen to it in music.

Bo Diddley

I try to say things in my music that men sometimes have difficulty saying to women.

Jeffrey Osborne

People buy emotion. That's helped me, because I've never been a great technician. I play with some heart and convey that to the listeners through the recording groves.

Guitarist Chet Atkins

ABOUT ENTERTAINERS

Entertainers with the highest incomes:

1.	Bill Cosby	$58,000,000
2.	New Kids on the Block	$54,000,000
3.	Kevin Costner	$50,000,000
4.	Oprah Winfrey	$42,000,000
5.	Johnny Carson	$30,000,000

As reported in "Forbes"

Michael Korda, whose new novel, *Curtain,* is about the stormy marriage of Laurence Olivier and Vivien Leigh, thinks that Olivier was the heel who may have destroyed his fragile wife when she learned of his alleged dalliance with Danny Kaye.

Columnist Frank Swertlow

He looks great and feels great, has lots of money, gives to good causes, is in love with his wife, races cars, is incredibly happy, and still has a face....After having dinner with him, I wanted to shoot myself.

Robert Redford
on Paul Newman

Kim Basinger is the most self-indulgent, dumb, most irritating person I've ever met. She's dumb as a shoe.

Jonathan Van Meter

When angels want to please God, they perform Bach. When they want to please themselves, they perform Mozart—and God puts his ear to the keyhole and listens.

David McDonald Broshar
on the bicentennial of Mozart's death

We never get sick of each other. That's how sick we are.

Roseanne Barr
on her relationship with husband Tom Arnold

Julia Roberts' career increasingly resembles Dolly Parton's: she does wonders at the supermarket checkout racks, but not necessarily at the box office.

Celia Brady

Everything that happened to me happened by mistake. I don't believe in fate. It's luck, timing, and accident.

Merv Griffin

I don't like Vanilla Ice, because he's too arrogant and talks too much shit. He says he's street. He ain't from no street—what street's he from, "Sesame Street?"

Rapper Ice-T

I don't think making me a sex symbol would ever happen. That's not our show...I'm no sex symbol. I can see the article in "People" now—Chris Noth...body by Budweiser.

Chris Noth
star of "Law & Order"

I was short, dumpy, got C's and never expected to be on bedroom walls.

Actor Michael Fox

If life was fair, Elvis would be alive and all the impersonators would be dead.

Johnny Carson

Everyone probably thinks that...I have an insatiable sexual appetite, when the truth is, I'd rather read a book.

Madonna

It was all a rumor. I never met the woman.

Actor Sean Penn
on his marriage to Madonna

I don't smoke, I don't drink, and I don't do drugs. I never did. And that's because of my upbringing. I was taught the difference between right and wrong. As a rap artist, it's important to me to share that with the kids who listen to my music. The family is key in learning how to be a positive person.

Rap star Biz Markie

She's Having His Beatty: First, the Soviet empire collapses. Now, Warren is going to be a dad. What next?

Headline in "People"

I'm not Elvis Presley; I'm Vanilla Ice. I don't know anything about him except he made movies and was a superstar. I never bought any of his records.

Rapper Vanilla Ice
sometimes referred to as the "Elvis of Rap"

Things are very bad when kids have to write to an actor for advice. I can't tell anybody what to do. I'm just as screwed up as the next guy.

Actor Johnny Depp

She's unusual for a television journalist—she's got a brain.

Novelist Tom Clancy
on talk show host Linda Ellerbee

When I was a kid, I hung out with 15 guys on my block in Oakland and 10 of them ended up in jail. My loves—music and dance—provided an escape route from my neighborhood where drugs and gangs were common.

Rapper M.C. Hammer

Am I just cynical, or does anyone else think the only reason Warren Beatty decided to have a child is so he can meet babysitters?

Talkshow host David Letterman

I'm now using the name Twiggy Lawson to make me sound more like a human being not just some kind of pet animal.

Former fashion model Twiggy

I'm still doing that thing you do when you're a kid, when you're 11 1/2 and you tell everybody you're 12. It's because of my appearance—this pituitary nightmare that is my life.

Michael J. Fox
on turning 30

What is this—MC squared?

Mark Burstein
on the decision of M.C. Hammer to give up harem pants
for tailored suits

TELEVISION

I've jumped from a pool of testosterone to a pool of estrogen. There's no more male place than "Saturday Night Live."

Actress Jan Hooks
on moving from "Saturday Night Live" to "Designing Women"

Right now, the unmet spiritual needs of the American people is the subtext of the '90s. We all have a genetic, God-given capacity for wonder that's being starved, and that's what I'm interested in exploring.

Producer Norman Lear
on his current projects

The stories we do are real. We don't do aliens eating babies.

> *Maureen O'Boyle*
> *host of "A Current Affair"*

We're looking for new people in the cast. Possibly an Asian or Hispanic, just to broaden who we can make fun of.

> *Keenen Ivory Wayans*
> *executive producer of "In Living Color"*

It is just four weeks into the new television season, and already you can't tell the pregnancies, the false alarms, and the in-vitro fertilizations without a score card.

> *Caryn James*

One day on the talk shows:

> Sally Jessy Raphael: Porn stars' mothers
>
> Jenny Jones: Wives of gynecologists
>
> Maury Povich: How the family of a man who executed 14 persons coped with the situation
>
> Donahue: People who say they all lived in the same town in a past life
>
> Geraldo: Men who have been raped

[The purpose of my talk show] is to humanize people who have suffered. it becomes a vehicle for examining our prejudices.

> *Talk show host Phil Donahue*

[My talk shows are demonstrations of] man's triumph over adversity.

> *Talk show host Sally Jesse Raphael*

Call-in talk shows, an American idea now beginning to spread globally...are the electronic answer to the town meeting. For the price of a phone call, citizens try to change the world. Politicians are among the listeners. They know the sound of a populi when it voxes.

> *Commentator Ben Wattenberg*

There were far too many unannounced knocks on the door. I kind of regret that. Unfortunately, we thought it was out of a sense of fun, but I don't think the celebrities thought it was too funny.

Maury Povich
on his stint on "A Current Affair"

I had the idea that the world of inner thought was being ignored. We have so drifted into a secular way of thinking that we've ignored the things that really matter: wonder, mystery, love, gratitude.

Norman Lear
defending his T.V. show "Sunday Dinner"

"I hate waiting in lines, but I'd do it.

David Letterman
when asked if he planned to firebomb NBC

Today the three broadcast networks pretty much look alike. To stay in business they will have to find a way to be distinctive. [By the end of the decade], they may look different. One may emphasize news programming, another sports, and another dramatic programming.

Robert Pepper
of the Federal Communications Commission

All the networks are struggling now with their desire to put on live executions, if they could, to get the ratings. I think the difference is that Fox would put on naked live executions.

Producer Gary David Goldberg

In the fifth season of "Star Trek: The Next Generation," viewers will see more of shipboard life in some episodes, which will, among other things, include gay crew members in day-to-day circumstances.

Executive producer Gene Roddenberry

10

RELIGION

Prepackaged Communion Service—coffee-creamer-looking communion cups. Each sealed receptacle contains a serving of grapejuice. They cost only 10 cents each and require no refrigeration.

According to "Your Church"

Belly Dancing and Women's Spirituality: Learn to use muscles you never knew you had, wear exotic costumes, and enjoy moving all parts of your body to sensual Middle Eastern rhythms.

Seminar offered at Harvard Divinity School
according to "The Nave"

Five years ago, God told Bob Haifley to build a life-size figure of Jesus out of toothpicks. This summer, after 2,500 hours and 65,000 toothpicks, Haifley finished.

According to **The Los Angeles Times**

The Bible is now printed in 1,946 languages and dialects, understood by more than 80 percent of the world's population.

According to **United Bible Societies**

They now have a 900 number for atheists. When you call, nobody answers and you get charged for the call.

Unknown

Tammy [Bakker] says this is a great victory for Christians. I told her it was a Jew that did it, so let's call it a great victory for religious freedom in America. She agreed.

Jewish Lawyer Alan Dershowitz
after having won an appeal for Jim Baker

A symbol, with the very effect of being a symbol, has not one sole or absolute meaning. It throws out light in every direction. Meaning comes pouring from it.

P. L. Travers

We are seeing in our lifetime the collapse of the objectivist worldview that dominated the modern era, the worldview that gave people faith in the absolute and permanent rightness of certain beliefs and values. The worldview emerging in its place is constructivist. If we operate from this worldview we see all information and all stories as human creations...within a universe that remains always beyond us and always mysterious.

Author Truett Anderson

For sex, I mean that's why he stopped me, that's what I do, I'm a prostitute.

Rosemary Garcia
who was riding with evangelist Jimmy Swaggart when
he got three traffic tickets

I think he will step out of the ministry at this point.

Rev. Don George

Pope offers qualified praise of capitalism
  Chicago Tribune, May 3

Pope assails capitalist evils
  Chicago Sun-Times, May 3

Free market gets Pope's blessing
  The Washington Times, May 3

Pope warns against godless capitalism
The Washington Post, May 3

> *Headlines for articles on Pope John Paul's new encyclical*

Louisiana Gov. Buddy Roemer has been excommunicated by the Orthodox Catholic Church of Louisiana because in the past two years, he vetoed three bills banning abortion before the Legislature overrode one of the vetoes. Roemer, a Methodist who does not belong to that church, said "I don't like being excommunicated, no matter whose organization it is."

> *As reported by Steve Marshall*

That was the beginning of the end. That's what started the whole frozen food thing. It ruined American cuisine. As far as I'm concerned, Mrs. Swanson is the Antichrist.

> *Jeff Smith, the Frugal Gourmet*

Pope John Paul II has authorized the use of his name and picture on the box of "Catechic," a new board game in which players answer questions about religious culture.

> *Columnist Leah Garchik*

It is true that God's children in Africa suffer because there is less freedom in their countries than during the colonial times.

> *Archbishop Desmond Tutu*

The program, nicknamed "Dial-a-Pope," permits callers around the world to dial a 900 number, or similar special-cost line, and hear a recording from one of John Paul II's recent speechs or sermons.

> *According to the Associated Press*

ABOUT BELIEFS

God ordained the killing of animals. He himself killed animals to provide skins for Adam and Eve after they sinned.

> *District Judge Warren Litynski*

[Near-death experience] could be a process that's already to go in our brains, like a function key on a computer. At the point of death or under some other great stress, the brain hits the key and lets the experience happen.

Dr. Melvin Morse

Once again, the Lord has been struck across the face—this time, by the ordination of an active lesbian in the Episcopalian Church....By ordaining a practicing homosexual, some liberal Christians seemingly want the world to approve sin.

Larry Blandino

One mark of the church's wholeness must be a willingness to receive and live with the unfashionable wounded, the truly insufferable, the difficult, the wounded who make you want to cross the street to avoid them.

John Garvey

Here's Satan's agenda. First, he don't want anyone having kids. Secondly, if they do conceive, he wants them killed. If they're not killed through abortion, he wants them neglected or abused....One way or another, the legions of hell want to destroy children because children become future adults and leaders.

Randall Terry

Psychiatrists who are members of the Christian Medical and Dental Society definitely felt that drug therapy was the best treatment for major mental illnesses such as schizophrenia, but they preferred use of the Bible and prayer to treat lesser problems such as suicidal intent, grief, or alcoholism.

According to a survey published in the "American Journal of Psychiatry"

Coming of age about sexuality requires affirming a diversity of responsible sexualities in the church, including the lives of gay men and lesbians, as well as new patterns among nontraditional families.

*From the majority report of the **Presbyterian Church (USA)'s Special Committee on Human Sexuality***

We don't feel that marriage, by itself as a legal entity, ought to be the sole norm for legitimizing sexuality.

John Carey
Chair of the Presbyterian Special Committee on Human Sexuality

After three years' work, a commission of the Episcopal Church recommended that the way be cleared for ordination of homosexuals to the priesthood.

Associated Press

It is not enough to save the drowning babies from the river. Someone must go up the river to stop those who are throwing the babies in.

Bishop Barbara C. Harris

Christ never promises peace in the sense of no more struggle and suffering. Instead, he helps us to struggle and suffer as he did, in love, for another.

Novelist Frederick Buechner

About 80 percent of the words attributed to Jesus are thought not to be his own.

According to the 200 member "Jesus Seminar"

Spirituality is that place in us where the utterly intimate and the vastly infinite meet.

Rick Fields

Key problems the churches must grapple with:

1. Morality

2. Aging adults

3. Youth issues

4. People's lack of time

5. Lack of money

*According to a survey of clergy by the **Barna Research Group***

Religion has been important in supporting human-centered ethics, as in the civil rights movement. When churches came into the civil rights movement, they strengthened it, gave it continuity, and carried it through for 30 years. Now we are moving toward the idea that the natural world also has rights which must be respected.

Mary Evelyn Tucker

Yesterday I was on the golf course, and as I tee'd off I was reminded that we must follow through in life.

Opening line of a sermon by **Charles Whitney Gilkey**

Forgiveness is God's invention for coming to terms with the world in which, despite their best intentions, people are unfair to each other and hurt each other deeply.

Myra Marshall

Throughout most of our history, a stranger represented the divine or a friend; today a poor person, unknown and hungry, represents evil and stands as an enemy.

Ed Loring

The obligation to earn one's bread by the sweat of one's brow, also presumes the right to do so....A society in which this right is systematically denied, and which economic policies do not allow workers to reach satisfactory levels of employment, cannot be justified from an ethical point of view, nor can that society attain just social peace.

Pope John Paul II

To insist upon maleness as an essential attribute of priesthood...is to commit the fundamental error of making the maleness of Christ more significant than his humanity.

Archbishop of Canterbury George Carey

A tragedy of humanity in our time is the certainty that what we see is what alone exists, what we create is alone worthy...We suffer the peculiar blindness of those who see only the visible.

David Wolpe

AIDS was caused in this country by promiscuity and casual sex. It is not traditional values that have brought us to where we are.

John Walsh

We cannot deny the importance of religion in shaping our culture; therefore, the time has come for women and men to recognize the existence and importance of the female deity.

Carisia H. Swital

In biblical times, current psychological understanding about sexual orientation was unknown. Biblical writers presumed that everyone was heterosexual; therefore same-sex relations by persons who were regarded as heterosexual were considered abnormal...We cannot simply transfer texts from ancient cultural worlds to our own.

From the report by a study commission of the United Methodist Church

We have a teenage client dying with AIDS right now. No one told him about AIDS, condoms, or homosexuality. If you deny young people information based on your morality, you are sentencing them to death. Nothing is more immoral than that.

Frances Kunreuther

The Goddess is not just the female version of God. She represents a different concept. [The Goddess is located] with each individual and all things in nature.

Merlin Stone

A developing life in the womb does not have an absolute right to be born, nor does a pregnant woman have an absolute right to terminate a pregnancy.

From a statement by the Evangelical Lutheran Chruch

Gays and lesbians are feared because erotic passion between persons of the same gender is a sharp break with socially conventional patterns of male dominance and female subordination.

The Presbyterian Church (USA) report on human sexuality submitted last May

That happiness is to be attained through limitless material acquisition is denied by every religion and philosophy known to humankind, but it is preached incessantly by every American television set.

Sociologist Robert Bellah

I shall know there is a heaven on earth when our moral alternatives stop being the lesser of two evils and start becoming the better of two goods.

Paul D. McNamara

Virtue may not be its own reward, but it can be its own worse enemy. Among life's perpetually charming questions is whether the truly evil do more harm than the self-righteous and wrong.

Jon Margolis

Human life in all phases of its development is God-given and, therefore, has intrinsic value. The strong Christian presumption is to preserve and protect life. Abortion ought to be an option only of last resort.

From a statement by the Evangelical Lutheran Church

What the church says must never be determined by the "market" for its teaching or by opinion polls.

From the "Minority Report"

Meditation taught me many things, but it didn't acquaint me with my feelings. I didn't know if I was angry, sad, or happy unless it was very obvious. I spent 10 years using therapy, along with meditation, to reclaim my capacity to feel.

Jack Cornfield

The search for God will herald the dawn of the 21st century, and physical evidence will alter our view of God, but we must redefine God in terms of physics.

Frank Tipler

Abortion, euthanasia, eugenics, and hostility to the radically handicapped—these are among the signs today of a culture of death that is destroying millions of human lives and corrupting our society.

Roman Catholic Cardinal John J. O'Connor

We are relieved that the armed conflict in the gulf region has ended but must state categorically that there is little cause for jubilation. Thousands of civilians have died as a result of Iraq's illegitimate aggressions against Kuwait, the coalition's subsequent war against Iraq and the Iraqi government's suppression of revolts by groups within that country.

Joint statement of the National Council of Churches and the Union of American Hebrew Congregations

RELIGION AND RELIGIONS

Seminary enrollment outside the United States and Canada is rising sharply, especially in Africa. Africa boasted a 138% increase but Canada and the U.S. together reported a 31% loss.

According to a Vatican report on seminarians

Life doesn't lend itself to this Christian bureaucracy, where the Father, Son, and Holy Ghost are like the FBI, and the Virgin Mary intercedes for you like the executive secretary in the office.

Carolyn See

How overjoyed Pope John Paul II must have been to watch as his religion reestablished itself in his homeland, Poland, and in the neighboring nations that he knew so well. He led no armed battalions, but he did lead a powerful aggregation of ordinary citizens who longed for freedom and who recovered it.

Novelist James A. Michener

Going to bed with Episcopalians is like ecclesiastical necrophilia.

Rev. Walter Sundberg on relations between Lutherans and Episcopalians

In Chicago, a Chicago detective paid $3.00 for his dog, Fluffy, to receive ordination as a minister of the American Fellowship Church through a mail-order program.

According to **USA Today**

In the Catholicism I was brought up with, grace is terribly important, and how to get it is tricky.

David Plant

Roman Catholic Church employees receive a few benefits and earn wages 17.5% below the median income of the general population.

According to a task force of 15 church agencies
as reported in **Lutheran**

Preaching is not the only thing a minister does, like passing is not the only thing a quarterback does. But if the quarterback can't pass, he won't make it.

Reverend Haddon Robinson

There's been a rebellion against mysticism in the Protestant tradition going back to the Reformation, and there's still a lot of resistance. They've never been comfortable with the idea that you can strive to attain union with God.

Rev. Sharon Peoples Burch

What we have in most white churches today is so boring. It's just dead. Worship does not have to be that way.

Rev. Matthew Fox

Anti-Christian bigotry is the safest bigotry still exercised in American life. If people made simplistic characterizations of Jews, Blacks, or women the way the media routinely do about evangelicals, they'd be ripped apart in the public press.

Richard Land

"Thelma and Louise" has a message for the men who run the churches. Even imperfect decisions made by imperfect women are more liberating than watching men in the churches create God in their own image.

Barbara Reynolds

There will be a huge increase in the number of believers. It will be part of a general rediscovery of Russian culture. The church played a vital role in the development of Russia.

Former Communist Party member Vasily Bayangin

When I speak at denominational universities, I'm often asked what I think of the organized church. My answer is, "I think it stinks, but it's all we've got." You can't do it in isolation.

Madeline L'Engle

Top religious television shows:
1. "Hour of Power"
2. "World Tomorrow"
3. "Oral Roberts"
4. "Kenneth Copeland"
5. "Larry Jones"

According to **Nielsen Media Research News**

"Mommy," said the little boy, "Why does the pastor get a month's vacation in the summer when daddy gets only three weeks?" "Well, son," answered mommy, "if he's a good minister, he needs it. If he isn't, the congregation needs it!"

From "Homiletics"

For many years, American Jews have depended on Israel and the Holocaust for their Jewishness. Young Jews today are looking for a belief in God.

Rabbi Randall Konigsburg

England itself may need missionaries to come to us with the same verve and fervor as they did 100 years ago to this land.

Archbishop of Canterbury George Carey

If Men Got Pregnant, Abortion Would Be a Sacrament

Title of a book by **Helen Forelle**

Frankly, some of this will never be addressed by preventive steps because there will always be a small segment of ministers who are in fact sexual predators.

Rev. **Marie Fortune**
author of the pioneering book on clergy sexual misconduct,
Is Nothing Sacred?

Scientists in Milan announced that a mixture of iron chloride and calcium, which looks like dried blood, can duplicate a phenomenon that has long been regarded as the miracle of St. Januarius. A vial believed to contain blood from the 4th century priest is kept in Naples, where several times a year the contents spontaneously liquefy and return to a powdery state.

"Newsweek"

Based on interviews and reports...nearly 50% of Roman Catholic priests in the United States are either temporarily or permanently not observing strict celibacy.

Jack Dominian

The way religious groups use athletes to sell religion isn't much different from the way Gillette sells razors.

J. Gordon Melton
of the American Institute for the Study of American Religion

The appropriate salary for a pastor is $29,999 or less.

According to a **Gallup Poll**

Religion is not obeying rituals, rules, and social action. It is a means to a transformative interior life.

Professor Jacob Needleman

Religion tends to be part of the family tradition. If people do switch religions, they tend to change to a similar sect.

According to **Prof. Barry A. Kosmin**

The closest I have ever come to a spiritual awakening was having a baby, but it was close enough for me to realize that moments of over-powering insight are possible and real.

Jean O'Reilly

I began to see that cults form and thrive not because people are crazy, but because [people] have two kinds of wishes. They want a meaningful life, to serve God or humanity; and they want to be taken care of, to feel protected and secure, to find a home.

Arthur J. Deikman
in The Wrong Way Home: Uncovering the Patterns
of Cult Behavior in American Society

Just because a building is called a church doesn't mean that God's there or that the people there are really even interested in God. By and large, our churches seem to be cultural places for brief social gatherings. Business is much more of life-and-death matter these days; people are spending much more time there. It may be more approriate, actually, to build community in business than in churches.

Scott Peck

The page of history has turned, a new era is beginning. The bitter years of Golgotha...have passed.

Ukrainian Cardinal Myroslav Lubachivsky
on his return home after 50 years of exile

Two monks were crossing a bridge. One asked the other, "What is Zen?" The second monk picked up the first and threw him in the river, telling him to swim in it, become one with it but not ask about it because words don't mean s——.

Action movie star Steven Seagal
explaining the meaning of Zen

On an average Sunday, the Shiloh True Light Church of Christ receives about $7,500 in offerings. On National U.S. Debt Retirement Day, the church received $247,635.

According to the **Willington Morning Star (NC)**

Church leaders normally do not take positions based on what their constituents think. Church leaders try to think and reflect thoughtfully and allow their motivations to come from the teachings of the Gospel of Jesus Christ.

United Methodist Bishop Melvin Talbert

BELIEVERS

We have no right to reconstruct [Christianity] as we like or choose. We are not authorized to change Our Father into Our Mother.

Cardinal John J. O'Connor

[For Robert] Bly, one God is as good as any other, for none exists in the objective world. Anyone can believe all of them. Religion is simply a form of auto therapy.

Charlotte Allen
on Iron John

For the first time, most American Christians belong to Churches that are theologically committed to environmental concerns. This change represents the largest shift in church policy since churches began to stand against slavery 200 years ago.

According to a survey by the North American Conference
on Christianity and Ecology

Church members who give the most: Mormons, Seventh-Day Adventists, Church of God, and Assembly of God. Those who give the least: Roman Catholics, Evangelical Lutheran Church in America members, Episcopalians, and Unitarian Universalists.

As reported by the Star Tribune

Four out of every ten Americans go to church in a typical week.

According to a Gallup Poll

Make sure it is God's trumpet you are blowing—if it is only yours, it won't wake the dead; it will simply disturb the neighbors.

Major W. Ian Thomas

Eighty-one percent of Americans believe prayers can be effective in a situation like the one in the Persian Gulf.

*From a **Gallup Poll***

People who attend worship regularly give 3.8% of their annual household income to charitable causes. Those who would attend less often give about 0.8% of their income.

*According to a report from "**Relgion in American Life**"*

There are 1,795,900,000 Christians; 962,423,280 Muslims; 17,865,180 Jews; 700 million Hindus, 300 million Buddhists.

*According to **David B. Barrett***

Among denominations Unitarians have the highest rate of divorce; Greek Orthodox have the lowest.

*According to "**National and International Religion Report**"*

About 15% of those who were raised Catholic are no longer Catholics, a proportion that has not changed appreciably since 1960...About half of that group are people who leave Catholicism for another Christian denomination at the time of marriage...the other half for reasons having to do with matters of sexuality and authority.

Andrew M. Greeley

As our economic situation becomes worse, I expect many people will turn to God for help because they have nothing else.

Soviet engineer Olga Shmilova

I rap for Christ, no crossin' the line
I don't water down lyrics or forget the spine
I gotta come bold,
'cause I been sold
On the word that'll never grow old

Christian Rapper Toby McKeehan

Eighty-seven percent of Americans claim to be Christian, 1.8% say they are Jewish, 0.5% say they are Muslin.

According to a City University of New York survey

One of the reasons people show up on Sunday morning [is] an inarticulate yearning and wishfulness for a lost communion.

Theologian Walter Brueggemann

Sixty percent embrace the concept of Hell today, compared to 48% in 1958.

According to a 1990 Gallup Poll

Almost 1 American in 12 has no religious affiliation. Members of these groups are likely to be affluent, well-educated young men who live in urban areas.

Susan Krafft

The most affluent religious affiliation is Jewish, with an average household income of $36,700 in 1989. They are followed by Unitarians ($34,800), Agnostics ($33,300) and Episcopalians ($33,000).

Susan Krafft

I don't believe in jewelry because that's stuff from the natural world and I don't live there anymore.

Dodger Darryl Strawberry
on his new religious perspective

Fifty-two percent of Jews who married since 1985 have gentile spouses, 72% of children in intermarried families are being raised with no religion or a religion other than Judaism, 90% of children of intermarriage are marrying non-Jews.

According to the 1990 National Jewish Population Survey

Pentecostal and charismatic churches worldwide now count 382 million members, or one of every five Christians. They gain 19 million members per year and they donate $34 billion to Christian causes.

According to the "International Bulletin of Missionary Research"

The majority of Americans—about two out of three—say they believe in life after death.

According to a **Gallup Poll**

That the "conservatives" think they are winning proves very little. Conservatives always think they are winning. That the "liberals" think they are losing proves even less. Liberals always think they are losing.

Andrew M. **Greeley**

Overall, Latin America is 10 percent Protestant and, given the weak practice of most Catholics, they represent the majority of consistent churchgoers.

John A. **Coleman**

We're just three young brothers who were willin' to serve
Took a stand, threw the devil a curve
By usin' our talent for the Almighty Lord
When he gave us a gift, he gave us a chore
Called the Great Commission, it's like fishin'
But, souls are the goal of this Christian mission.

Christian Rapper Toby McKeehan

At Harvard Divinity School, where I studied, Jewish responsibility for patriarchy became a new dogma among the feminists....The radical, post-Christian feminism...was not all that radical, nor all that post-Christian, since it retained classical anti-Semitic motifs found in Christian theology.

Suzannah Heschel

Only 64% of younger Americans between the ages of 18-29 know why Easter is celebrated.

According to a **Gallup Poll**

11

SCIENCE
AND TECHNOLOGY

The authors also report that longer sperm can indeed swim faster than their shorter brethren, and may also be able to penetrate the egg more easily—that is, size does matter.

"Nature"

Halocarbons emitted from industrial sites in the greater Los Angeles area are dispersed into the Nevada and Arizona deserts and show up a day or two later, after traveling as far as 240 miles.

According to a study led by scientists from **Washington University**

It is a measure of the degree to which we have polluted our skies that while almost every one has heard of the Milky Way, surprisingly few people in the developed countries have seen it.

Chet Ramo

About 570 million years ago today's South Pole was probably less than 1000 miles from the shore of California.

According to geologists **Ian Dalziel and Eldridge Moores**

Other scientists have said that the ice sheet has been stable for around 20 million years. We're saying that the ice sheets come and go every few million years, that Antarctica 3 million years ago was cool, but experienced some periods of warmth.

Peter Webb

The core motivation for human beings to venture where they can, and to send robotic proxies where they cannot, is as sublimated but as real and ultimately unerring as the one that guides snow geese, salmon, and other migrators on their own image journey...We go because of a profound urge to leave our imprint on the universe.

William E. Burrows

Newspaper has a nutritive value of 35 to 40% TDN [total digestible nutrients]....Cattle are ruminants, and they can use the fiber. Newspapers should make up no more than 30% of a cow's diet, though.

Barry Stevens
proposing a way to recycle newspaper

On 2 June, the state-owned All-India Radio embarked on a massive science popularization program—a 130-part serial on human evolution. Aired every Sunday in 17 languages from 51 radio stations, the serial will run for 2–2 1/2 years.

K. S. Jayaraman

It took educated people to make a hole in the ozone layer. It will take even better educated people to correct it.

From an advertisement for **Sallie Mae**

Acid clouds filled with chemicals derived from car exhausts pose more of a threat to East Coast forests than acid rain. Rain is less acidic than the cloud and contaminates groundwater supplies, rather than the leaves themselves.

According to **Barrett Rock**
director of the National Oceanic and Atmospheric Administration
Cooperative Institute

The United States' world lead in technological research is diminishing. In engineering, technology, and applied sciences, those research areas most closely linked to industrial competitiveness, the citation of U.S. papers has fallen by 6.9 percent, relative to the world average.

Peter Alhous

For all its talk of fashioning a new consciousness that will bring humans into balance with the environment, ["Biosphere politics"] does little to advance understanding of what the species must do to slow the apparently head-long race toward extinction. Nor does it help to illuminate how Western societies, while obtaining food, shelter, and a degree of comfort, can minimize their impact on the plants and animals that share the planet.

Gina Maranto

The spectacular view of the night sky that our ancestors had above them on clear, dark nights no longer exists.

Astronomer David Crawford
regretting the pollution of the sky with light and radio waves

If all goes according to plan, the Mars probe, called Planet B, should arrive at Mars in September, 1997 and will orbit the planet at distances ranging from 150 to 34,000 kilometers.

According to Koichiro Tsuruda
of Japan's Institute of Space and Astronautical Signs

The most important step we can make toward Mars is to make significant progress on earth. Achieving even modest improvements in the serious, social, economic, and political problems that our global civilization now faces could release enormous resources, both material and human, for furthering space exploration and other worthy goals.

Carl Sagan

Nobody wants the Galapagos to become another Hawaii. Galapagos is one of the last places where it's still possible to control damage from tourism.

Lisa Minischiello

If the sun were the size of a soccer ball, the earth would be the size of a pea.

"Omni"

ANIMALS AND HUMANS

There are between 1.84 and 2.57 million species of insects on earth.

According to a new study by ***I. D. Hodkinson***
and C. Casson

A controversial new system for protecting endangered species is being proposed by some conservationists: a computer model, which would function as a global "megazoo," for managing animals in the wild. Proponents believe that an international data network would enable scientists to mate, move, and otherwise supervise the animals.

"New Scientist"

A few [scientists] have begun to conclude that it can no longer be dismissed out of hand. With luck and ingenuity, they say, geneticists might one day recover enough dinosaur DNA to create a beast that is reasonably close to the original.

The New York Times

The polar bear is the Arctic incarnate. When you watch one sauntering across the ice and it's 30 below, he looks as comfortable as someone in a pair of shorts on the beach in Hawaii.

Ian Stirling
on the admiration scientists have for polar bears

A male moth confuses infrared radiation given off by hot candle wax with similar infrared signals that are given off by a female moth. Thinking that the infrared radiation from a candle is coming from a female, the male moth heads for the candle and gets burned.

According to entomologist ***Philip S. Callahan***

We must find methods of saving our forests, of saving threatened species, of maintaining a healthy ecological balance on earth. If there is any spare effort left over from these absolute necessities of scientific advance, we can put them into other projects—otherwise not.

Isaac Asimov

Recent work in the United States and Switzerland has documented that young kittens that have regular exposure to people in their early weeks of life, 3-9 weeks of age, grow into adult cats that more readily approach people in a friendly way and remain longer when held.

Lynette A. Hart

All the wild, wild stories you hear about these [killer?] bees are nonsense. You don't hear about them killing people, or animals, or other bees in Africa or Brazil...only in the United States.

Entomologist Roger A. Morse

Globally, biopesticides account for only 1% of the sales volume of $25 billion.

According to **Michael E. Hochberg**

COMPUTERS

Searching for information among the millions of documents stored in today's huge and numerous databases can be like looking for a needle in a haystack. Many scholars can tell you about first-hand experiences with this problem. They and their counterparts in business and industry are learning that, if you can't find information, it might as well not exist.

Mark H. Chignell

Personal computer security is still an oxymoron.

Daniel White

"Viruses" that disrupt computer functions are drawing the interest of military planners, who consider them potential weapons. Because the ultimate targets would be powerful, heavily secured mainframe computers, designers are focusing on ways to infect smaller systems, such as those on combat aircraft, with links to the mainframes.

Suddeutsche Zeitung

MusicWriter, Inc. has developed a computerized kiosk for music stores that allows customers to make customized copies of sheet music that are reproduced on the spot with a laser printer. The music is stored on optical discs, each capable of holding up to 17,000 songs.

Journalist Dawn Clark

Personally, when I want to experience virtual reality, I take drugs.

Rock singer Todd Rundgren

In the near future, your telephone, fax machine, photocopier, color printer, and computer won't be separate items, but, rather, integrated components in an information appliance...The appliance, in effect, will be an information jukebox that shuffles 10 billion or 100 billion-byte capacity optical laser discs—the same laser discs or CDs you now use to listen to music.

Samuel Bleecker
a business technology consultant

At some point, we'll all have a computer on our desk and a phone in our shoe, but who will pay for it?

Sherrie P. Marshall

"Terrorists Group Profiles" — a computer disc containing detailed information, statistics and chronologies of some of today's most dangerous organizations.

Developed by Wayzata Technology, Inc.

If you have bad handwriting, this is great. You only have to write well once.

Prannoy Roy
on his new software "MyScript," which translates
typewritten letters into your own handwriting.

THE SOLAR ECLIPSE

It's a reminder of how the earth and planets are so much bigger than we are. The more we humans can get away from trivial stuff and think about the whole cosmic picture the better.

Dan Shugrue
commenting on the solar eclipse

The wide sheet of clouds mantling Mauna Kea's (Hawaii) stark, frigid, cinder-covered peak contrasted with the blackened sun, encircled by a delicately rayed burst of coronal gases glowing white. The black disk was topped with a cloud of denser pink gases blown explosively out into the corona in a huge "prominence" shaped vaguely like the letter M, rising at least 50,000 miles above the solar surface.

One description of the eclipse

You know God is in charge when you see this.

Janet Krupnick
commenting on the solar eclipse

I wanted to come and see it, considering it will be the last one this century, and now that I have, it's time to go shopping.

Cathy Murray
commenting on the solar eclipse

GENERAL SCIENCE

The largest-ever Search for Extraterrestrial Intelligence (SETI) [is] scheduled to begin on Columbus Day 1992 in honor of the 500th anniversary of Columbus' discovery of America.

Stephanie Sanson

Gamma-ray bursts have been observed for 25 years, but the source of these bright flashes in the sky remains a mystery. If they are beyond our galaxy, then the energy released in the brief one-second flash of gamma rays is many times the total energy released when a star explodes as a supernova.

Neil Gehrels

The scientist's subculture of the last 200 years has...developed a creation myth, though it undergoes major changes every decade or two as new ideas and new facts compete.

William H. Calvin

IBM® scientists have constructed an electrical switch whose only moving part is a single atom. This atomic switch is the latest of several recent advances by IBM in the infant field of molecular engineering—building machines consisting of just a few thousand atoms.

Kenneth Chang

Sometimes science has to take a time-out when its goals collide with the moral and ethical concerns of society.

Bernadine Healy
the new director of the National Institutes of Health

Cutting old-growth forests and replacing them with younger trees will not reduce atmospheric carbon dioxide levels. An old-growth forest includes dead woody debris, snags, litter on the forest floor, dead roots, and other decayed material that can store as much or more carbon as the trees themselves.

According to a study at Oregon State University

With the genetic engineer's increasing dexterity in manipulating pigmentation, who says the leopard still cannot change its spots?

According to "Nature"

Nature may respect a new, hitherto unseen symmetry, called supersymmetry and there may be a new form of matter.

G. G. Ross

With what we know now, it certainly seems logical that hurricanes will be stronger because of global warming. But it's a complicated problem. We're just beginning to answer some of the questions.

Jay Hobgood

The consensus so far after 10 years of research nationwide is that there is no documentation for believing that acid rain is causing widespread harm to North America's commercial forests.

Ivan Fernandez

The cardon cactus is the first cactus, and one of the first plants ever, to be discovered to be trioecious (having three sexes)—male, female, and hermaphrodite.

According to biology professor **Ted Fleming**

So four men and four women have sealed themselves off inside Biosphere 2. No contraceptives are allowed and if a woman gets pregnant she's expelled. This is progress? Sounds more like high school in the 1950s.

Christopher Blinden

Alison Brooks and her colleagues found that certain amino acids in ostrich eggshells decay at a constant, predictable, and very slow rate...Brooks believes that pinpointing the age of an ostrich eggshell can help determine the ages of the tools found alongside it.

According to **"National Geographic"**

The protective ozone layer in the earth's atmosphere is disappearing about twice as fast as previously thought.

According to researchers at the **National Aeronautics and Space Administration**

British and German scientists have discovered a gene that is responsible for making an unborn child a boy instead of a girl.

According to **"Current Science"**

One of Evolution's most intriguing operations is described by what might be called the Law of Used Parts. Everything Evolution makes, he makes from used materials. To make a lizzard, he had to use the frog; to make a bird, he started with the lizzard...That is how Evolution always works. Bending this, compressing that, lengthening, expanding, inflating, dividing, engraving, sanding, polishing.

William Jordan

The center of the Milky Way appears to be primed to explode in the profusion of star formations leading to the expulsion of vast amounts of matter from our galaxy.

According to **A. Stark**

Whereas there is an inherent and overriding philosophical commitment to create manned programs before precise missions are found for them, the exact opposite is true in science and exploration, where there is an abundance of potentially valuable and clearly defined missions but not a commensurate philosophical committment to support them.

William E. Burrows

Each cubic meter of lunar soil contains the chemical equivalent of lunch for two—two large cheese sandwiches, two 12-ounce sodas with sugar, and two plums with substantial nitrogen and carbon left over.

Geochemist Larry Haskin

Any time we lift a student's self-esteem, everything improves. Technology has the ability to do that. It offers a lot of hands-on, interactive activity that these kids need.

Kathleen Duplantier

Investment in academic research has an average annual rate of return to society of about 28%.

According to researcher Edwin Mansfield

The major climate changes of the past 1.80 million years can be understood entirely in terms of changes in ocean circulation.

According to calculations by D. Rind and M. Chandler

Astronomers have detected a quasar that may be the oldest, most distant object yet discovered, an enigmatic powerhouse born less than 1 billion years after the birth of the universe.

Frances Ann Burns

Molecular machines could be used to rebuild damaged organs, make cosmetic alterations, or provide people with wholly new parts capable of dramatic powers. Missing limbs could be regenerated. Defective eyes and ears could be restored to perfect function or even enhanced.

Technology researcher Jon Roland

Surely there is some point at which the national economy is in such dire straits that sending people to Mars is unconscionable. The only difference there might be between me and other enthusiasts for human missions to other worlds is where we draw the line. But surely, such a line exists, and every participant in such a debate should stipulate where that line should be drawn, what fraction of the GNP for space is too much.

Carl Sagan

Recent research by American astronomers supports the 200-year-old theory of the existence of Lagrange points, areas in space where weigh stations for interplanetary travel could be parked....Anything placed in the Lagrange point would stay in that pattern, rotating around a common center of gravity, using little or no fuel.

According to astrophysicist **Kim Innanen**

I would say the current situation is that we have no believable theory of galaxy formation. What has happened in the last year or so is that a theory that many people took very seriously, the cold dark matter theory, has collapsed.

Cosmologist Ethan Vishniac

These days there's a 95% chance that earthbound satellite-watchers will see a piece of junk instead of a spacecraft passing overhead.

David Talent
on the increasing debris in space

Solar, wind, and thermal energy are expensive only if you ignore the environmental, health, and the safety costs of fossil and nuclear fuels.

Lisa Aug

PRODUCTS AND PROCESSES

The Watchman lightbulb has a back-up filament that burns for about a week after the primary filament burns out.

Developed by **Philips Lighting Co.**

A new window allows glass to transmit light when voltage is applied through a light switch. Without the current, the glass is frosty.

Developed by **Taliq Corp.**

Environmentally safe BIO-T, a golf tee which when moistened melts into an organic brown goo within 36 hours.

Developed by 13-year-old **Casey Golden**

Ricoh's PF-1 is the world's smallest fax machine capable of sending and receiving 8 1/2 x 11 inch documents.

According to the **Guiness Book of World Records**

The Car Bar, a portable personal kitchen, plugs into your car's cigarette lighter to chill fresh fruit or heat home-cooked meals.

Developed by **Motoring Accessories**

When you enter your skin type and the rating of your suntan lotion, SunWatch measures the strength of solar U.V. rays and calculates how long you can safely stay in the sun.

Developing by **Saitek Industries Ltd.**

A Japanese lingerie maker has designed a brassiere with a tiny memory chip that plays 20 seconds of Mozart's music, to honor the bicentennial of Mozart's death.

According to **Reuter News Service**

Seeding epoxies and polymers with particles that produce a microscopic swiss cheese texture increases the fracture resistance of the material by up to 300 percent.

According to **Professor Albert Yee**

Despite unexpected headwinds and thunderstorms, the aircraft Sun-Seeker completed a 2,467 mile route across the Southern United States in less than 120 hours powered only by the battery-charging solar cells spread over its wings plus updrafts.

According to **Popular Science**

MicroStraight—a portable device that trains people to correct their own curvature of the spine.

*Developed by **Rockefeller University researchers***

Broccoflower, a cross between cauliflower and broccoli, is becoming more available across the country. It is more nutritious than cauliflower, which it resembles.

*"**University of California at Berkeley Wellness Letter**"*

Toyota is working on air bags that are mounted in the doors to protect against side impacts, to be available in 1996.

*According to "**Car and Driver**"*

Biojector—an alternate to injection by needle, uses pressurized carbon dioxide to force a jet of medication through the skin at close to the speed of light.

*Manufactured by **Biojet, Inc.***

The Attorney VooDoo Doll.

*Developed by **Voodoo To You***

CompCap—a voice-activated computer that you wear.

*By **Park Engineering***

When one of its four heat detectors senses a fire, The Guardian releases a fire extinguishing chemical and shuts off your stove. Normal cooking conditions won't activate the system.

*Manufactured by **Twenty First Century Interntional Fire Equipment and Services Corp.***

Pop-out nozzles beneath the headlights provide a high pressure spray that cleans headlights without wiper blades in less than one second.

*Developed by **Audi of America***

Designed specifically for decorating, the new [Elmer's GluColors] comes in neon shades of blue, green, red, yellow, orange, and pink. It can be applied with a brush or toothpick or straight from the applicator-tip bottle.

*Robert **McMath***

As thin as a credit card, the Card Lite flashlight weighs less than one ounce.

*Manufactured by **Tekna***

The "Perfectie" has a zipper that runs along the loop that goes around the wearer's neck, through the knot and down the narrow back part of the tie, allowing it to be tightened or loosened.

*Developed by **World Tie Corporation***

Huffy, maker of bicycles in the $70 to $250 range now offers customized hand-built bikes from $7,000 to $10,000.

*According to **Popular Science***

A California firm, Columbia Laboratories, has reportedly received a patent for a means of timing the release of flavorings in chewing gum over several hours. The control is achieved through the use of polymers added to the gum base.

*According to **"World Monitor"***

Used in conjunction with the car's rear-view mirror, The Lane Changer lets you see both sides of your car without turning your head, eliminating the blind spot.

*Manufactured by the **The Lane Changer, Inc.***

Peppermint scent really does stimulate the brain's electrical activity, resulting in better job performance in a control group.

*According to researchers at **Catholic University***

British researchers have developed a computer and light box interface that measures a patient's height, weight, volume, and percentage of fat, and proceeds to give the patient advice and helpful hints on how to lose weight.

*According to **The Science Teacher***

Researchers at Carnegie Mellon University have invented a micromechanical "velcro" that some day may be used to suture blood vessels, attach a pacemaker, or act as a mechanical adhesive for electronic devices.

According to **The Science Teacher**

Researchers at Thermoscan have developed an ear thermometer that takes a person's body temperature in two seconds. When the thermometer is inserted in the ear, it measures the infrared radiation, or heat, in the ear.

According to **Science News**

About 400 Hallmark stores in the West are being equipped with computers that can add personalized messages in a minute or two to colorful, factory-printed cards.

John Eckhouse

Within five to seven years, we will have a lot of service robots cleaning buildings and toilets, or helping out in hotel kitchens. Within 10 years...every home will have them.

Lin Kye Young
Korean robotics researcher

The Staywell 21 Electronic Cat Door emits a radio signal that is interrupted by a "key" collar worn by your pet, releasing the latch.

Developed Heath Co.

Interactive Network, Inc. of Mountain View, makes a system of the same name that lets viewers play along with such game shows as "Wheel of Fortune" and "Jeopardy," call plays in football, baseball, and basketball games, and express an opinion on talk shows like Phil Donahue.

Larry Hicks

It's almost like having a little cook in the microwave.

Patricia Smith
of Sharp, on a new microwave that can mash, blend
and stir food in a built-in bowl

Ra Ra II is the first solar-powered car in Japan to get a license plate. The single-seat open vehicle has a top speed of 27.5 m.p.h. and weighs 453 pounds.

Developed by **Toyota**

The Electronic Swing Groover calculates the force of your golf swing and displays the distance your ball would travel if untethered. The ball's swinging motion indicates an overslice.

Manufactured by **Dennco, Inc.**

New products for children:

Fun 'n Fresh, a solid deodorant for kids as young as 7

Gregory, a boy's cologne for $15.50 an ounce

Kidsmetics, a line a cosmetics for kids

The Simpsons Toiletry Collection, which includes such products as "Radical Hair Stuff"

Microwave dinners by Banquet's Kid Cuisine and Tyson's Looney Tunes Meals

The Little Operator Easy Dialer Picture Phone, with a grandma, a firefighter, and other adults depicted on speed dial buttons

Lisa J. Moore

A revolving driveway which rotates so that you won't have to back-up into traffic, costs $30,000 to install.

Developed by **Hovar Systems**

The Australian biotechnology company Calgene Pacific estimates that it will be marketing blue roses by 1997, now that it has successfully isolated a blue pigmentation gene from other flowers. Such a rose cannot be produced by normal breeding techniques since roses do not have the necessary pigment.

Mark Lawson

The dark age spots that exposure to the sun's ultraviolet rays causes in an estimated 75 percent of Caucasians can now be effectively removed with the "Pigmented Lesion Laser" developed by Candela Laser Corporation.

According to **The New York Times**

In Tokyo, 62,000 Coca Cola vending machines will soon "talk" directly to the bottling company's office, ordering more soft drinks or reporting malfunctions. In the experimental system, radio waves will link the machines to a central Coke computer.

"Japan Economic Journal"

Jockey for Baby—urethane-coated nylon diaper covers with elastic waistbands. Itty-Bitty Jockeys (worn over environmentally-safe cloth diapers), come in pink and blue for gender-identification. It is also available in white for no-gender bias.

Elizabeth Snead

MicroFridge—a combination refrigerator, freezer, and microwave.

Manufactured by Sanyo

Sensors on the "Fuzzy" microwave measure variables such as food weight and moisture content enabling the oven to make decisions on timing, power, and cooking procedures. Built-in blades mix or mash foods.

Manufactured by Sharp

CoverAge, a stucco-like wall covering made from recycled paper and wood chips, replaces replastering to smooth over wall and sealing imperfections. It is applied like wallpaper and painted over.

Developed by CoverAge, Inc.

Development of a new compound from discovery to FDA approval takes an average of 12 years and costs an average of $230 million. At any time during that process, after the investment of years of research and many millions of dollars, a drug that initially seemed promising may be abandoned. Even after approval, the life cycle of a new product may be cut unexpectedly short by a further therapeutic advance.

Charles A. Sanders

Scientists Bob B. Buchanan and Karoly Kobrehel reported that they have identified the system of natural enzymes that, in combination with water and kneading, turns wheat flour into the sticky elastic mess necessary to trap carbon dioxide bubbles and cause dough to rise.

Charles Petit

Environmental economists have shown time and time again that [radioactive wastes generated by nuclear power production] should not be generated in the first place because, under logical benefit cost scenarios, the benefits of nuclear energy cannot exceed its costs when the potential damages from an accident and waste storage are considered.

W. Dougliss Shaw, Jr.

A Dutch research center has developed a tiny heart pacemaker thinner than a ballpoint pen weighing only about 6.5 ounces, it can be implanted without major surgery, and it runs off of a battery with the life of seven-and-a-half years.

As reported in **Die Presse**

Flavr Savr—a tomato containing a specially inserted gene that slows deterioration, allowing it to be picked when it's ripe and still reach the store in good shape and in good taste.

Developed by **Calgene Inc.**

The phonocardiograph enables physicians to watch the computer image of the heartbeat at the same time as they are listening to the sound. Because the sensitivity of the human ear is supplanted by the ability of the human eye to recognize patterns, this method will make it easier to detect heart problems.

Physicist William Bennett, Jr.
on his recently developed software program

To break down materials for recycling, microwaves are used to break the bonds that join atoms to other atoms. Materials are reduced elements such as iron, oxygen, carbon and sulfur. Most of these materials can then be reused.

According to **Science News**

Using a highly advanced Swedish machine called a gamma unit or "gamma knife," doctors...can now perform bloodless brain surgery. The gamma unit...uses radiation to repair lesions, or damaged tissue in the brain without cutting into a patient's skull.

According to **Jean-Yves Nau**

Automobiles that get the best fuel economy:

1. Geo Metro
2. Honda Crx
3. Suzuki Swift
4. Daihatsu Charade
5. Volkswagen Jetta Diesel

According to the **Environmental Protection Agency**

A thin TV screen that can be hung on a wall like a picture is now being sold in Japan. The screen, about one inch thick, was developed by the Sharp Corporation.

According to **Science News**

The walk-in bathtub makes bathing easier for the elderly or handicapped. Its watertight door opens inward; when its closed, the water pressure creates a tight seal. An internal lock helps prevent leaks.

Developed by **BathEase, Inc.**

Radioluminescent lights can be fashioned into cubes, sticks, or virtually any shape. They require no electrical power supply, can produce almost any color, operate for years without maintenance, and are solid-state and unbreakable, containing no liquids or gases.

According to the **American Chemical Society**

Iceberg lettuce that tastes like its larger cousin, but grows only to the size of a tennis ball has been developed by isolating a growth hormone-producing gene.

According to the scientists at **U.S. Department of Agriculture**

The Pro-One Instant Thermometer measures heat in the ear canal, recording in less than two seconds a temperature more accurate than an oral thermometer.

Developed by ***Thermoscan, Inc.***

The airlock bicycle intertube contains a viscous sealant that blocks and seals small punctures before air can escape.

Manufactured by a ***Specialized Bicycle Components***

Using peat moss instead of synthetics, Johnson & Johnson has come up with a natural, extra-thin sanitary napkin that it says absorbs 12 times its weight in liquid.

Associated Press

I think its a tough sell, a brown sanitary napkin.

Bonita Austin
Household products analyst

Mobilstar. A single-ear headset provides hands-free communication for cellular phone users.

Developed by Plantronics, Inc.

I'm happy to be the first woman, but I doubt I'll be the last.

Nobel Prize winner Gertrude B. Elion
about being voted into the National Inventors' Hall of Fame

A B-52 bombing from 30,000 to 40,000 feet is very accurate. They hit the ground every time.

Retired Adm. Eugene Carroll

12

SOCIETY

The soul of our quest for the simple life...reflects a need to reestablish control of our lives.

Peter V. Fossel

The average consumer will eat 72 potato chips, about four ounces, at a sitting.

According to research by Frito Lay

However incredible the UFO experience seems, and whatever it might actually be, it is not in any obvious way the product of serious psychopathology.

Psychologist James S. Gordon

Shoe salesman: Do you want to wear them, or are you buying them for investment purposes?

From a cartoon by Cochran

How could he possibly be a good psychiatrist? He couldn't even tell when I was lying.

From a cartoon by Machlis

Major institutions such as the police who use gangs to get to other areas of organized crime; or politicians who use gangs to do political work like the old political machine used to do; or government agencies whose budgets are dependent on the existence of gangs; or entertainment industries, which sell the romance of gangs from Jesse James on, all keep gangs going.

Author Martin Sanchez Jankowski

One man to another: they will never really crack down on air pollution until it interferes with television reception.

From a cartoon by Capelini

The great majority of passengers purchase discount tickets, which restrict their access to flights. It would be the same if subway riders could buy half-price tokens that would be valid only for every fourth or fifth train that enters the station.

Louis Uchitelle

Three out of four whites believe that Blacks and Hispanics are more likely than whites to prefer living on welfare. The majority of whites also believe that Blacks and Hispanics are more likely than whites to be lazy, violence-prone, less intelligent and less patriotic.

According to a survey by the National Opinion Research Center

If blacks, Jews, Asians, Indians, Hispanics, or Eskimos were portrayed in a movie the way males are portrayed in "Thelma and Louise," civil rights organizations would be all over it screaming bloody murder.

Richard Grenier

We are now equals of society and we believe this telethon still emphasizes our helplessness, our pitifulness and, by application, our uselessness to society.

Laura Hershey
protesting the Jerry Lewis telethon

At 42, I desired to retire from medicine and begin Ph.D studies in mathematics. I settled in a small college town ten miles from the nearest interstate. The kids can walk to school; I bike to class. Life can truly be a feast.

Robert Ingle

These people are not successful—they're losers...horrible losers in life....They're crafty, not crazy. They have intense need for power....They lack a conscience, remorse, any capacity for empathy.

Criminologist James Fox
on serial killers

We can modify the form, the size can be bigger or smaller. But it must be round, contain a chocolate base and vanilla cream, and fit Oreo's personality...fun and playful.

Oreo spokesperson Sandy Putnam
on the new one-inch diameter "Mini Oreo"

Twenty-seven percent of American households contain at least one Scrabble set and more than 100 million sets have been sold worldwide.

According to the National Scrabble Association
on the 60th anniversary of the game

I love them with a passion, and I want them to stay together after I'm gone.

Philanthropist Walter H. Annenberg
announcing his bequeathal of $1 billion worth of paintings to the
Metropolitan Museum of Art

Annual phone calls per person:

1. Americans	1,800 calls per year
2. Canada	1,500 calls per year
3. Denmark	907 calls per year
4. Australia	510 calls per year

According to Siemens Corporation

The better society—the most civil, humane, democratic society—exists when individual rights and community needs are in careful balance.

Social scientist Amitai Etzioni

There's a kind of lovable defiance about wearing a baseball cap. It's become common for straitlaced business people to put on baseball caps as a sign of knocking off, time away from work.

Prof. Stuare Ewen
on the growing fashionable interest in baseball caps

Otherwise healthy, seemingly well-adjusted Vietnam veterans still have violent nightmares, even 10 or more years after combat.

According to a study by Cynthia A. Loveland Cook

One good thing can be said for all airline food: It's served in small portions.

Sam Ewing

Seventy-two percent of Black Americans prefer to be called Black; 15% opt for African- American; 3% choose Afro-American; 2% choose Negro.

According to a survey by the Joint Center for Political and Economic Studies

Glacier water [is] tapped from the melting snow flats of British Columbia's glacier tundra. The refreshing, crisp character of this just-arrived Canadian product is reportedly the result of the water cascading 7,000 feet—rendering it highly oxygenated—before being captured.

Tom Sietsema

A limo out here is like a second car.

Phill Lewis
on moving to Southern California

Never get into a car with a man with a gun. "If you say 'No, I'm not going,' and then walk or run away, approximately 98% of the time, the man will not shoot. However, if you get into the car with him, statistics have shown that approximately 98% of the time, a woman will not survive her attacker and a man will not survive nearly 100% of the time.

Edward Welch

In sheer numbers, fish are the most common pet. The American Pet Products Manufacturers' Association found 78 million fish in home aquariums.

Diane Crispell

Dogs and cats alone consume over $7 billion worth of food in a year, and pet owners spend another $2 billion on flea collars, litter boxes, aquariums, and other pet paraphernalia.

Diane Crispell

The average right-handed person lives 75 years, while the typical leftie dies at 66.

As reported by "Popular Science"

Adding a new street to a jammed network can make traffic flow even more slowly. In congested situations, drivers apparently will head towards the new route, jamming it and the other streets.

According to **The New York Times**

The average American throws away 17.7 pounds of batteries every year.

According to "Garbage"

Americans eat 90 acres of pizza every day.

According to **American Health**

The most popular bottled waters:
1. Arrowhead
2. Sparkletts
3. Poland Spring
4. Perrier
5. Hinckley and Schmitt

As reported in **Health**

The latest fashion accessory for those who like to stay in touch is the beeper cover, available in quilted, metallic, or even mock-crocodile leather.

At $22 and $26, the cover is a hot item at Macy's and other department stores.

"Newsweek"

Rock star Rod Stewart put his two-story Beverly Hills mansion on the market for $14.5 million. The house includes master suite with two fireplaces, ballroom with 50-foot ceilings, minstrel gallery, and two family rooms.

Thomas D. Elias

Fourteen million households now possess a computer.

According to the Census Bureau

By the year 2000...Americans will do most of their shopping at neighborhood strip shopping malls...With increasing demands on their time, they will choose speed and convenience instead of the elegance and variety offered by large regional malls.

Chip Walker

The surest way to hold down the amount we drive is to stop building new roads and to remove other economic incentives that encourage businesses to locate farther from where people live.

Russell Reagan

In 1982, the average domestic new-car price topped $8,000. For 1992, the average price has more than doubled to top $17,000.

Jim Mateja

Average T.V. viewing hours per week for various age groups:

    1. 2-5: 21 hours, 50 minutes
    2. 6-11: 20 hours, 5 minutes
    3. 12-17: 23 hours, 24 minutes
    4. 18+: 24 hours, 28 minutes (men)
        28 hours 58 minutes (women)

From a recent survey

I don't need caffeine to wake me up...I keep my underwear in the freezer.

From a cartoon by **Edgar Argo**

More than 3,000 teenagers and children start smoking each day in the U.S.

According to the **American Academy of Pediatrics**

$12.6 billion is spent annually on kitchen renovations.

According to the **National Association of Home Builders**

One of the most disconcerting aspects of old age is that we usually haven't the vaguest notion of when it will end, or how.

Columnist **Page Smith**

Cheating individuals account for 75 percent of each year's tax shortfall, compared with 25 percent for corporations.

According to **Money**

You could write a one-page book on how not to get a ticket. It would say "obey the law."

New York State Police Officer Raymond Dutcher
responding to word of the book
A Speeder's Guide to Avoiding Tickets

EDUCATION

Tuition, room and board now top $20,000 on 69 U.S. campuses, up from 39 last year.

According to the **College Board**

Public school officials in Michigan must inform all students in the 6th through 12th grades that they can seek an abortion without their parents' knowledge or permission by petitioning a probate court for a waiver of the consent requirements.

According to **The New York Times**

I know white people put the drugs in the neighborhood but you don't have to buy them...Drug dealers don't advertise. They are not in easy to find places, they're in the worst spots in the world.

Chris Rock

Shani is tomorrow's African-American woman. She's young, strong, beautiful, and fresh. She exemplifies every attitude insinuated by her Swahili name, which translates as "marvelous."

From the promotional material for "Shani,"
a new line of African-American fashion dolls by **Mattel**

In just two years, we have seen a dramatic shift in teen attitudes. In addition to becoming less materialistic, teens also proved to be more globally concerned than they have been in the past.

Peter Zollo
president of TRU (Teenage Research Unlimited)

The message of ["Teenage Mutant Ninja Turtles"] is always "Might is Right." But kids need to learn to value human life, and that there are ways to solve problems without killing people off.

Principal Desirée Ford

Children of divorce perform less well in school, have more behavioral and psychological problems, and a greater tendency (once they become adults) to divorce than children raised by both biological parents.

Reporter Paul Taylor

More than 780,000 students transfer to a new college each fall. Over 500,000 move to a four-year institution and about 280,000 enter two-year schools.

According to the **College Board's Annual Survey of Colleges**

ELIZABETH TAYLOR

I always said I would get married one more time, and with God's blessings, this is it, forever.

Elizabeth Taylor

It may be obvious that I'm the marrying kind. But every time I got married I had hoped that it would be forever. It's like when you make a film—you don't make a film hoping it's going to be a disaster.

Elizabeth Taylor

Knot Again, Liz!

Headline from "Entertainment Weekly"

I'm signed up all over the world.

Elizabeth Taylor
on where she is registered for bridal gifts

She's part of the family. Now it's like, "Hi Elizabeth," — she doesn't like to be called Liz.

Lisa Fortensky
on her cousin-in-law, Elizabeth Taylor

I would do anything for Elizabeth. I truly love her. We're so much alike, you know. She and I, we're exactly alike. It's hard being a child star and having to grow up, but she and I understand each other and all about it.

Michael Jackson
on his role in Liz Taylor's wedding

With this ring I make you a promise that from this day forward you shall not walk alone. My heart will be your shelter and my arms will be your home.

From the marriage vows

This is the first time she has married a regular worker.

Eddie Fisher

It was a beautiful, beautiful ceremony. There was a feeling of intimacy. It's nice that you can get married at that age and make it a sacred moment.

Diane Von Furstenberg

Larry is solid, sensitive, direct, delightful. [Liz] was real smart to marry this man.

Officiating minister Marianne Williamson

Graham Sharp of William Hill Bookmakers gives 8:11 odds that the marriage will last one year. But it's 15:8 against wedded bliss enduring three years, and 12:1 the newly weds never celebrate 10 years.

Karen Thomas

This isn't a wedding—this is a commerical for Liz's new perfume and Michael's new album.

Anonymous **National Enquirer** *employee*

I survived Liz Taylor's 8th Wedding and Media Circus.

T-Shirt
sold at the wedding by a photographer

MARRIAGE AND FAMILY

Marriage in the United States has fallen to its lowest popularity level in two decades.

According to the National Center for Health Statistics

Married men live longer than single men, but married men are a lot more willing to die.

Johnny Carson

The federal numbers show that about 3.7 million of the 9.9 million single mothers in the nation received partial or full child support payment in 1989. Of the 6.2 million women who didn't get any money, about 1.2 million of them were "stiffed"—they had court orders but fathers simply didn't pay

Ramon G. McLeod

Number of times women age 15–65 have been married:

Once   50 million

| Twice | 10 million |
| Three+ | 2 million |

According to the U.S. Census Bureau

The median amount of discretionary money the average American household has is just $108 a month.

*According to the **Roper Organization***

You know your children are growing up when they stop asking you where they came from and refuse to tell you where they're going.

P. O'Brien

If you want a preview of what kind of husband a man will make, look at his relationship with his mother. If the man in your life had a cold, rejecting mother, or one who ran hot and cold on him, watch out.

*According to **Dr. Lynn Miller***

Mixed marriages matter to African-American women because high prison rates, death rates, and jungle fever (Spike Lee's word for interracial love) have made eligible black men scarce.

Columnist Barbara Reynolds

Thirty-five percent of all births to currently and formerly married women are unintended.

*According to the **National Center for Health Statistics***

Almost one in five Americans grew up with an alcoholic family member.

Medical Tribune News Service

A national survey on sex found that nearly all married people polled say they are faithful to their spouses and about three-fourths consider sex outside marriage always wrong.

Associated Press

Motherhood and homemaking are honorable choices for any woman, provided it is the woman herself who makes those decisions.

NOW president Molly Yard

The cost of raising a single child from birth to 18 years averages $200,000.

According to the U.S. Department of Agriculture

Fathers can do anything for their children that mothers can do. The parenting role is one of compassion and caring; therefore, the ability to parent is not gender-linked.

Dr. Charles V. Willie

A good marriage is like a good trade: Each thinks he got the better deal.

Ivern Ball

The worldwide habit of mothers cradling a baby on the left side developed in the distant past when humans lived in the wild. Holding a baby on the left side gave the baby a better chance of surviving because the mother could keep a closer eye on the child and react more quickly in an emergency.

According to anthropologists Andrew Chamberlain and John Manning

Dennis Quaid and Meg Ryan are expecting a child in March. And get this—they're even married! (Meg and Dennis quietly got hitched last Valentine's Day in Los Angeles.)

Liz Smith

Although a good relationship with their father after divorce is consistently found to help children's adjustment, most of all divorced men have limited or no contact with their children as they grow up.

According to sociologist Peter Uhlenberg

There was an old woman who lived in a shoe, she had so many children she ran out of names to call her husband.

Ann Landers

Outcomes of unmarried couples who lived together:

1. Successful marriage—40%

2. Broke-up—37%
3. Marriage dissolved—13%
4. Still living together—10%

As reported by **USA Today**

Studies of children raised by parents of the same sex indicated that the adults' homosexuality does not influence the youngsters' sexual orientation.

According to **Lawrence Hartmann**

If you're with a man who cheated in his first marriage, you can't make him faithful, no matter how special you are. Assume he'll cheat, and come to some decision about whether it would be tolerable to you.

Psychologist Judith Sills

The most common measures of success among Americans:

1. Being a good spouse and parent
2. Being true to yourself
3. Being true to God
4. Having friends that respect you
5. Being of use to society

According to the **Roper Organization**

As women increasingly claim the money, power, and position that used to be male prerogatives, they're also seizing the right to choose a younger partner. And as women empower themselves, younger men are increasingly attracted to them.

Sociologist Constance Ahrons

More marriages end by divorce than by death, and more than twice as many marriages end with death of the husband as with death of the wife.

Barbara Foley Wilson

Voluntary sterilization is the No. 1 contraceptive choice for married couples older than 30.

Dr. June M. Reinisch

Divorced and widowed people in most age groups remarry at higher rates than single people do, regardless of their sex.

Barbara Foley Wilson

The wedding present men would most like to receive: a microwave oven.

According to a survey taken by Robert Krups

I think marriage is a strange relationship. It's very trying to be living in the same house with someone all the time if you're a grown-up person.

Katharine Hepburn

Two decades ago, babies were commonly seen as social embarrassments. Now they are seen as personal statements.

According to "American Demographics"

Engaged couples spend $10 billion a year on weddings and receptions. For a comparative figure, the entire music industry generates $7 billion a year in sales of records, tapes and compact disks.

Reporter Shann Nix

If I want to spend Friday evening at his house, I make an appointment. If he's already booked, I either request another night or...talk to the other wife and we work out an arrangement. One thing we've all learned is that there's always another night.

Lawyer Elizabeth Joseph
whose polygamist husband has nine wives

Black women are willing to take on the responsibility of a child because they believe they can do it. But they don't want to take on the baggage of a man.

Brenda Reid

Children of divorce perform less well in school, have more behavioral and psychological problems and a greater tendency (once they become adults) to divorce than children raised by both biological parents.

Reporter Paul Taylor

There were nearly 2.4 million weddings in 1988. Some 10.7 percent were divorced men marrying never-married women. But a greater number, around 10.9 percent, represented unions between divorced women and previously unwed men.

*According to the **National Center for Health Statistics***

When spouses join counseling sessions, alcoholics have a better chance of beating the habit or at least cutting down.

*According to **Dr. Thomas G. Bowers***

Children in single-parent families are economically disadvantaged and that [hurts] their opportunities. It makes it harder for Black children to achieve economic mobility.

Sociologist Christin Moore

The only thing I want to inherit is his frequent-flier miles.

Robyn Phelps
on her recently deceased husband, who was married to two other women at the same time

Adults whose mothers and fathers were warm and affectionate were able to sustain long and relatively happy marriages, raise children, and be involved with friends and recreational activities outside their marriage at mid-life.

*According to research reported by the **American Psychological Association***

Preferred anniversary celebrations:

1. Eating at a romantic restaurant
2. Revisiting honeymoon site
3. Checking into hotel for the night
4. Having champagne breakfast in bed
5. Throwing a party
6. Renewing wedding vows

*According to a survey by **Bruskin Associates***

Americans believe that children are the most fun between the ages of 5 and 8 and are at their worst between the ages of 15 and 17.

*According to a **Gallup Poll***

A baby born out of wedlock is as deserving of a baby shower as one born of married parents. And probably more in need of one.

Abigail Van Buren

Society teaches us to lie. One of the first things parents teach kids is that they should try to look like they like a gift whether they do or not.

Social psychologist Robert Feldman

My mother abused me from the time I was an infant until I was 6 or 7 years old. She did lots of lurid things...My father molested me until I left home at age 17. He constantly put his hands all over me. He forced me to sit on his lap, to cuddle with him, to play with his penis in the bathtub.

Roseanne Barr
as reported in People

THE SEXES

Those yuppies who are scaling down are simply taking early retirement.

Crystal Jarek

The activities most liked by men: Getting together with friends, watching a movie or entertainment on TV, watching a sports event on TV.

According to **Playboy**

Worst-dressed women of the year:

1. Sinead O'Connor
2. Ivana Trump
3. Glenn Close
4. Queen Elizabeth
5. Julia Roberts

6. Carrie Fisher
7. Kim Basinger
8. Laura Dern
9. Kathy Bates
10. Barbra Striesand

According to **Mr. Blackwell**

The worst-dressed women of the past three decades:

1. Cher
2. Roseanne Barr
3. Elizabeth Taylor
4. Queen Elizabeth II
5. Barbra Streisand
6. Shelley Winters
7. Dolly Parton
8. Mia Farrow
9. Jayne Mansfield
10. Sinead O'Connor

According to **Mr. Blackwell**

The worst-dressed list had nothing to do with women I don't like. If I didn't like them, they'd never make the list. The fact that they don't know how to dress has nothing to do with my personal feelings toward them. I mean, I think Dolly Parton is an absolute doll. She's everybody's dream of a fantasy woman. But I think she dresses like a garbage pail.

Mr. Blackwell
creator of the annual best- and worst-dressed list

Once you've done everything possible physically, the next logical step is plastic surgery. If you look better than the next guy, you'll do better socially, get a better job, and be happier.

Glenn Cannon
on the increase in cosmetic surgery among men under 30

It used to be that only 10% of my face lift patients were under 50—now it's about half.

Dr. Fritz Barton
a Dallas plastic surgeon

[Plastic surgery] has become a status symbol. It's like saying, "Come look at my new car!" The "me" consciousness of the '80s hasn't ended. The men of the '90s want to be noticed for their looks, their bodies.

Plastic surgeon Richard Ellenbogen

Society devalues and desexualizes older women. It would have us believe that we are no longer sexual creatures. In my heart of hearts, I feel myself as thirty, maybe thirty-five at best.

Sexagenarian actress Joanne Woodward

Men are perilously close to becoming pets. Women are starting to see that their lives can go on quite famously without them. Men are no longer the only breadwinners in society.

Watts Wacker

Younger adults are driven by "ego values" such as intellect, reason, objectivity, morality, competition. Mature adults increasingly respond to "being values" such as intuition, feeling, subjectivity, reality, cooperation, and influence.

According to **Dr. Jonas Salk**

The median age of all Americans over the age of 65 is 72, and two-thirds are women.

According to the **Fact Book on Aging**

A jury convicted a woman with several personalities of heroin charges, rejecting her lawyer's contention that she could not be held responsible for the actions of her drug-using identity.

Chronicle Wire Services

Kids do what they see, not what they know. We tell kids not to have sex and then we use sex to sell everything.

Richard P. Keeling

Most unwanted presents are alcohol, clothing, and tickets to sporting or entertainment events. Most wanted gifts are flowers or jewelry.

*According to a **Gallup Poll***

Regardless of how many dates, how many drinks, how many walks on the beach, whose apartment you may be in, the time of night or day, if a woman says no, the man should stop. No debate is needed.

Joe Chizmas

Ten and a half million Americans are alcoholics; 76 million more are affected by alcohol abuse, having been married to an alcoholic or problem drinker or having grown up with one.

*According to a study by the **National Center for Health Statistics***

Women are more skeptical of advertising's message than men are.

*According to "**Adweek**"*

HE: Thirty years ago I was egotistical, shallow, and totally immersed in the quest for money and power. SHE: You were ahead of your time, Earl.

*From a cartoon by **Bill Lee***

Stop thinking of the over-50 population the way that your grandmother was 30 years ago. Stop thinking about ages and think instead about stages of life.

Tom Richman

The estimated worldwide sales of the hair-growth product in 1990, $140 milllion; in 1991, $200 million.

*As reported in **USA Today***

Men who have lost their hair are considered less assertive, less likely to be successful and less likable.

*According to a study by psychologist **Thomas Cash***

Beauty is a conspiracy of pain forced upon women. In the boardroom and in the bedroom, women are entrapped by a cult that is the equivalent

of the iron maiden, a medieval torture instrument that impales its captive
on spikes.

Emily Mitchell

Older is becoming better....Forty now is what used to be 30, 50 is now
what used to be 40, 65 now is the beginning of the second half of
life, not the beginning of the end.

Faith Popcorn

I'm proud to be living in a free, democratic country like America,
where men are men, women are women and whatever's left is on
"Geraldo."

Johnny Carson

The male image for the 1990s:

    Optimal weight: 185 pounds

    Optimal suit size: 42 long

    Optimal waist size: 34 inches

    Optimal height: 6 feet

    Optimal age: 41

    Optimal recreation: power walking

    Optimal lunch drink: anything in cranberry juice

    Optimal subject for conversation: bad 1991/good 1992

According to "Esquire"

The average bust size, once 34B, is now 36C.

According to consumer affairs writer Bernice Kanner

Eighty-eight percent of women wear shoes that are too small for their
feet.

*According to a survey by the American Orthopaedic Foot
and Ankle Society*

The problem [of battered women] won't be solved by just giving women
a place to live. We have to get at the root of the problem and find
a way to help the abusers, too.

Miss America 1991 Marjorie Judith Vincent

The average male owns eighteen pairs of socks, 16 ties, six pairs of shoes, 15 shirts, 5 suits, eight pairs of pants, 12 pairs of undershorts, and 25 T-shirts.

"Details"

The same traits that allow him to make money make it difficult for him to get close. Women are dazzled by...success. But at a deeper level, successful men are often cut off from their personal selves.

Psychologist Herb Goldberg

Subjects of most interest to men:
1. Money
2. Family
3. Sex
4. Sports

Subjects of most interest to women:
1. Family
2. Money
3. Health
4. Reading

According to a survey by **Sports Illustrated**

Household duties performed most often by men: Putting out the garbage, household repairs, washing the dishes.

According to a survey by **Sports Illustrated**

The rule of thumb is, if you're old enough to remember it, you're already too old to wear it.

Fashion consultant Ellin Saltznin

I realized in our culture if you don't have a penis, the only true contribution you can make is to lose 20 pounds. Any of your accomplishments pale in comparison. Ask Oprah Winfrey.

Actress Tyne Daly

In some cases, males will participate in a rape even though they're aware it's wrong and won't be condoned. But the worst thing for them is to lose face and lose respect among the group. That's primary, more primary to them than respecting the laws of the country. It turns into a performance for one another.

Claire Walsh

Unmarried men per 100 unmarried women:

Under 25	111
25-29	127
30-24	125
35-39	99
40-44	83
45-64	60
65+	29

According to the U.S. Census Bureau

I love the differences between men and women. No matter how liberated we all get, they will always be there, thank God. I just think it's time we stopped operating full time out of fear and boundaries and old images, and stepped out and showed ourselves. Why can't that be sexy too?

Actress Ali MacGraw

These days it's not easy to tell a Republican from a Democrat, AM from FM, clothes from underclothes—or a cigarette from a sanitary napkin.

Mary Roach

For males, a good laugh represents the essence of intimacy, for to be intimate for men is not to be connected, but to be with, in the same frame of mind, coming from the same source, from the same point of view.

Don Eric Curtis

If life was fair for men, women would divorce you when you're ten, make passionate love to you when you're 18, and squeeze your cheeks and give you candy when you're 79.

Johnny Carson

It is now accepted in the social sciences that males and females perceive verbal and nonverbal cues in different ways and therefore are exceptionally good at misunderstanding one another.

John Leo

Ours is the love that has historically not spoken its name. Today is the day we speak it proudly and we speak it loudly.

Gay San Francisco Supervisor Harvey Britt
at the first official ceremony registering couples as
"domestic partners"

The persons most admired by teens:
1. Paula Abdul
2. Mom
3. Michael Jordan
4. Dad
5. Barbara Bush
6. Oprah Winfrey
7. Nelson Mandella
8. Donald Trump
9. George Bush
10. Tom Cruise
11. Janice Jackson

*According to a poll by **World Almanac***

Scandals are those things prominent people deny until they can brag about them when they write their memoirs.

Gil Stern

Until women take more responsibility for how they manipulate men with their sexuality, the date-rape problem will persist.

Joe Nicassio

The average American would like to live to be 85.

According to the **Gallup Poll**

SEX

Twenty percent of the population has little or no desire for sexual intercourse.

The American Psychiatric Association

Sneezing is better than sex. It's a mini-instant orgasm. You keep your clothes on, you don't get involved, you can do it in public and when you're done, perfect strangers bless you.

Dentist and standup comic Mark McMahon

The entire American dating system is basically oriented toward a man wearing down a woman's resistance until she finally gives in. We need to make [men] understand that when a woman says no, she means no.

John Furze

The average adult had 1.16 partners in the past year. Married people had sex 67 times; divorced and never-married singles, 55 times; separated adults, 66 times; widowed adults, 6 times.

Men said they had sex 66 times a year on average; women 50 times.

1.5 percent of those married had affairs in the past year. Since marriage, 65 percent of women said they were faithful, 30 percent of men.

As reported in "Family Planning Perspectives"

There are too many boys who consider girls their personal sex labs for gaining manly experience and prestige.

Samantha Johnson

I think amateur adult videos are very positive because people are taking into their own hands the redefinition of sexual conduct. They are not letting the priests, the feminists, the therapists, tell them what sex should be. These people are rejecting the moralistic Judeo-Christian attitude

toward sex, which is that sex is a problem and the more you can wipe it from yourself the closer to God you are.

Writer Camille Paglia
on the new wave of amateur adult videotapes

We're getting a really good cross-section of people. A lot of everyday people, with pot bellies, in their 40s, 50s and 60s.

Mickey Blank
vice president of Homegrown Videos on the new wave
of amateur adult videotapes

The highest form of sex appears to be the imagination, and imagination demands theater, lingerie is theater.

Leon Wieseltier

If love is blind, why is there lingerie?

Elizabeth Snead

Orgasm is very important to all of us. It is a great feeling to get a man one day who is impotent and make him potent another day.

Sex expert Marilene Vargas
at the first global conference on orgasm

A great concert is like great sex. You get wild and frenzied, then turn that around quick to something gentle, tender and slow, and then get wild and crazy again and just keep doing that over and over until one of you drops dead.

Singer Garth Brooks

Although an alarming number of young males are having extreme difficulty staying clear of the law and making a future for themselves through honest work, all too many are having no problem whatsoever making babies.

Virginia Governor Douglas Wilder

Why do women fake orgasms? Because men fake foreplay.

Unknown

Feminism is not antisexuality; on the contrary. It says that sexuality shouldn't be confused with violence and dominance and that it should be a matter of free choice. It shouldn't be forced on you by economics, including dependence on a husband, or by pressure.

Publisher Gloria Steinem

We know many kids are having sex too early, too often, with too many people. We ought to figure out how to divert them from that conduct.

Gary Bauer of the Family Research Council

Remember when safe sex meant your parents had gone away for the weekend?

Rhonda Hansome

Adolescents have the greatest probability of losing their virginity during their summer vacations.

According to psychologist Joseph Lee Rogers

Despite AIDS, two in three adults ages 27–45 see nothing wrong with premarital sex. But 70 percent of these baby boomers are now parents and they also favor earlier sex education, laws banning sex-talk 900 lines, and less sexual freedom for their teenagers than they themselves enjoyed.

Larry Hugick and Jennifer Leonard
reporting on a new Gallup poll

More than half of American women ages 15–19 have had premarital sex, and nearly three-quarters of sexually active young women have had more than one partner.

According to a survey by the National Centers for
Disease Control

13

WORK

I gave youse $300,000 in one year. Youse didn't defend me...You're plucking me. I'm paying for it. Where does it end? Gambino crime family? This is the Shargel, Cutler, and who-do-you-call it crime family.

*Reputed Gambino crime family boss John Gotti
about the work of his defense team, Shargel, Cutler, and Pollok*

People in the USA throw away enough office and writing paper each year to build a wall 8 1/2" wide and 7 feet high from Los Angeles to New York City.

According to Franklin Associates

The top lunchtime favorite for females is salad, for males a sandwich.

According to a survey by Western Temporary Services

A generation ago most men who finished a day's work needed rest. Now they need exercise.

Mrs. P. D. Brothers

The 80s are over, along with the clutter and toomuchness.

Louis Oliver Gropp

Don't give up. Keep going. There is always a chance that you will stumble onto something terrific. I have never heard of anyone stumbling over anything while he was sitting down.

Ann Landers
quoting Charles F. Kettering

By the year 2000, we will all be talking into our word processors instead of typing.

Jan Galvin
director of assertive technology at the
National Rehabilitation Hospital

Let us set the record straight: the work ethic is not (a traditional value). It is a johnny-come lately value...In ancient times, work was considered a disgrace inflicted on those who had failed to amass a nest egg through imperial conquest or of the forms of organized looting.

Barbara Ehrenreich

I believe in the work ethic, just not the hard work ethic.

From a cartoon by Cottiaon

Even though unions are recognized as legitimate, they are still relatively weak compared to other groups in the polity, such as employers. They have to renegotiate their status every time their contract expires. Union members resort to violence when they feel their organization's existence is threatened.

Professor Don Grant

In terms of earnings and employment levels, at least, industries that are protected show no improvement over those that aren't. And in certain industries (including leather shoes, color televisions, and automobiles), stock returns and numbers of employees declined significantly after protective policies were enacted.

*According to a study by **J. Kimball Dietrich and Victor Canto***

By the time Toyota closed its deal to build an assembly plant in Georgetown, Kentucky, the state's taxpayers had contributed $300 million—the plant's entire wage bill for two or three years.

Professor Candace Howes

"Voluntary Death and Dismemberment Plan"
Title of a report sent to all U.S. Leasing employees

HOLLYWOOD

Sigourney Weaver complains that she's not making as much money as Paul Newman. Well, some of us are not making as much as she is, and we're just as good.

Actress Whoopi Goldberg

I find myself leaning more toward light comedy, because I have a two-year-old. I don't really want to come home every day thinking about the Vietnamese girl who was raped, murdered, and thrown off the bridge. It makes it tough to play with my son. I don't have aspirations to change the world, just to make a nice, simple movie.

Actor Michael J. Fox

I do it six days a week. On Sunday, I rest. I go to church and make love to my wife. With this schedule, everybody's happy.

Actor Jean-Claude Van Damme
on his workout schedule

It's hard for my wife to watch women actually shove their hands down the back of my pants. And while I know how uncomfortable it is for me, it's hard for anyone else to understand that this kind of adulation is more persecution than pleasure.

Actor Patrick Swayze
on being a sex symbol

Being an actor is like being a currency in the currency exchange. Today they are going, "Hey, you're the deutsche mark"...Then they turn around and say, "Hey, somebody else is the deutsche mark. You're the peso."

Actor Alec Baldwin

In show business, women have it hard. Just imagine if I had to wear skintight pants and take my clothes off in almost every film I did. Women have to do this every time. It's what they're expected to do. I think if I were a woman, I'd be a whore.

Actor Bruce Willis

I couldn't get any jobs, and when that happens, you get so humble it's disgusting. I didn't feel like a man anymore—I felt really creepy. I was bumping into walls and saying, "Excuse me."

Actor Joe Pesci

The most important thing you need to make a hit band is promotion...The second thing you need is a pretty good song...Third—last and least—what you need to have is talent.

Maurice Starr
creator of New Kids on the Block

I enjoy singing every kind of song and in different languages. If anything, I think my success has been my ability to learn how to entertain people with different kinds of music.

Shirley Bassey

I've never been so relieved and have never crossed myself so fervently and thank God as much as when ["Sister Kate"] got cancelled. I don't mind being upstaged for a good cause, you know, but timing comedy with children is one of the most painful things you can possibly do, either as an actor or a human being.

Actress Stephanie Beacham

African Americans have traditionally been shut out (by Hollywood), and our report shows they still are—in the main—shut out. We found that several factors have combined to produce this result: nepotism, cronyism, and racial discrimination.

According to a National Association for the Advancement
of Colored People study

Arnold Schwarzenegger was paid $15 million for his role in "Terminator 2," and spoke 700 words. That's $21,429 per word. Such classic lines and their monetary value: "Hasta la vista, baby," $85,716; "I insist," $42,858; and "Stay here, I'll be back," $107,145.

As reported by "Entertainment Weekly"

I don't generally look at scripts....I don't care what [a film] is about. At $200,000 a week, what do I care what it's about?

Actor Mickey Rooney

I'm an artist; art has no color and no sex.

Actress Whoopi Goldberg
on being the first black woman to win an Oscar in over 50 years

I wasn't a poor little thing. I don't know what I would have done if I'd had to come to New York and get a job as a waiter or something like that. I think I'm a success, but I had every advantage—I should have been.

Actress Katharine Hepburn

As a heterosexual ballet dancer, you develop a thick skin.

Ronald Reagan, Jr.

In the industry, it's very easy for a record company to tell you they want you to sound like so and so. And it's very difficult to establish a sound of your own. As a matter of fact, sometimes the road is a lot longer but it pays off because you have a stronger foundation and you know deep down inside what you're about.

Dianne Reeves

The part jumped straight off the script into my mind like the Alien. I immediately knew Lechter's voice, how he looked. I understood his complexities. It was easy. I use to make heavy weather of acting. Now I just learn my lines, show up and do it. No need to torture myself.

Actor Anthony Hopkins
describing his role as Dr. Hannibal Lechter in
"The Silence of the Lambs"

This part came very easily—which doesn't say much for my mental health.

Anthony Hopkins
on his role as Hannibal the Cannibal

Because it covered her zits better than color—no kidding.

Director Alek Kenshishian
on why he shot portions of "Madonna: Truth or Dare"
in black and white

A number of sources tell us that for starring in the film ["A Few Good Men"] as a military lawyer [Tom] Cruise will receive a $12.5 million paycheck. These same sources have told us that [Jack] Nicholson's salary, for playing a base commander and working all of two weeks on the project, will be $5 million.

People

It took a long time to come to the realization that I loathe acting. And, unless someone tempts me with a vast sum of money to secure my daughter's future, I'll never do it again.

Actor/director Sean Penn

What writers do is very solitary, and what actors do is very collaborative. And it's frustrating and hurtful to an actor when writers won't listen.

Actress Julia Duffy

I can't sit around worrying about how smart or pretty people think I am, or how lucky. I do my work. I enjoy my work. I love my life.

Mary Hart
of "Entertainment Tonight"

Comedy is something I've come to slowly and rather reluctantly. It's the most difficult of the things we do and very easy to fail at.

Actor Peter O'Toole

With a play, I have only two people to please—myself and the director. With this movie, it was 19 executives, a director who'd never done anything but animation before, and two stars who would tell you what lines they'd say and what lines they wouldn't say.

Neil Simon
on making "The Marrying Man"

It's a very strange time for men's roles these days. To be a contender, a man must be sort of half John Wayne, half Shirley MacLaine, and that's really hard to show in a 30-second commerical.

Barbara Lippert
discussing the right image for marketing men's perfume

I'm often asked why I like directing more than acting. Simple. Because you can arrive on the set with dirty, stringy hair. You don't have to look pretty and well-groomed to direct.

Actress/director Penny Marshall

There aren't so many scripts for women as for men. That's life. We don't make as much money as men do. But I make so much money from this that I can't bellyache about it.

Actress Cher

LABOR

Fifty-eight percent of all married couples are dual earners.

Particia Braus

Ronald Reagan has held the two most demeaning jobs in the country—President of the United States and radio broadcaster for the Chicago Cubs.

Columnist George Will

Ratio of the average CEO's salary to that of a blue-collar worker in 1980: 25 to 1. Ratio today: 91 to 1.

According to "Harper's"

Everyone is elated and eager to return to work. This is a great victory for the working men and women of America.

Labor leader George McDonald
on the purchase of The New York Daily News *by*
British publisher Robert Maxwell

Being the Playmate of the Year was good for me. A lot of the girls don't get anywhere. But, of course, you don't know what roles you didn't get.

Playmate of the Year, Shannon Tweed

Pregnancy discrimination is the No. 1 topic on our job-problem hot line.

Barbara Otto
a spokeswoman for the advocacy group 9 to 5.

Why does a hearse horse snicker/Hauling a lawyer away?

Martin Kirby
quoting Carl Sandburg

Pregnant women who use video display terminals in their work are no more likely to suffer miscarriages than women who do not.

According to a report by the National Institute for
Occupational Safety and Health

I feel like a guy in an open casket at his own funeral. Everyone walks by and says what a good guy you were. But it doesn't do any good. You're still dead.

Exbaseball manager Tom Trebelhorn
on what it's like to be fired

In view of the link between work and mental health, job-training programs don't just put bread on the table—they contribute to the mental health of a community.

Professor Julian Rappaport

If life is a jigsaw puzzle, the lawyer's job is to place a handful of pieces on the table and convince his viewers they saw a complete picture.

Chris Goodrich
in Anarchy and Elegance: Confessions of a Journalist
at Yale Law School

Despite unique personalities and positions, professional women are facing a remarkably similar set of challenges as they break into all-male fields. [They] are jumping through the same sets of hoops in an almost identical order.

Beth Milwid
author of Working with Men

Nine out of ten white collar workers say they have it as good or better than people working in other companies.

*According to a **Gallup Poll***

Younger women are nearly as segregated into traditionally female jobs as middle-aged and older women.

*According to a study by the **Older Women's League***

We seem to be able to mobilize the resources of our country for Desert Storm and bailing out the savings and loans, but we haven't been doing it for our unemployed workers.

John Sturdivant
president of the American Federation of Government Employees

One out of every 160 employed Americans work at the Postal Service. People are 83% of our cost. Up to 14 different hands handle each piece of mail. If we make a house call on every home and every business six days a week we do it for 29 cents, plumbers charge 58 bucks.

Postmaster general Anthony Frank

When measured by international standards, most American workers are not well-trained...Our major foreign competitors place much greater emphasis on developing workforce skills at all levels...American manufacturing and service workers have the skills for yesterday's routine jobs.

*According to **Congress's Office of Technology Assessment***

Medical studies have found that about one-fourth of patients who develop a job-related dermatitis cannot be cured with medical therapies or by changing the way in which they work. These people may be forced to change careers because of a skin disease.

Dr. C. G. Toby Mathias

Professions ranked by heart attack risk, in descending order:

1. Bartenders
2. Laundry and dry-cleaning operators
3. Public Adminstraion
4. Food service workers

5. Private child-care workers

6. Bus drivers

*From a study by **Professor J. Paul Leigh**
of 8,130 full-time workers*

Many professionals are unable to take time out from their schedules to travel to a therapist's office. I make it convenient for them, so that a one-hour session can be substituted for a lunch break. We drive around the city and discuss their problems.

*New York psychotherapist **Alice Fox**
who sees patients in her limousine*

Electrocution is the fifth leading cause of work-related deaths.

*According to the **American Society of Safety Engineers***

In nearly 51% of married couples, both partners worked outside the home.

*According to "**Work In America**"*

To date, 38 women have earned more than a million dollars in commissions during their Mary Kay careers.

*From an advertisement for **Mary Kay cosmetics***

Repetitive motion cumulative trauma disorders are now the most common occupational illnesses, accounting for about one-half of all job disorders.

Barbara Goldofstas

Benefits valued by workers:

1. Health insurance coverage for employee

2. Health insurance for dependents

3. Pension plan

4. Retirement savings plan

5. Vacation

*According to a **Northwestern National Life Insurance
Company** survey*

The average workweek in:

Japan	46.8 hours
U.S.	41.0 hours
West Germany	40.5 hours
U.S.S.R.	39.0 hours

According to "Country Forecasts"

The five least stressful jobs:

1. Forester
2. Bookbinder
3. Telephone line worker
4. Tool maker
5. Millwright

According to the American Institute of Stress

Industries with the largest number of occupational injuries and illnesses:

1. Meat products manufacturing
2. Motor vehicle manufacturing
3. Nursing homes
4. Trucking and courier services (except air)
5. Wholesaling grocery products

"Monthly Labor Review"

More than five million drug abusers work at small businesses.

According the the Small Business Administration

Women really must have equal pay for equal work, equality in work at home, and reproductive choices. Men must press for these things also. They must cease to see them as "women's issues" and learn that they are everyone's issues—essential to survival on planet Earth.

Writer Erica Jong

America's fastest-growing jobs:
  1. Paralegals
  2. Medical Assistants
  3. Radiological Technologists
  4. Homemaker — Home Health Aids
  5. Medical Record Technicians
  6. Medical Secretaries
  7. Physical Therapists
  8. Surgical Technologists
  9. Securities and Financial-Services Representatives
  10. Operations/Research Analysts

From the "The Futurist"

The U.S. won't have a competitive workforce unless it creates opportunities for youth trapped in an urban pit of hopelessness, anger, and despair.

John E. Jacob

Spies are different from spycatchers. Spies do healthy things, collecting information and analyzing it. Spying is still important; the old targets are still valid...We have to make certain that no half-wit nationalist does something stupid.

Tom Mangold

What satisfies employees the most:
  1. Being treated with fairness and respect
  2. Pay
  3. Job security
  4. Benefits
  5. Recognition for performance

*According to a study by **International Survey Research Corp.***

The Bureau of Labor Statistics estimates that there were 15.3 million Americans aged 55 and older in the U.S. workforce last year, compared with 14.3 million in 1975.

Beatrice Motamedi

People think modeling's mindless, that you just stand there and pose, but it doesn't have to be that way. I like to have a lot of input. I know how to wear a dress, whether it should be shot with me standing up or sitting. And I'm not scared to say what I think.

Top Model Linda Evangelista

More than 7,200,000 Americans—6.2% of the workforce—hold two jobs, the highest level in three decades. In addition, daily absenteeism in America's offices and factories is 3.5%, compared with 8.14% in northern European countries.

According to **USA Today**

You can teach a friendly person to be a waiter. You can't teach a waiter to be a friendly person.

Restauranteur Allen J. Bernstein

Given the choice between two jobs, identical except that one offers flexibility and benefits, 90% of working Americans would choose the employer offering flexibility.

According to the **Employee Benefit Research Institute**

If you want creative workers, give them enough time to play.

John Cleese

It's not a pay raise; it's a pay equalization.

Senator Ted Stevens
on the $23,200 raise in Senate salaries

Fifty-four percent of adults polled would prefer a change from eight-hour shifts and five-day workweeks to ten-hour shifts and four-day workweeks.

According to the **Gallup Organization**

The basic right to strike has been turned on its head—from a tool of workers in their effort to improve their conditions to a weapon of employers in their efforts to eliminate unions.

Greg Tarpinian

Forty-one percent of Americans said leisure was "the important thing" in their lives; only 36% put work first. Among college students, 47% put leisure ahead of labor.

*According to a **Roper Organization** survey*

Occupations where current workers are 50% more likely than average to have symptoms of depression:

1. Law
2. Apparel sales
3. School counseling
4. Typing and secretarial work
5. Supervising sales staff
6. Operating computer equipment

Occupations where current workers are 50% less likely than average to have symptoms of depression:

1. Teaching secondary school
2. Treating illness
3. Testing goods
4. Precision textile work
5. Miscellaneous repair and mechanical work
6. Repairing electrical equipment

*According to **The Journal of Occupational Medicine***

Of all job-related illnesses, the largest single group is skin disease.

*According to the **Bureau of Labor Statistics***

Most families headed by baby boomers and younger adults get ahead of their parents by living in a dual-earner household, by delaying marriage and childbirth and by spending more years in school.

Joe Schwartz

Pregnant women who have jobs that require prolonged standing are more likely to give birth prematurely.

*According to a **Yale University** study*

The General Accounting Office has calculated that, including only pay, medical, and retirement benefits, military compensation is now 27% higher on average than that of comparable federal civil-service employees.

James F. Dunigan and Albert A. Nofi

Playboy's centerfold Playmate of the Month is paid $15,000; Penthouse's Pet of the Month is paid $5,000.

According to **M inc.** *magazine*

Playmate averages, 1977–1990:

    Bust size—35 inches

    Waist size—23 inches

    Hip size—34 inches

    Weight—113 pounds

    Height—5 feet 6 inches

    Age—22

According to **Playboy**

The person 50 and over is regarded as someone who buckles down to the task at hand and devotes his or her full attention to the job, and does not move frequently from job to job.

James Challenger

Despite all those years at home with Dagwood and the kids, Blondie's earning capacity won't be much worse than that of other women. If she is typical, her earnings will peak at about age 40–50 at $22,000....Just about what the average man earns between 25 and 29.

Columnist Ellen Goodman

When equally qualified young men, one black and the other white—apply for entry-level job openings, the white advances higher in the hiring process one out of every five times.

According to a study and analysis of hiring by the **Urban Institute**

Legal training doesn't create selfish, aggressive people—but it does provide the intellectual equipment with which recipients can justify and give force to beliefs and actions most people would wholeheartedly condemn.

Chris Goodrich

Although fewer than 20 percent of the employees said that coworkers and the grapevine were their preferred source of information, 95 percent most frequently got their company news and information from them.

According to a survey by Deluxe Data Systems

The most successful person is the one who understands in totality what he is doing. That's what makes Magic Johnson such a great basketball player. He understands every position on the court, not just his position. You need that kind of complete understanding to be good at what you do, be it music or any other profession.

Wynton Marsalis

The traditional Orthodox Jewish matchmaker charges on a sliding scale from $500 to $5000. She is paid after the engagement and before the wedding ceremony.

According to "New York Woman"

It wasn't just a victory about make-up—this was about company prerogative and personal choice.

Teresa Fischett
a Continental Airlines' employee fired for refusing to wear
make-up, after getting her job back

The greatest way to serve is to give someone a job and make him independent.

Andrew Young

Most home office workers are men, approximately 35 years old with at least two years of college. He is presently earning $24,000 annually and wants to earn an additional $20,000 per year.

According to the American Institute of Computer Technology

More than three-fourths of the people surveyed said they prefer to take a number of brief vacations during the year—less than a week or just a long weekend.

According to the **American Productivity and Quality Center**

Although blacks make up 12 percent of the U.S. population and more than 11 percent of all magazine readers, they appear in only 4.5 percent of all magazine advertisements and constitute a little more than 3 percent of the characters in those advertisements.

Reported by **The New York Times**

Sampling of big name speaker fees:

Margaret Thatcher	$60,000-65,000 plus private jet
Ronald Reagan	$50,000-60,000
Tom Peters	$45,000
Ted Koppel	$30,000
Henry Kissinger	$30,000
Dianne Sawyer	$20,000
Tommy Lasorda	$15,000
Dr. Joyce Brothers	$ 8,500

According to **Capital Speakers, Inc.**

Honorable police officers, who are in the majority, do themselves and the whole criminal-justice system a great disservice any time they fail to speak out against acts of unwarranted violence by their colleagues.

Joe H. Hamilton

Between 1973 and 1987, the percentage of men earning less than the poverty line—approximately $12,000 for a family of four a year—grew from 8.4 percent to 13.2 percent for whites, from 24.9 percent to 33 percent for African-Americans, and from 19.6 percent to 33.9 percent for Hispanics.

According to a study by the **Institute for Research on Poverty**

[Women police officers] are less authoritarian and use force less often than their male counterparts. They gain compliance without excessive force on the average more than men do...and they respond more effectively to incidents of violence against women.

Eleanor Smeal

In South Africa, they fire you for striking. In America, they replace you for striking. There is no difference, my friends—it's apartheid in America!

Cecil Roberts

No matter which direction I turn, I end up at the refrigerator. This is one of the hazards of the home office.

Columnist Jon Carroll

One out of every eleven Americans works at a shopping mall.

According to "Harper's"

The fastest growing segment of the labor market is mothers of infants....By the year 2000, 90% of the women entering the workforce will be dealing with the maternity and child care issues at some time during their careers.

Evelyn Block

You have to come up with a funny idea a day for the rest of your life. Then you have to execute it in 25 words or less, in a small space.

Nancy Nicolelis
on being a successful cartoonist

Merit pay is not merit pay. The differences may be caused by the system. It's rewarding the circumstances. The same thing as rewarding the weatherman for a pleasant day.

W. Edwards Deming

The average age of farmers is 52. There are now twice as many farmers over the age of 60 as there are under the age of 35. Over the next ten years, farmers will be retiring in record numbers. Who will grow the nation's food then?

Leland Eikermann

The survey found that nearly one in six employed adults now works a second job. More than one in three works regular evenings or weekends, up from one in four in 1989. Elements of job satisfaction have dropped 3 to 8 percentage points during the same time.

*According to a new **Gallup Mirror of America** poll*

Living in our society is like living in a very tall building. The rich live on the top floors. The poor live on the lowest floors. And only cops travel to all the floors. Only a cop sees it all.

Detective Ted O'Connor

I make good money. That's why I do it, and that's why I've been doing it since I was 15. If I worked at McDonald's for minimum wage, then I'd have low self-esteem.

An anonymous prostitute

We are overpaid. And we're a little embarrassed by what we make. Because the salaries are not why anyone gets into this business. And we don't determine the market.

Dianne Sawyer
who earns a reported $1.5 million as an ABC newswoman

Does America really need 70 percent of the world's lawyers? There is one lawyer for every 335 people in the U.S., as opposed to one for every 9000 people in Japan.

Vice President Dan Quayle
before the annual meeting of the American Bar Association

There is something deeply wrong when the metropolitan Washington, D.C., area has nearly four times as many lawyers by itself as the entire nation of Japan, or that we have 26 times as many lawyers per capita as Japan, and 2 1/2 times as many as Germany, our two biggest competitive rivals.

Warren T. Brookes

MANAGEMENT

On an average business day, 2,200 people are laid off.

Mark Memmott

Employees for the most part, tend to drift to the level of work ethics and productivity of the corporate culture they're in. It wo..ld be extremely hard to discipline another employee for not reporting to work when the V. P. doesn't show up either.

Sarah Thornton

Of course women will have trouble getting to the top. They were not made for it.

Romance writer Barbara Cartland

Leading methods used by companies to avoid lay-offs:
1. Hiring freezes
2. Salary freezes
3. Intracompany transfers
4. Early retirement plans

American Management Association Survey

Rightsizing, smart-sizing—Terms substituting for "downsizing"; Work force adjustment, redundancy elimination, requested departure, negotiated departure, premature retirement, vocational relocation, coerced transition, personnel surplus reduction—Terms substituting for firing employees.

As reported in the "Marin Independent Journal"

Fortune 500 companies with the highest percentage of top executives who are women:
1. International Paper
2. Georgia Pacific
3. Eastman Kodak
4. Dow Chemical
5. Mobil

According to the Feminist Majority Foundation

Less than 3 percent of the top jobs at Fortune 500 companies were held by women in 1990.

Associated Press

I can comfortably speculate that if, a year from now, the show ["Real Life with Jane Pauley"] is not on the air, I will not be clutching my chest in despair. But when you've got a show that has your name attached to it, you are responsible for a lot of jobs, and hat sends shivers through me. When I think about all those families I am supporting, I get tension headaches and grind my teeth.

Jane Pauley

Operating a hotel is, I think, a woman's business. It's knowing food, keeping a room clean—it's running a house on a larger scale.

Hotel owner Leona Helmsley

Women in Alaska are almost three times more likely to own a business than a women in Mississippi.

According to "American Demographics"

Small-business owners work an average of 52.5 hours per week, compared to 43.5 hours per week by Americans in general.

According to the National Association for the Self-Employed

Employee empowerment requires fostering a culture in which employees are encouraged to make decisions. The role of managers is to set parameters for how, when, and where those decisions are made.

American Society for Training and Development

We are so imbued with the superlative player that we forget that there are people supporting the organization that are not superstars but they're good solid people. We have not ignited or excited the people who are the meat and potatoes of the business.

John Knappenberger

A lot of managers get trapped because they're threatened by good people. Therefore, they're constantly reinforcing their own paradigm—that if it weren't for me this place would go downhill.

Scott Gibson

Congress has changed pension laws 15 times in the last 10 years. Small- and medium-sized employers increasingly are reluctant to offer adequate retirement plans because of frequent changes and the added complexities of compliance.

James A. Curtis

The top factor that makes their organization successful according to senior managers in large companies:

1. United States   customer service
2. Japan   product development
3. Germany   work force skills

As reported in "ComputerWorld"

It's the most important thing that entrepreneurs have going for them: brazen stupidity.

Mo Siegel

Corporations have a lot of cats and dogs working for them. The dogs are eager, enthusiastic, good-natured, clumsy team players. The cats are quiet, competent, thoughtful, even-tempered individualists. So who gets promoted? The dogs, of course...If you want to get to the top, be smart like a cat and act like a dog.

Al Ries and Jack Trout

The most popular perks:

1. Company car/limousine
2. Disability coverage
3. Entertainment expense account
4. Telephone credit cards
5. Company car for personal use

According to the National Institute of Business Management

We have a workplace that focuses on control versus management, surveillance versus supervision. Companies need to invest in human consultants.

Barbara Otto

First, corporations introduced child-care services for employees' kids. Next came "eldercare" for workers with older parents. Now a handful of companies are bucking the recessionary trend and adding some new twists to family benefits. They're offering frazzled working parents guidance on their kids' education or counseling couples who want to adopt a child.

Larry Reibstein

By sheer force of their growing numbers in management ranks, women will force open the door to the executive suite over the next two decades.

Joseph F. Coates, Jennifer Jarratt, and John D. Mahaffie
from their book, Future Work

SEXUAL HARRASSMENT

He talked about pornographic materials depicting individuals with large penises or large breasts involved in various sex acts. On other occasions, he referred to the size of his own penis as being larger than normal and he also spoke on some occasions of the pleasures he had given to women with oral sex.

Anita Hill

I can only say that I think this is part of the frustration that I am experiencing and a lot of women are experiencing—that these kinds of claims and statements are not taken seriously, that this is not an issue that men can deal with necessarily without a lot of different supporting documentation, and that just does not happen in most cases.

Anita Hill
on the "Today" show

As I told the Federal Bureau of Investigation of Sept. 28, 1991, I totally and unequivocally deny Anita Hill's allegations of misconduct of any kind toward her, sexual or otherwise. These allegations are untrue.

From the signed affidavit of **Clarence Thomas**

Language thoroughout the history of this country, and certainly throughout my life—language about the sexual prowess of Black men, language about the sex organs of black men and the sizes, etc....That kind of language has been used about Black men as long as I've been on the face of this Earth.

Clarence Thomas

If you want to track through this country in the 19th and 20th centuries the lynchings of Black men, you will see that there is invariably a relationship with sex and an accusation that person cannot shake off. That is the point that I'm trying to make...that this is a high-tech lynching.

Clarence Thomas

From the very beginning, charges were leveled against me from the shadows, charges of drug abuse, antisemitism, wife beating, drug use by family members. This is not American, this is Kafkaesque. It has got to stop. It must stop for the benefit of future nominees and our country.

Clarence Thomas

Today, now, is a time to move forward, a time to look for what is good in others, what is good in our country. It is a time to see what we have in common, what we share as human beings and citizens.

Clarence Thomas
on being sworn in as the nation's 106th Supreme Court justice

In its broadest definition, [sexual harassment] is sexual pressure that you are not in a position to refuse. In its verbal form, it includes a working environment that is saturated with sexual innuendos, propositions, advances...In its physical form, it includes unwanted sexual touching and rape.

Catharine A. MacKinnon
author of Sexual Harassment of Working Women

Sexual harassment, like rape, has nothing to do with sex. It's about power. It's about a man who asks a coworker out and is rejected, but decides he won't take no for an answer. He will prevail.

Jean Reid Norman

Capitol Hill is not just a place where you can bounce checks with impunity...It's a place where men can listen to Clarence Thomas' straight-faced claim that he had no opinion on abortion, and then question Anita Hill's credibility.

Columnist Ellen Goodman

In a sense, Anita Hill is every woman trying to make it in a man's world. She is your wife, your sister and your daughter.

"Newsday"

I understand what she feared...that the focus would not be on what Clarence Thomas did to Anita Hill, but on what Anita Hill did to Clarence Thomas.

Anna Quindlen

It is difficult to feel polite, knowing the (politicians) are more concerned about how this looks for them, for their party, for their procedures and their political prospects than in discovering what really happened.

Anna Quindlen

There really are "sexists" and "sexual harassers" today, men who (like, say, Ted Kennedy) have been taught, often by their fathers, that women are merely vessels for their animal pleasures, and if occasionally a woman must pay with her reputation or her health or even (as with a certain famous politician) her life, well, that's just the price women have to pay for the pleasure of these men.

Wes Pruden

Date rape assumes a different perspective on the part of the man and the woman. His date, her rape. Sexual harassment comes with some of the same assumptions. What he labels sexual, she labels harassment.

Columnist Ellen Goodman

There is no proof that Anita Hill has perjured herself, and shame on anyone who suggests that she has.

Senator Edward Kennedy

To compare his predicament to that of thousands of Black men who lost their life during lynching was a shameful affront to the legacy of the civil rights movement and to the memory of these men.

Rep. John Lewis

It is not Black women who have lynched Black men. It is white racism that has been tolerated for so long by many of Judge Thomas' supporters. It is a problem that will not be addressed by attacking and demeaning Black women.

Rep. Craig Washington

Ironically, a man who has said over and over again that if you work hard, if you're smart, you can achieve success in this country, a man who has said that you don't need affirmative action, a man who has said that it has nothing to do with being Black or white, that if you're good at what you do, then you can rise to high levels in this country, resorted to a Black defense.

Rep. Maxine Waters

What this says to harassing men all over the country is that your record of harassment is a time bomb that can be brought out at any time. The legal statute of limitations is short but the moral statute of limitations is long. And the higher you go, the more likely it is to come up.

Sociologist Lee Bowker

The theory that this has somehow been a seminar on sexual harassment is undercut by the depressing realization that this is what happens to women who stand up and complain. She was the target of a massive attack quarterbacked by the White House. Frankly, the lesson for women is pretty grim.

Columnist Molly Ivins

It is important to note that among Afro-Americans, Black Americans, that the support [for Clarence Thomas] is very, very strong. That is significant and I think highly important.

President George Bush

Women across the country understand why Anita Hill stayed at her job, why she kept phoning Thomas. They understand that you need to put up with harassment, that this is your job and your life. But men don't understand, because they have options that are far better and far greater.

Dr. Frances Conley

Men don't understand that caged feeling. But women know what sexual harassment is. It's when your neck hairs stand up, when you feel like you're being stalked.

Sociologist Susan Marshall

Fighting sexual harassment is in everyone's best interest. In past studies, 15% of men surveyed said they had experienced sexual harassment on the job. As women gain power in the workplace, those numbers will increase. Women are not above abusing power.

Jean Reid Norman

Sexual harassment complaints filed with the EEOC in 1981—3,661; in 1990, 5,694.

As reported in "Newsweek"

Unacceptable workplace activities:

1. Kissing
2. Ethnic jokes
3. Sexual jokes
4. Swearing
5. Short skirts

According to a survey conducted by "Working Smart"

Men don't learn a lot of different ways of relating to women other than in sexual or flirtatious ways.

Richard Meth
author of Men in Therapy

There is a tendency for men to feel "She wasn't fired. She wasn't hit. It's not that big a deal." Actions are what count for men, not words. Women seem to give more emphasis than men to the power of words, and they expend great effort to avoid conflict and confrontation or hurting anyone's feelings.

Catharine A. MacKinnon

Many men are sensitive and do know where the line is drawn between acceptable and inappropriate behavior. But for those men who are still, quote, groping, unquote, we may see an increased reluctance to express compliments or share even a modicum of their personal lives with their employees.

Karen Walden
editor, "New Woman"

Senate Judiciary Committee: "Gosh, we didn't think it was an example of sexual harassment. We thought it was an example of natural law!"

From a cartoon by Wright

14

SIGNS OF THE TIMES

Fantasia Unlimited runs home parties, but instead of Tupperware, the company sells underwear and other products to make sex more pleasurable.

Reporter Constance Walker

Minnesotans can pick their lottery numbers through their Nintendo video game equipment. The state is testing this method by letting 10,000 residents pick lottery numbers at home, using the game and a state lottery cartridge.

USA Today

My friends and I all want romance in our lives, but we're not sure whether it really occurs. We've seen too many long-term relationships that did not work. I think what it must have been like to go home and to dream about a woman instead of just to go home with her.

Twenty-six-year-old interviewee, Paul

Department store chain Sears Canada, Inc. has agreed to stop selling women's boxer shorts that have NO!NO!NO! printed in black all over them, which changes to YES!YES!YES! in the dark.

Reuters

You owe it to the women in your life to keep their best interests in mind....Don't burden yourself and someone you care for with a child neither of you is ready to bear.

From the revised **Boy Scout Handbook**

Consensual nonmonogamy

Term currently being used to describe wife-swapping or swinging

The number of teenagers "huffing" or inhaling household products is reportedly higher than the number abusing cocaine.

According to the **National Institute on Drug Abuse**

If your newly found love won't use a condom, you are in bed with a witless...and uncaring person.

From **The New Joy of Sex**

Dial-A-Map—offers its subscribers directions by phone for 48,000 cities in the U.S. and Canada.

Unknown

There was a message from my youngest son: "I am the son you're looking for. My brother and I have been looking for you for many years.

Robert Switzer
who used CompuServe to contact his two long-lost sons

"The Great Doonesbury Sellout Catalog"—a catalog of items related to the "Doonesbury" comic strip.

Developed by **Garry Trudeau**

FAXable greeting cards—100 separate FAXes conceived for a wide variety of occasions.

Developed by **Workman Publishing**

My health is good and my English You can see here. I have the wife and the daughter and I'd like to work to keep them. I'd agree with

the very dirty work that You'll can to offer me and I'm ready to be everywhere You'll need me (without my family).

*From a resume of a Byelorussian
received by the Massachusetts Institute of Technology*

Sun Spots—small, adhesive yellow spots that indicate when sunscreen is no longer effective.

Made by **Sun Du Jour**

Next-day-mail is now obsolete.

According to a spokesman for **The Fax Exchange**

Viewers will see more of shipboard life in some episodes, which will, among other things, include gay crew members in day-to-day circumstances.

Gene Roddenberry
the producer of "Star Trek"

Ann M. Munson and Marie A. Hanson joyfully celebrated their loving and committed relationship of 13 years by officially registering their domestic partnership on February 19, 1991, with the Minneapolis City Clerk's Office. The event was attended by friends and loved ones followed by a congratulatory breakfast at Ruby's Cafe.

An announcement appearing in the **Minneapolis Star Tribune**

Our bowls and plates are made of oatmeal and can be eaten or thrown away after use. Unlike plastic foam, they won't cause any pollution because birds and dogs can eat them.

Lin Wan-jung
spokesman for Taiwan Sugar Co.

Subway Smell—an aerosol blend that lets you close your eyes and pretend you're back in the undergound tunnels of the Big Apple.

The Los Angeles Daily News

Everyone puts in voice mail to save time and money, but what happens is that they waste other people's time and money by making them listen to stupid messages. Eventually, there is so much voice mail that everybody ends up wasting the time and money they were trying to save.

Mark Foster
of Consumer Action

In this small Midwestern city, a 42-year-old woman is pregnant with her own grandchildren. The woman, Arlette Schweitzer, is carrying twins produced from her daughter's eggs, fertilized in a laboratory dish with sperm from her daughter's husband.

Gina Kolata

Born: To Arlette Schweitzer, 42, acting as a surrogate mother for her daughter who was born without a uterus, twins, a boy and girl... Oct. 12.

"Newsweek"

If a married man has an affair, it may not be with a woman.

*From an ad about AIDS by the **Health Education Authority***

From waking up in the morning to going to bed at night, my son does nothing but play Ninja Turtles. He has Turtles on his underpants, Turtles on his lunchbox, and he wears a Turtle mask for most of the day. Sometimes I worry that he'll grow up warped in some way. I mean, just how much time can you spend communing with turtles?

Anonymous mother of a four-year-old

A couple who were arrested after a neighbor viedotaped them having sex face charges of lewd and lascivious conduct in Tampa, Fla. because nearby children allegedly saw them through the open blinds of a condominium.

Associated Press

You begin to grow up the moment you die.

Graffito

TV is king and we are its court jester.

Grafitto

The macrograffiti expresses a political perspective, and it does so in a way that it can't be ignored. It's a written form of screaming.

Sociologist Gary Fine

Eat dessert first, life is uncertain.

Motto of the Pacific Dessert Company

Woodfinisher's Pride [is] a product that works just as well as conventional paint and finish removers with one big difference—it is biodegradable and does not contain methylene chloride.

Tom Graham

Rain-insurance policy—guests pay $5 for each $100 of insurance and can collect up to $500 for each rainy day.

For hotels, offered by Lloyd's of London

"Nothing—Eau de Cologne Imaginaire, a subtle blend of scent-free ingredients, imaginary essences, and air."

Gag gift

Casket Fit for a King—an Egyptian sarcophagus made of reinforced fiberglass, adorned with artwork and gold paint, for $7,500.

Retailed by Don and Margaret Northway

Slackers—a new breed of social drop-outs and post-Reagan beatniks, born in the late 50s and 60s and faced with bleak economic prospects. They can't see much sense in joining the lunatic bandwagon known as "the real world" but haven't discovered an attractive alternative, either.

Journalist Edward Guthmann

Kitty Video—a 30-minute cat video for cats, featuring colorful birds fluttering and chirping.

Reported in The San Francisco Chronicle

I don't want to encourage women to buy guns but to promote training and education for those who already have them.

Sonny Jones
editor of the new publication, "Women & Guns"

The Sheriff's Department has proposed moving its headquarters from downtown to the Kearny Mesa area to get away from city crime.

According to the Associated Press

The plot on "Northern Exposure" is one that at one time would have been impossible to get past the network censors as Holling (John Cullum) decides to get circumcised to please Shelly.

David Moore

An annual $39.95 payment ensures monthly delivery of 10 condoms, including periodic "seasonally themed" condoms such as glow-in-the-dark for Halloween.

The Condom of the Month Club

$500 Reward. "Sterling," a gray Persian cat, no claws. Was wearing rhinestone collar w/name and electronic cat door opener.

According to the **Reno Gazette**

BUMPER STICKERS

A state law banning bumper stickers with lewd or offensive messages wrongfully restricts a motorist's right to express themselves.

According to a ruling by the **Georgia Supreme Court**

Winning isn't everything, eating is.

Bumper sticker

Not All Dumbs are Blond.

Bumper sticker

Columbus had a Norwegian map.

Bumper sticker

Enjoy life. This is not a rehearsal!

Bumper sticker

Extinct is forever.

Bumper sticker

I love Pavarotti.

Bumper sticker

Save a pig. Roast an activist.

Bumper sticker

Sexism a Social Disease.

Bumper sticker

Congressional corruption "A renewable resource."

Bumper sticker

The more hair I lose the more head I get.

Bumper sticker

This vehicle stops at all dinosaur crossings.

Bumper sticker

I love my country—I fear my government.

Bumper sticker

THE PERSONALS

Three Musketeers. Loving, hardworking couple seek same in bisexual female, age 30–45 to share our home and souls with. Relocatable animal lover a plus. Permanent relationship desired.

Personal ad

Looking for financially secure woman to take care of me. I am art student, 23, S[ingle] W[oman]. Will be your escort, companion, lover.

Personal ad

White Male 35. Athletic, non-smoker, married, seeking outside relationship w/ female to age 65.

Personal ad

So you've been naughty! Now you must be spanked until it aches! S[ingle] W[hite] M[ale] tutor (28) seeks devoted pupil who is 18–21 pretty.

Personal ad

Married professional 52 W[hite] M[ale] with problems at home seeks romantic liaison with married or single female.

Personal ad

Lymphatic drainage massage. Will trade for herbal colon detoxification program.

Personal ad

Dial An Insult—Take 5 min. of insults and you will earn a FREE t-shirt. Call 1-900-896-2800.

Personal ad

Docile white male, 40, seeks take charge-type female who prefers the dominant role in a relationship. He promises to love, honor and obey. Age unimportant.

Personal ad

Eccentric, queen-sized, extraterrestial female, 42 (according to Terran [earth] definition of time), loves long walks, black cats...Her interests include UFOs, dream analysis, hypnosis, linguistics, creative writing and most aspects of psychology and metaphysics in general.

Personal ad

Tall, beautiful, active 41-year-old male to female transsexual with original plumbing seeks nonsmoking, trim liberal(s).

Personal ad

Unconventional, bisexual, 40, petite, sensual, fun, seeks pretty, sexy younger woman 18–27 for intense, nonmonogamous relationship.

Personal ad

I don't think 5'4" is that short, and anyway I've got enough interests for two six-footers. I'm a single nonobservant J[ewish] M[ale], 29, 140 lbs.

Personal ad

A Superb Massage While-U-Wait.

Ad in the "Bay Area Reporter"

W[hite] F[emale] 44 yrs, married wants discrete (sic) outside relationship with similar partner-professional.

Personal ad

Mature S[ingle] W[hite] M[ale] seeks lonely, open-minded lady for friendship and exciting telephone romance.

Personal ad

Attractive W[hite] F[emale], 29, married, seeking attentive professional gentleman, married, for dignified quality relationship.

Personal ad

LICENSE PLATES

UPPA US

License plate

4KEN A

License plate

YMINLA

License plate

74IPMOR

License plate

2SCROOO

License plate

6E Izzy

License plate

PHK ME

License plate

4NIC8R

License plate

FKMALL

License plate

FFOCUSS

License plate

GASHAWK

License plate on a Mercedes 280SEL

UZ2BNVS

License plate

YY UUUU

License plate

I FX DX

License plate

1 KPT WMN

Licence plate

OH2BINSF

New York license plate

I POP BAX

License plate

SIGNS

The original sexual harrasment cost one rib.

Sign outside a church

In northern San Diego County, Caltrans officials have posted four new signs warning motorists on Interstate 5 that there's a danger of illegal immigrants running across the road. The signs include the word "Caution" and the silhouetted logo of a family in flight.

Columnist Leah Garchik

Testosterone Kills. Give Estrogen a Chance.

Sign in a window

Fine Automotive Dining.

Sign at a drive-through restaurant

People have died for it. All you have to do is sign for it. Register to vote today!

Sign at a rally

"Paper of color" "Paper of pallor"

Signs over paper recycling bins

Who decides? You decide!

Sign at a proabortion rally

The movie poster is to movies what seduction is to sex: No come-on is too devious, no promise too glittering or empty, if it entices succesfully.

Owen Edwards

Safe Spex

Name of an eyeglass boutique

Men who love men sometimes abuse the men they love.

Sign for an organization called Men Against Violence

If you are smoking in this shop, you better be on fire.

Sign in a retail store

We serve no swine before its time.

*From the marquee of the **Pigout Barbecue Restaurant***

We pawn cars—classic cars, RVs, motorcycles, limos, airplanes.

The sign in front of Opera Motors

She's only 16. She doesn't do drugs. But she does have a dealer.

Billboard in Atlantic City warning of teenage gambling

Ciao Mein

The name of an Italian-Chinese restaurant

Anal warts? Fissures? Hemorrhoids? Call 1-800-MD TUSCH

Advertisement in N.Y. subway

Choice means quality!

Sign at a prochoice rally

Authentic Reproductions of Endangered Animals Made with Genuine Fur and Leather.

Sign in a store window

T-SHIRTS

Homophobic and Proud of It.

T-shirt

I don't dial 911.

T-shirt

Club Faggots, Not Seals.

T-shirt

Veni, Vidi, Visa—I came, I saw, I shopped.

T-Shirt

Trespassers at the Kennedy compound will be violated.

T-shirt being sold in Palm Beach

2QT2BSTR8

T-shirt

900 NUMBERS

1-900-773-SUDS

1-900-B-INFORMED

1-900-XXX-1-ON-1

1-900-XXX-3SEX

1-900-XXX-LIVE

1-900-XX-NASTY

1-900-XXX-LICK

1-900-XXX-DEEP

1-900-INFO-SEX

1-900-XXX-BI-BI

1-900-XXX-TV-TS

1-900-XXX-HOTT

1-900-XXX-SWAK

1-900-XXX-EASY

1-900-LOVE-HIM

1-900-XXX-BURN

1-900-LOVE-GUYS

1-900-HOT-LEATHER

1-900-VIP-STUD

1-900-TIGHTEND

15

FAR OUT

In a century or two people will appreciate the Beatles as much as Beethoven or Mozart today. I don't believe there is any difference in status between the great composers. This may sound arrogant, but you never amount to anything unless you believe in yourself.

Singer Paul McCartney

What a great saving!

Former Chilean dictator Gen. Augusto Pinochet
upon being told that victims of his bloody 1973 coup had been
buried two to a coffin

I have buck teeth. I sucked my thumb until I was 11...and then I went on to suck other things.

Actress Rosanna Arquette

You allow me to license and regulate marijuana, I'll fill every hotel and motel room in the state of Kentucky.

Gubernatorial candidate Gatewood Galbraith
explaining that legalizing pot would boost tourism

Fashion retailer Benetton apologized for shocking Londoners with an advertisement showing a newborn baby girl covered with blood with the umbilical cord still attached.

As reported by Mark Lundgren

If Doogie Howser finally got the chance to do it for the first time, then there's hope for me too.

Fred Savage
on losing his virginity on "The Wonder Years"

Don Johnson's not the Duke. He's not even a pimple on the Duke's ass.

Producer Jere Henshaw
comparing Johnson to John Wayne

I want to play in a movie with a lot of frontal nudity and sex scenes. When I see a movie, I rate it on how many times I see people undressed. "Henry & June" gets 55 stars, but "GoodFellas" none.

Actor Paul Hipp

This isn't a hobby. There's too much fanaticism involved. This is closer to a religious cult.

Leonard Nathan
on bird-watching

What I want him to do is to go to New York and hang-out for a week with the House of Xtravaganza [a drag-queen group].

Madonna
on how she would remake Michael Jackson's image

We're human. We doo-doo in the toilets and do everything people do.

Jonathan Knight
New Kids on the Block singer

Put your lips on my big chocolate Twinkie!

Line from "She Swallowed It" by N.W.A.

Having less people than needed leads to a greater load on those who are in the army, which is against the principles of social justice.

Soviet Defense Ministry
on ordering the Red Army into secessionist republics
to enforce the draft

Madonna—she's like toilet paper. She's on every magazine cover in the world. Devalued.

Director Oliver Stone

They stuff the meat full of hormones and all sorts of chemicals. It tastes delicious, but when I'm getting my period, I'm like Freddy Krueger...At first I thought it was the television that was making me like that, but it's the meat.

Singer Sinead O'Connor

During his rambling two and one-half discourse on nothing in particular, [Journalist Hunter] Thompson and his companion, a red-headed woman in cowboy boots whom he introduced to his audience of 500 as his "interpreter" consumed the better part of a liter of Chivas Regal scotch. He also arrived thirty minutes late, in a white Lincoln Continental, and displayed a stun gun, which he referred to as his "weapon of choice."

Mitchell Fink

I think men should sleep with as many women as they can before they get married...A man who doesn't feel he's had his wild days will be uncomfortable with a long-term relationship like marriage.

Actor Kevin Bacon

Major porn star Al Parker was so displeased with his recent circumcision that he had a foreskin stiched on.

Columnist Herb Caen

A beautiful woman without a brain in her head can still be exciting.

Director Oliver Stone

Women who wield power in business or politics look not unlike women weight lifters or bodybuilders, a parody of their sex.

TV commentator Andy Rooney

Net worth equals self-worth.

A Wallstreet banker as quoted in **The New York Times**

Today, women are trying to create a "new man"—a sensitive man...Someday soon, women won't mate with any other kind of man—by the third date, men will have to have cried. Soon we'll have classes to teach them crying on demand.

Actor Patrick Bergin

I want to have a baby and I want Peter Jennings to be the father. I want him to read to our son or daughter, the newspaper. The kid would be so smart....I know he's married, but we could just have a cheap and tawdry affair.

Singer Sheena Easton

It pisses some people off that I can act so easily. My incredible intelligence makes it possible.

Actress Sean Young

I've fallen, and I can't get up. But now that I'm down here..."

Singer Madonna

Joan, I've seen and taped all your shows, but I have nothing of you nude. Could you please send me a tape of you naked?

Fan letter sent to Actress Joan Van Arc

I don't know about you, but winning a Grammy sure helped me get laid.

Singer Bonnie Raitt

The only difference between a pit bull and a cheerleader's mother is lipstick.

A school official

I don't talk to people when I'm naked, especially women, unless they're on top of me or I'm on top of them.

Detroit Tigers' pitcher Jack Morris

If I want somebody, I want them. I want to have the joy in my heart of just to, like get out of the car and, like, "remember me" and then

just shoot him. I don't want to be just shootin' up his house and hopin'
I get him, and might get his mama or his father. I want him. I want
that person. I don't want to be like the nigger who blasted the wrong
family. That's a stupid nigger, and what he did is scandalous.

G. Roc
a Los Angeles gang member featured in the book, "Do or Die"

You don't love me. If you loved me, you'd do this so you could be
with me.

*Allegedly spoken by convicted teacher **Pamela Smart***
*to her 15-year-old lover **William Flynn***

My drinking now is very intermittent. I'll have a little something four
days a week and once every two months, I'll binge. In the past, I
binged for years.

Actor Sean Penn

There's gonna be guns, there's gonna be all kinds of stuff like that.
Real stuff that goes on in my life. Whew, God, I could make a bad
one.

Rapper Vanilla Ice
on his second movie

Oprah Winfrey greeted as her guests a couple, Bonnie and Bruce Lambert,
who were suspected of murdering their four children.

Columnist John Carmon

After finding no qualified candidates for the position of principal, the
school department is extremely pleased to announce the appointment
of David Steele to the post. David was the best choice.

Phillip Streifer,
superintendent of schools in Barrington, Rhode Island

I do have big tits. Always had 'em—pushed 'em up, whacked 'em
around. Why not make fun of 'em? I've made a fortune with 'em.

Singer Dolly Parton

Dream symbols for sex: Flying, snakes, a train in a tunnel, women's shoes, goats, dragons, bulls, eggs, climbing stairs, playing ball, dancing around a Maypole, losing your pants, catching a butterfly, hiding in a cave, playing the guitar, putting a key in a lock, plowing a field, putting on gloves, lighting fireworks, eating bananas or asparagus or tomatoes.

According to "Playboy"

I wish I looked like Robert Redford and had a 12-inch cock, but that isn't the way it worked out, okay?

Actor Kurt Russell

It's impossible for me to remember everybody I've made love to...I try and point them out if [my wife] Rachel and I are out together and we bump into someone I've dated before.

Singer Rod Stewart

I have a wife and a mistress. From my wife I get love and understanding and sensitivity. From my mistress I get love and passion and sensuality....Ees a very Italian way. My wife understand that like a child I need to be always in the center of some interest. It demands great sacrifices of the woman...What? Guilt? We won't talk about thees.

Sixty-six year old actor, Marcello Mastroianni

Cambodia says it wants to help find remains of Americans missing from the Vietnam War, but the task is difficult becaues the country has so many bones.

USA Today

I rowed us to a secluded spot...Right there, the estranged First Lady of Canada lent new meaning to the term "head of state."

Geraldo Rivera
on his alleged affair with Margaret Trudeau

Robert Martinque complained of "right angulation," pain, and inability to have sex [after a penile implant operation]. He said that one doctor told him he risked having his penis explode if he tried to have sex.

As reported by Reuters

Two American brothers from Florida were sentenced yesterday to each have one hand and one foot amputated for robbing $3,365 from a bank in Pakistan.

Chronicle Wire Services

You showed concern and consideration by wearing a contraceptive.

Words to a convicted rapist by **British Judge Arthur Myerson**
justifying his light sentence

I don't screw around. If I'd done one third of what people say I have, if I'd had half the women, I'd be a great man. But I haven't. I wish I had.

News anchor **Dan Rather**

An Irish company is making personalized condoms for rock bands to give to fans at concerts.

Mark Lundgren

Always remember, the weak, meek, and ignorant are always good targets.

From a company memo for **Lincoln Savings and Loan**

Please read and reread these presentations until the detailed verbiage...flows from your mouth like carbon monoxide from the exhaust of a Mack truck.

From a company memo for **Lincoln Savings and Loan**

We are unimportant. We are here to serve, to heal the wounds, and to give love. We want men...to look after us.

Marike de Klerk
wife of South African President F. W. de Klerk

The only time I use them, they're either naked or dead.

Movie producer Joel Silver
about women in his films

We dated in 1984 but I knew going out with a white person wasn't cool careerwise, so I told her we had to eat at McDonalds and keep it low-key.

Arsenio Hall
on his relationship with Emma Samms

Huey Lewis is the biggest and Peter Frampton is the smallest.

Groupie "Little Rock Connie"
on the endowments of the rock stars she's known

His hyperdramatic vocals, invariably pushing the ceiling of his range, drove his turgid songs into a kind of pseudo-passion posing as genuine emotion. He underlined this intense delivery with the strained expression of someone trying to pass a difficult bowel movement.

Critic Joel Selvin
in a review of singer Michael Bolton

It's a morbid observation, but if every one on earth just stopped breathing for an hour, the greenhouse effect would no longer be a problem.

Writer Jerry Adler

She's not a bimbo. She reads books. Hardbacks.

Line from the TV sitcom "Step by Step"

We wanted to call this "Eight Peaks," but they wouldn't let us.

Ron Cowen
producer of "Sisters," a show about four women

I've uncovered numerous examples of fathers getting steroids for their kids because they wanted them to be better athletes.

Assistant U.S. Attorney Phillip Halpern

Catholicism is a mean religion and incredibly hypocritical. How could I support it? I think they probably got it on, Jesus and Mary Magdalene.

Madonna

New cereals for kids:

Prince of Thieves, with crunch, fruit-flavored, multicolored arrows

Bill and Ted's Excellent Cereal, with orange, lilac, and yellow marshmallow musical notes

Reported by **Paula Span**

I've never tried to hide the fact that I'm a chick. I like whorey-looking shoes, with little stiletto heels. I love perfume. I love guys, man. If I'm walking down the street and I see a cute guy, I will make a two-block diversion to follow him, just to have a look.

Singer Chrissie Hynde

There was nothing to do.

Fifteen-year-old Terance Wade
on why he and his friends attacked and murdered
a Boston woman on Halloween

A service of Blessing of the Animals, to be followed by a barbecue.

Church announcement

The latest Hollywood pastime is tuning into everyone else's cellular phone conversations, which can be picked up by radio scanners.

According to **"Mirabella"**

Let me tell you something about intelligence. You can get that from men. When I go into the bedroom with my woman, I don't want a bunch of educated crap.

Actor Jim Brown

Christie Hefner, Brandeis University graduate and president of Playboy Enterprises, has been elected to the university's board.

According to the **San Francisco Chronicle**

Dear Madam: This is a warning to your husband, which we are sending through you because we want you to know that you could soon be a widow.

A letter sent to the wives of members of the
South African National Party

Ten percent of America's dog owners say they are as attached to their dogs as they are to their spouses.

According to a survey sponsored by **Frosty Paws**
a manufacturer of canine frozen treats

Authorities say that at least 17 other men did not get away; that Dahmer drugged their drinks, strangled them and cut up their bodies with an electric buzz saw; but he discarded bones he did not want in a 57-gallon drum he had bought for that purpose; that he lined up three skulls on a shelf in his apartment, but only after spraying them with gray paint to fool people into thinking that they were plastic models....Once, he told police in Milwaukee, he fried a victim's biceps in vegetable shortening and ate it.

The New York Times
reporting on mass murderer Jeffrey Dahmer

I've got nothing against middle-aged women, but younger women are the only ones willing to give everything up and follow a lifestyle that I have.

Peter Arnett

I just have a hard time laying all the blame on him. I don't see how he could take up with her. She was such a pitiful woman.

Judge Kenneth Leffler
on his decision not to send an admitted rapist to jail

Dear Beth: My friend and I have both been seeing the same man—and he's much older. She says that we could get pregnant, but he said he had an operation. I can't pronounce it, but it starts with "v." He showed us his scar, but we have never heard of this in our health classes. Is he lying to us?

Robyn

Officials [at the Cleveland Zoo] plan to ship Timmy to the Bronx Zoo to mate with four female gorillas as part of an interzoo program to preserve endangered species. But Timmy already has a significant other, an infertile female named Kribi Kate, and animal-rights advocates say that separating the pair could be emotionally devastating. They hired Cleveland lawyer Gloria Homolak to block the move.

Newsweek

A woman carrying a Torah is like a pig at the Wailing Wall.

Orthodox rabbi Meir Yehuda Getz

The winner of a recent Oprah Winfrey look-alike contest in "Ladies' Home Journal" was revealed to be a man...who says he is planning to have a sex-change operation.

Kevin Kerr

If you can pick women, you can pick cattle. You look for good angularity, nice legs and capacity.

Hockey star Bobby Hull

It's obvious if someone did commit a crime and put a body in a trunk, they wouldn't leave a hand hanging out for the public to see.

West Virginia policeman, N.K. Davis
on a popular gag gift: arms that dangle from car trunks

I think it's a very healthy thing to hit the person you love. I hit, and I've had it done to me. I'm not talking about abuse.

Actress Valerie Perrine

Lead-lined coffins termed health risk.

Headline in **The Washington Times**

Smugglers are saturating clothing in heroin that has been diluted in water. The garments are then dried and packed in suitcases, which are carried through customs. The clothes are then washed and the discharge water is collected and evaporated, leaving the heroin.

According to **Jet**

I'm an atheist, so it was actually a joy. Spitting on Christ was a great deal of fun—especially for me, being a woman. Let's face it, the atrocities done in the name of Christ and Christianity to women throughout the history are horrific—inhuman, really.

Actress Amanda Donohoe
on spitting on a crucifix in a film

Whaddya mean we haven't done anything for the homeless? How about all those overpasses?

Overheard

He picks his nose. I saw him pick his nose lots of times.

Jim-Jim, 5
on working with Arnold Schwarzenegger in "Kindergarten Cop"

Q: If I told you one of [your sons] was an informer, a police informer, gonna put somebody in prison, and I told you, you must kill them, would you do that for me without hesitation?
A: He has to go.

From a tape recording of the Mafia's secret initiation rite

Feminism was established to allow unattractive women access to mainstream society.

Talk show host Rush Limbaugh

He had been drinking some tea during the interview, and after it was over he got up and left. I went over, looked in the cup, and the tea was, like, half a cup still there! I picked it up and drank it. I didn't care if I got a disease—I wanted to. If it was from Paul McCartney, that'd be okay.

MTV's Martha Quinn

[G.G. Allin, lead singer of the defunct group Toilet Rockers] who defecated on stage and tossed excrement at his audience was convicted in Milwaukee by a jury that rejected his argument of artistic freedom.

David Landis

The Harley, it is difficult to say. It means freedom. When someone asks you if you believe in God, you don't know why, but you do. It is like that with Harley.

Manuel
of the Hell's Angels, on Harley-Davidson motorcycles

Air Force Barbie is the perfect role model for young girls....Captain Barbie epitomizes everything that women can do today.

From "Barbie Bazaar"

I think women force men to be unfaithful. Men are unfaithful by nature occasionally, but not as constantly as I was.

Actor Anthony Quinn

Available in Japan, "Unchi-Kun, The Defecating Doll," for $500. You insert a pellet into the designated area, light and stand back.

*As reported by San Francisco writer, **Ron Gluckman***

Nintendo epilepsy—convulsions triggered by flashing images in video games.

Don't worry about being excommunicated. You are dead.

Death threat received by federal Judge Patrick Kelly
from an antiabortion protester

Men are scum....excuse me. For a second there, I was feeling generous.

*Greeting from a **Hallmark card***
that was withdrawn from circulation

The rationale was to come up with a method of silencing you through killing you.

Watergate conspirator G. Gordon Liddy
telling columnist Jack Anderson of their plans for him

One time, I had gone to the movies with my mother, in Georgia, and I was in the bathroom. All of a sudden this voice says, "Excuse me? The girl in stall No. 1? Were you in 'Mystic Pizza'?" I said yeah, and she goes, "Can I have your autograph?" and slides a piece of paper under the stall door. I just said, "I don't think right now is the time."

Actress Julia Roberts

I'm from South-Central [Los Angeles], fool, where everything
    goes
Gang-bangers don't carry no switchblades
Every kid's got a Tec 9 or a hand grenade
Thirty-seven killed last week in a crack war
Hostages tied up and shot in a liquor store
Nobody gives a fuck

From the "New Jack City" soundtrack by
rapper Ice-T

Bitches getting raped, niggers getting murdered
Adults fucking kids in numbers unheard of

Lines from a rap song

I have a morbid fascination with violent actions....So lyrics like "Shoot you in your face" turn me on. Is that wrong?

Rapper Ice-T

Now in '91 you want to tax me
I'll remember the sonofabitch used to ax me
Hanging men by a rope until my neck snaps
Now the sneaking motherfucker wants to ban rap

From the rap song "I Wanna Kill [Uncle] Sam" by
Ice Cube

It pleases me to have you touch me there
I think you know it gets to me
Stop! Don't stop! Ecstasy!

From "How Do I Love Thee" by
rap artist Queen Latifah

Rap is an art form. It is not just putting lyrics that rhyme to a melody. These [record company] execs are naive, thinking that any

Black man could rap. Just like those who think any Black man has a big U-know-what.

Rapper Heavy D.

On Oct. 1, Donald Trump called a taping of "Geraldo" and accused exprospective flame Kim Alley of capitalizing on his good name.

People

You know, it really doesn't matter what [the media] write as long as you've got a young and beautiful piece of ass.

Entrepreneur Donald Trump

Number 1: Couldn't decide who was the most shallow.

*From **David Letterman's**
top 10 list on why Donald Trump and Marla Maples broke up*

INDEX

A

Aaker, David, 107

Aaron, Hank, 20

Abdullah, Hazhar, 39

Abdul-Rahman, Assad, 38

About Faces, 41

Adamovich, Ales, 92

Adams, Randall, 3

Adams, Russell, 77

Adelman, Rob, 63

Adler, Jerry, 308

Adweek, 251

Aetna Life & Casualty, 65

The Age, 49

Ahrons, Constance, 245

Ajaye, Franklyn, 187

Alan Guttmacher Institute, 124

Albee, Edward, 142

Albretch, Mark, 46

Alderson, Sandy, 157

Aldhous, Peter, 121

Alepin, Andrei, 92

Alexander, Lamar, 4

Alexis, Kim, 10

Alhous, Peter, 215

Allain, Mary Francoise, 12

Allen, Charlotte, 208

Al-Nadwa, 52

al-Nashef, Mohammad, 39

Alsobrook, Cannon, 69

Alston, Jonathan, 34

Alter, Jonathan, 130

Alvarez, Wilson, 176

Al Watan al Arabi, 85

American Academy of Pediatrics, 239

American Association of Retired Persons, 110

American Booksellers Association, 131

American Cancer Society, 127

American Chemical Society, 231

American Demographics, 246, 279

American Health, 237

American Hospital Association, 127

American Institute for Computer Technology, 274

American Institute of Stress, 269

American Journal of Psychiatry, 198

American Management Association survey, 278

American Medical Association, 113, 121

317

American Orthopaedic Foot and Ankle Society, 252

American Productivity and Quality Center, 275

American Psychiatric Association, 256

American Psychological Association, 247

American Society for Training and Development, 279

American Society of Safety Engineers, 128, 268

Amis, Kingsley, 139

Anderson, Sparky, 154, 164

Anderson, Truett, 196

Angell, Roger, 173

Annenberg, Walter, 235

Anrig, Gregory, 74

Archives of General Psychiatry, 115

Argo, Edgar, 239

Armey, Richard, 72

Arnett, Peter, 43, 137, 310

Arnold, Lanny, 153

Arnold, Tom, 9

Aronson, Marc, 135

Arquette, Rosanna, 301

Asimov, Isaac, 216

Associated Press, 25, 74, 103, 104, 111, 135, 159, 168, 197, 199, 232, 243, 279, 290, 292

Atkins, Chet, 189

Atkins, Linda, 62

Atwater, Lee, 21

Audi of American, 225

Aug, Lisa, 223

Austin, Bonita, 232

Automotive Information Council, 117

B

Bacon, Kevin, 303

Bacon, Michael, 25

Baer, Donald, 76

Baghdad Radio, 42

Baker, James, 21

Balanlova, Olga, 91

Baldrige, Letitia, 28

Baldwin, Alec, 261

Ballantine Scotch Whiskey ad, 102

Ball, Ivern, 244

Barbie Bazaar, 313

Barkley, Charles, 176

Baron, Buddy, 63

Barrett, David, 209

Barrow, Robert, 34

Barr, Roseanne, 190, 248

Bartlett, Neil, 16

Barton, Dr. Fritz, 250

Barzun, Jacques, 130

Baseball America, 158

Bassey, Shirly, 262

Bass, Pamela, 65

BathEase, Inc., 231

Bauer, Gary, 258

Bayangin, Vasily, 205

Beacham, Stephanie, 262

Beblo, Wojciech, 86

Becker, Boris, 166

Beckman, Martha J., 14

Beguelin, Mike, 36

Belkov, M. Ann, 59

Bellah, Robert, 71, 202

Ben Bridge Jewelers ad, 102

Benfield, John, 125

Bennett, William, Jr., 230

Bentsen, Lloyd, 56

Bentzlin, Carol, 35

Ben Yahmed, Bechir, 49

Berendt, John, 110

Berey, Mark, 96

Bergalis, Kimberly, 114

Bergin, Patrick, 304

Berkeley Wellness Letter, 116, 225

Berkow, Ira, 138

Berman, Morris, 87

Bernays, Anne, 35

Bernstein, Allen, 271

Beschloss, Michael, 134

Biojet, Inc., 225

Blackwell, Mr., 249

Blair, Linda, 184

Blandino, Larry, 198

Blank, Mickey, 257

Blatz, William, 27

Bleecker, Samuel, 218

Blewer, Jim, 62

Blinden, Christopher, 221

Blizzard Mints ad, 101

Block, Evelyn, 276

Blodgett, Harriet, 131

Bloom, Harold, 130

Blount, Roy, Jr., 78

Bluestein, Susan, 6

Blumenthal, Susan, 136

Boggs, Wade, 154

Bonaduca, Danny, 182

Bonnell, Rick, 156

Boom, Faye, 69

Booz, Allen & Hamilton survey, 96

Bosworth, Brian, 168

Bouton, Jim, 161

Bovin, Alekandr, 84

Bowers, Dr. Thomas, 247

Boyd, L., 97, 112, 155, 171

Boy Scout Handbook, 288

Bozworth, Brian, 161

Bradish, Frank, 34

Bradlee, Ben, 136

Bradley, Jon, 78

Bradshaw, Terry, 161

Brady, Celia, 190

Brandes, Charles, 97

Branson, Richard, 188

Braus, Patricia, 265

Bray, Robert, 111

Brennan, Donald, 102

Breslow, Ronald, 121

Brett, George, 156, 164

Brindle, David, 87

British Medical Journal, 121

Britt, Harvey, 255

Brokaw, Tom, 136

Brookes, Warren, 277

Brookner, Anita, 149

Brooks, Garth, 182, 257

Broshar, David McDonald, 190

Brothers, Joyce, 132

Brothers, P. D., 259

Brown, Dale, 160

Brown, Dr. John, 121

Brownfield, Allan, 56

Brown, Jerry, 71

Brown, Jim, 309

Brown, Marie, 131

Brown, Paul, 100

Brown, Peter, 71

Brown, Rita Mae, 180

Brue, Bob, 163

Brueggemann, Walter, 210

Bruskin Associates, 247

Brzezinski, Zbigniew, 81

Bubka, Sergei, 177

Buchanan, Dr. James, 157

Buckner, Brentson, 162

Buechner, Frederick, 199

Bundsen, Jerry, 13

Burbach, Rodney, 126

Burch, Sharon Peoples, 204

Bureau of Census, 58

Bureau of Labor Statistics, 272

Burlington Industries ad, 101

Burns, Frances Ann, 222

Burns, George, 21

Burnstein, Mark, 192

Burrows, William, 214, 222

Burton, John, 32

Busch, Frederick, 150

Bush, Barbara, 3, 22, 23, 31

Bush, George, 2, 29, 30, 31, 32, 54-55, 67, 71, 75, 82, 87-88, 180

Business Recycling Manual, 61

Business Week, 125

Butler, Brett, 172

Butts, Claudia, 71

Byrd, Robert, 188

C

C & W frozen peas ad, 102

Cacero, Karen, 122

Caen, Herb, 46, 107, 303

Calder, Iain, 143, 144

Caldwell, Gail, 151

Calgene, Inc., 230

California Department of Health Services, 114, 125

California Egg Commission ad, 101

Callaghan, James, 157

Callahan, Daniel, 109

Callahan, Philip, 216

Calvin, William, 219

Cameron, James, 186

Campbell, Carroll, 62

Campbell, Elden, 171

Cannon, Glenn, 249

Cannon, Mike, 177

Canseco, Jose, 170

Canto, Victor, 260

Capelini, 234

Capital Speakers, Inc., 275

Caporale-Carabelli, Claudia, 43

Car and Driver, 225

Carew, Rod, 177

Carey, George, 200, 205

Carey, John, 199

Carmon, John, 305

Carnegie Mellon University, 123

Carroll, Eugene, 232

Carroll, Jon, 25, 276

Carson, Johnny, 28, 38, 55, 60, 69, 95, 116, 190, 242, 252, 255

Carter, Jimmy, 48, 105

Carter, Lynda, 103

Carter, Stephen, 56, 57

Cartland, Barbara, 142, 278

Casey, Caroline, 29

Cash, Thomas, 251

Casson, C., 216

Catholic University, 226

Cavin, Ruth, 148

Cayne, James E., 97

Census Bureau, 238, 243, 254
Challenger, James, 273
Chamberlain, Andrew, 244
Chandler, M., 222
Chandler, Sheryl, 64
Chandra, Prakash, 112
Chang-Chi Liu, 44
Chang, Kenneth, 220
Chase Lincoln First Bank ad, 99
Cheever, John, 143
Cher, 11, 135, 265
Cherney, Darryl, 118
Chignell, Mark, 217
Children's Defense Fund, 74
Chizmas, Joe, 251
Choice International Hotels, 40
Christi, Pat, 50
Chronicle Wire Services, 250, 307
Chruch, Norris, 18
Cioran, E.M., 138
Clancy, Tom, 142, 147, 191
Clark, Dawn, 218
Clark, Fred, 58
Cleese, John, 271
Clyde Robin Seed Co., 39
Cochran, 153, 159, 233
Cohen, Laura, 98
Cohen, Richard, 22
Cohen, Stephen, 84, 89
Cohn, Lowell, 172
Coleman, Dr. Gene, 174
Coleman, John, 211
Colitt, Leslie, 92
College Board, 239, 240
Collins, Joan, 6
Collinsworth, Cris, 161

Columbia University, 127
Comings, David E., 127
Computer World, 59
ComputerWorld, 280
Conde Nast Traveler, 58, 83
Condom of the Month Club, 292
Connard, Avril, 90
Conner, Melvin, 9
Conney, Allan, 121
Connick, Harry, Jr., 187
Connors, Jim, 177
Consumer's Digest, 57
Cook, Samuel DuBois, 16
Cook, Beano, 157
Cook, Cynthia Lovelend, 236
Cook, Harry, 45
Cool J, L.L., 18
Coombs, Dave, 163
Cooney, Frank, 172
Cooney, Michael, 70
Corman, Avery, 142
Cornfield, Jack, 202
Corrections Compendium, 64
Coste'Joel, 125
Cottiaon, 260
Country Forecasts, 269
Cousy, Bob, 169
CoverAge, Inc., 229
Cowen, Ron, 308
Crane, Phil, 67
Crawford, David, 215
Crayola crayons ad, 99
Crimmins, Barry, 37, 44
Crispell, Diane, 237
Cromartie, Warren, 164
Cronkite, Walter, 32, 43, 47

Cropp, Author J., 76
Crystal, Billy, 186
Cuomo, Mario, 8
Current Science, 221
Curtis, Don Eric, 254
Curtis, James, 280
Cusack, John, 183
Cuskley, Kevin, 96

D

Daily News Digest, 65
Daily, Robert, 106
Daly, Tyne, 11, 253, 308
Dalziel, Ian, 213
Dartmouth College Health
    Service, 122
David, Dennis, 164
Davies, Robertson, 143
Davis, N. K., 311
Davis, Ossie, 14
Dee, Kool Moe, 98
Deikman, Arthur, 207
Delahoussaye, Eddie, 153
DeLillo, Don, 140
Deluxe Data Systems, 274
Deming, W. Edwards, 276
Dennco, Inc., 228
Dennis the Menace, 3
Depardieu, Gerard, 4
Depp, Johnny, 191
Dern, Laura, 180
Dershowitz, Alan, 8, 196
Desai, Boman, 147
Details, 253
Developed Heath Co., 227
Dexter, Carolyn r., 37

Diamond, Dr. Seymour, 115
Dickerson, Eric, 175
Dickson, Peter, 105
Diddley, Bo, 188
Didsbury, Howard, Jr., 85
Die Presse, 230
Die Tageszeitung, 124
Dietary Guidelines for Americans, 115
Dietrich, J. Kimball, 260
DiMaggio, Joe, 176
Discover Private Issue credit
    card ad, 100
Dixon, Sharon Pratt, 18
Dobyns, Stephen, 150
Doghramji, Karl, 128
Dole, Bob, 91
Dole, Robert, 27
Dominian, Jack, 206
Donahue, Phil, 193
Donegan, Dorothy, 12
Donner, Judy, 41
Donohue, Amanda, 312
Dooven, K. Z. Don, 104
Dorfman, Bob, 102
Dornbierer, Anu, 46
Downtown Girl Perfume ad, 101
Draper, Theodore, 60
Dravecky, Dave, 178
Drees, Anthony, 34
Drennan, Denella, 38
Drewnowski, Adam, 116
Drucker, Peter, 5, 95, 106
Drug Control Policy Office, 62
Dubevich, Alexandra, 89
Duffy, Julia, 264
Du Jour, Sun, 289

Duke, Randolph, 107
Dunigan, James, 273
Dunlop, Robert, 49
Duplantier, Kathleen, 222
Durning, Alan, 11
Dutcher, Raymond, 239
Duva, Lou, 161, 165, 166

E

Easton, Sheena, 304
Ebert, Roger, 184
Eckerd College, 187
Eckhouse, John, 227
Economic Times, 124
Edmondson, Brad, 38
Edwards, Blake, 182
Edwards, Jonathan, 104
Edwards, Owen, 297
Ehrenreich, Barbara, 260
Eikermann, Leland, 277
Eisner, Robert, 149
Elias Sports Bureau, 165
Elias, Thomas, 26, 187, 238
Elion, Gertrude, 232
Ellenbogen, Richard, 250
Ellsberg, Daniel, 47
Emerging Hispanic Underclass,
      The, 72
Entertainment Weekly, 241, 262
Environmental Protection Agency, 231
Epstein, Edward, 57
Esquire, 252
Ettinger, Bob, 37
Etzioni, Amitai, 235
Evangelical Lutheran Church, 201, 202
Evangelista, Linda, 271

Everett, Jim, 172
Ewen, Stuare, 236
Ewing, Sam, 236

F

Fact Book on Aging, 250
Faisz, Ernest, 69
Faldo, Nick, 14
Family Planning Perspectives, 256
Fasso-Nicholson, Carlotta di, 52
Fax Exchange, 289
FBI Statistics, 59
Feagles, Jeff, 162
Federal Aviation Association, 55
Federal Highway Administration, 56
Feherty, David, 163
Felder, Raoul, 10
Feldman, Robert, 248
Feminist Majority Foundation, 278
Fernandez, Ivan, 220
Ferree, Jim, 163
Field, Sally, 16
Fields, Rick, 199
Fields, Rob, 35
Financial Post, 88
Fine, Gary, 291
Fingers, Rollie, 165
Fink, Michael, 303
Fischett, Teresa, 274
Fisher, Eddie, 241
Fisher, Henry, 36
Fisher, Marc, 158
FitzGerald, Tom, 160, 174
Fitzwater, Marlin, 30
Flaubert, Gustav, 133
Fleming, Ted, 221

Fletcher, Arthur, 3
Fonda, Jane, 9
Forbes, 5, 96, 98, 175, 189
Forbes, Peter, 140
Ford, Desire, 240
Ford, Eileen, 109
Forelle, Helen, 206
Foreman, George, 169, 174-175
Fortensky, Lisa, 241
Fortune, Marie, 206
Fossel, Peter, 233
Foster, Jodie, 17
Foster, Mark, 290
Fox, Alice, 268
Fox, Daniel, 126
Fox, James, 235
Fox, Matthew, 204
Fox, Michael J., 13, 60, 190, 192, 261
Frank, Anne, 133
Frank, Anthony, 267
Frankfurter Rundschau, 87
Franklin, Aretha, 188
Franklin Associates, 259
Frantz, Douglas, 113
Freeman, Morgan, 9
Frito Lay research, 233
Frosty Paws survey, 310
Furstenberg, Diane Von, 241
Furze, John, 256
Fusco, Frank, 138
Fussell, Samuel, 178
Futurist, The, 270

G

Gable, Greg, 106

Gabor, Zsa Zsa, 17
Galbraith, Gatewood, 301
Galeano, Eduardo, 20
Gallagher, Brian, 15
Gallup Poll, 19, 31, 129, 141, 180, 206, 208, 209, 210, 211, 248, 251, 256, 267, 271, 277
Galvin, Jan, 260
Garbage, 237
Garchick, Leah, 39, 297
Garcia, Rosemary, 196
Garfield, Charles, 95
Garr, Terri, 11
Garvey, John, 198
Gates, Daryl, 63
Gehrels, Neil, 219
Gendron, George, 108
General Accounting Office, 102
General Dentistry, 125
Gentry, Curt, 7, 140
George, Dave, 154
George, Don, 196
Georgia Supreme Court ruling, 292
Gephardt, Richard, 50
Gersh, Debra, 42
Getz, Meir Yehuda, 311
Gibbons, Dr. Lamar, 120
Gibson, Scott, 280
Giles, Larry, 103
Gilkey, Charles Whitney, 200
Gillick, Pat, 177
Gill, Vince, 183
Gioia, Dana, 139
Givens, Robin, 186
Gladwell, Malcolm, 57
Glanville, Jerry, 159
Glaspie, April, 38

Gleene, Joe, 155

Globe, 145, 146, 183

Gluckman, Ron, 313

Glynn, Tony, 175

GMC ad, 101

Goldberg, Gary David, 194

Goldberg, Herb, 253

Goldberg, Whoppi, 261, 263

Golden, Casey, 224

Goldman, Noreen, 83

Goldofstas, Barbara, 268

Goldstein, Avram, 62

Goldstein, Bernard, 118

Gooding, Cuba Jr., 186

Goodman, Ellen, 33, 78, 273

Goodrich, Chris, 266, 274

Gorbachev, Mikhail, 89, 91

Gordon, Bernard, 106

Gordon, James, 233

Gore, Albert, Jr., 47

Gotti, John, 259

Grachik, Leah, 197

Graffito, 290

Graham, Billy, 34

Graham, Tom, 291

Grant, Don, 260

Gravitt, Patrick J., 60

Greeley, Andrew, 209, 211

Greene, Joe, 161

Green, Roy, 176

Grelen, Jay, 13

Grenier, Richard, 234

Grier, Pam, 11

Griffin, Merv, 190

Grinta, Gloria, 23

Groening, Matt, 34

Gropp, Louis Oliver, 259

Groth, A. Nicholas, 62

Guest, Larry, 171

Guibert, Herve, 114

Guiness Book of World Records, 224

Guthmann, Edward, 291

Guthrie, A. B. Jr., 149

H

Hacker, Randi, 143

Hadley, Jack, 123

Haig, Alexander, 17

Halberstam, David, 106

Hall, Arsenio, 308

Hall, Karan, 53

Hall, Tony, 51

Halpern, Phillip, 308

Hamill, Pete, 42

Hamilton, Joe, 275

Hamilton, John Maxwell, 129

Hammer, M. C., 184, 192

Hampson, Rick, 123

Hanh, Thich Nahat, 7

Hannah, John, 155, 162

Hansome, Rhonda, 258

Harding, Chris, 130

Hardy, Charles, 185

Harkin, Senator, 70

Harper's, 53, 265, 276

Harrelson, Woody, 180

Harris, Barbara, 199

Harris, Cliff, 161

Harrison, Jim, 150

Harte, Mary, 264

Hart, Lynette, 217

Hartmann, Lawrence, 245
Harvard Divinity School, 195
Harvard Education Letter, 74
Harvell, Roger, 70
Harwood, Howell, 48
Haskin, Larry, 222
Health, 112, 237
Health After, 50, 115
Health Education Authority, 290
Healy, Bernadine, 220
Heath Line, 126
Heavy D., 315
Heflin, Howell, 11
Hefner, Hugh, 10
Heilbrun, Carolyn, 151
Hell's Angels manuel, 313
Helms, Jesse, 10
Helmsley, Leona, 279
Helprin, Mark, 147
Helton, Lon, 181
Heltzer, Mel, 68
Henderson, Brian, 122
Henry, Tom, 185
Henshaw, Jere, 302
Hepburn, Katherine, 2, 246, 263
HerbLock, 137
Herr, Harry, 78
Hershey, Laura, 234
Heschel, Suzannah, 211
Hester, Jim, 156
Heston, Charlton, 71
Hewitt, Jeanne, 33
Hiaasen, Carl, 118
Hicks, Larry, 227
Higginbotham, Naomi, 63
Hill, Andrea, 1

Hipp, Paul, 302
Hobgood, Jay, 220
Hochberg, Michael, 217
Hockswender, Woody, 108
Hodkinson, I.D., 216
Holden, Anthony, 20
Holland, Spencer, 14
Holloway, Wanda Webb, 20
Holt, Patricia, 23, 141
Holtz, Lou, 172
Homiletics, 205
Hooks, Jan, 192
Hope, Bob, 4, 33
Hopkins, Anthony, 263
Horner, Charles, 33
Horton, Miles, 7
House Select Committee on Children,
    Youth and Families, 82
Houston, Whitney, 52, 184
Hovar Systems, 228
Howe, Dr. Geoffrey, 122
Howe, Harold II, 72
Howes, Candace, 260
Hugick, Larry, 258
Hull, Bobby, 311
Humphries, Barry, 25
Humphry, Derek, 134
Hunter, Kenneth, 68
Hurd, Douglas, 48
Hussein, Saddam, 38
Hutton, Tommy, 165
Hynde, Chrissie, 309

I

IBM PS/1 ad, 100
Ice Cube, 314

Ice-T, 190, 314

Iglesias, Julio, 14

inc., 273

Ingle, Robert, 234

Innanen, Kim, 223

Institite for Research on Poverty, 275

International Bulletin of Missionary Reseach, 210

International Survey Research Corp., 270

Interplak ad, 99

Israel Government Tourist Office, 41

J

Jackman, Phil, 169

Jackson, Bo, 174

Jackson, Jesse, 12, 36

Jackson, Joseph, 5

Jackson, Julian, 171

Jackson, Katherine, 5

Jackson, Keith, 157

Jackson, Michael, 21, 22, 241

Jackson, Reggie, 171

Jackson, Thomas Penfield, 18

Jacob, John E., 32, 270

Jacobsen, Peter, 164

Jacobson, Dr. Terry, 120

Jagger, Mick, 117

James, Caryn, 193

James, Ian, 4

Jankowski, Martin Sanchez, 234

Japan Economic Journal, 229

Jarek, Crystal, 248

Jarman, Derek, 185

Javacheff, Christo, 179

Jayaraman, K. S., 214

Jerusalem Post, 47

Jesus Seminar, 199

Jet, 311

Jim-Jim, 5, 312

Johannesburg Sunday Times, 86

Johnnie Walker Red ad, 99

John Paul II, Pope, 200

Johns Hopkins Medical Letter, 164

Johns, Michael, 82

Johnson, Denise, 122

Johnson, Magic, 2, 166

Johnson, Michael, 69

Johnson, Samantha, 256

Johnston, Ed, 166

Joint Center for Political and Economic Studies, 72, 236

Jones, David, 113

Jones, Jerry, 7

Jones, Sonny, 291

Jong, Erica, 269

Jordan, Barbara, 20

Jordan, William, 221

Joseph, Elizabeth, 246

Journal of Occupational Medicine, The, 272

Journal of the American Medical Association, 112, 116, 125

Jovovich, Milla, 17

Joyner, Al, 173

Justice Department report, 64

K

Kanfer, Stefan, 57

Kathy B., 37, 45

Katims, Arthur, 45

Kaufman, Jackie, 143

Keeley, Don, 18
Keeling, Richard, 250
Kegal, Karen, 115
Keller, Bill, 92
Kelley, Cookie, 168
Kelley, Kitty, 22, 24
Kellwood Home Fashions, 40
Kelly, Leontine, 49
Kelly, Patrick, 313
Kemp, Jack, 58
Kennedy, John F., Jr., 57
Kenshishian, Alek, 263
Kent, Arthur, 42
Kerrey, Bob, 70
Kerr, Kevin, 158, 311
Khashoggi, Adnan, 51
Kids Count Data Book, 73-74
Kilpatrick, James J., 31
Kimbrough, Marjorie, 15
King, Coretta Scott, 49
King, Larry, 13, 162
King, Stephen, 143, 149
Kipper, Judith, 81
Kirby, Martin, 266
Kirt, Boris, 85
Kjellman, Samuel, 46
Klein, Robert, 25
Klerk, Marike de, 307
Knappenberger, John, 279
Knight Commission, 153
Knight, Jonathan, 302
Kolata, Gina, 290
Konigsburg, Randall, 205
Kornbouh, Felicia, 59
Kornheiser, Tony, 173
Kosmin, Barry, 206

Kozel, William K., 23
Krafft, Susan, 210
Krantz, Judith, 141, 142
Kriegel, Leonard, 19
Krupnick, Janet, 219
Krups, Robert, 246
Kunkel, Paul, 134
Kunreuther, Frances, 201
Kupelian, David, 60
Kushma, John, 43

L

Labao, Linda, 72
Lagerfeld, Karl, 4
LaJun Inc., 40
LaMotta, Stephanie, 16
Lancaster, John, 26
Landau, Saul, 86
Landers, Ann, 244, 260
Landis, David, 312
Landon, Leslie, 24
Landon, Michael, 24
Land, Richard, 204
Lane Changer, Inc., 226
Lange, Jessica, 14
Lansbury, Angela, 115
Lantos, Annette, 118
Latifah, Queen, 314
Laughlin, Tom, 69
Lawson, Mark, 228
Lawson, Twiggy, 192
Lear, Norman, 192, 194
Lee, Bill (Spaceman), 156, 251
Leeds, Marge, 26
Lee Jeans ad, 101

Lee, Stephen, 167
Lee, Thomas, 46
Leffler, Kenneth, 310
Legters, Llewellyn, 118
Leigh, J. Paul, 268
Lemmon, Jack, 184
L'Engle, Madeline, 205
Leno, Jay, 46, 64, 70
Leo, John, 255
Leonard, Jennifer, 258
Lepper, 117
Lerner, Michael, 77
Letterman, David, 38, 79, 192, 194, 315
Levine, Dennis, 104
Levi, Peter, 138
Levy, Frank, 66
Lewis, Anthony, 53
Lewis, Huey, 183
Lewis, John, 76
Lewis, Phill, 236
Liddy, G. Gordon, 313
Lily of France ad, 100
Limbaugh, Rush, 91, 312
Lincicome, Bernie, 169
Lincoln Savings and Loan, 307
Liney, Ruth, 184
Lin Kye Young, 227
Lippert, Barbara, 264
Little Richard, 3
Little Rock Connie, 308
Litynski, Warren, 197
Lloyd's of London, 291
Lockhart, Eugene, 158
Lorinez, John, 114
Loring, Ed, 200

Los Angeles Daily News, 289
Los Angeles Times, 195
Lott, Ronnie, 170
Lubachivsky, Myroslave, 207
Luciano, Ron, 159
Luckovich, Mike, 107
Lumina ad, 99
Lumina, Chevy, 99
Luna, Jorge, 83
Lundgren, Mark, 82, 301, 307
Lutheran, 204

M

McAdoo, Harold, 36
McCabe, Michael, 159, 171
McCarry, Charles, 147
McCarthney, Paul, 301
McClellan, Bill, 48
McClendon, Carl, 16
McCotic, 125
McCray, Kent, 24
McCulloch, Frank, 137
McDonald, George, 265
McGrath, Dan, 164
MacGraw, Ali, 254
Machlis, 233
McHugh, Richard, 154
McKeehan, Toby, 209, 211
McLeod, Ramon, 73, 242
McMahon, Mark, 256
McMaster, R. E., Jr., 37, 44
McMasters, Paul, 137
McMath, Robert, 226
McNamara, Paul, 202
McWilliams, John-Roger, 134

McWilliams, Peter, 134
Madden, John, 163
Maddox, Robert, 60
Madonna, 191, 302, 309
Mailer, Norman, 133, 140, 142
Mainichi Shimbun, 87
Malamud, Allan, 171
Maloney, John, 160
Mangold, Tom, 270
Manning, John, 244
Mansfield, Edwin, 222
Mantle, Mickey, 172, 176
Maranto, Gina, 215
Marcos, Imelda, 2
Margolis, Jon, 202
Marin Independent Journal, 278
Markie, Biz, 191
Marquez, Gabriel Garcia, 85
Marsalis, Wynton, 188, 274
Marshall, Myra, 200
Marshall, Penny, 265
Marshall, Sherrie, 218
Marshall, Steve, 197
Marshall, Thurgood, 77
Martinez, Bob, 65
Martin, R. Packard, 119
Mary Kay ad, 268
Mason, Dr. James, 113
Massachusettes Institite of
   Technology, 289
Massie, Robert, 59
Mastroianni, Marcello, 306
Mateja, Jim, 238
Mathias, Dr. C. G. Toby, 267
Matthews, Bob, 175
Matthews, Christopher, 8, 68

Matthiessen, Peter, 87
Mattingly, Don, 156
Mattox, William, Jr., 66
Maxwell, Robert, 136
Maybelline ad, 101
Mayo Health Clinic Letter, 116
Mazda MX-3 ad, 100
Medical Advertising News, 110
Medical Tribune News Service, 243
Meeks, Fleming, 141
Melton, J. Gordon, 206
Melville, Herman, 133
Memmott, Mark, 278
Men Against Violence, 297
Mencken, H. L., 135
Men's Health, 120
Merwe, Koos van der, 86
Meyer-Larsen, Warner, 62
Miami Herald, 99
Michelman, Kate, 76
Michel, Richard, 66
Michener, James, 203
Midgley, Mary, 131
Milken, Michael, 104
Miller, Dr. Lynn, 243
Milli Vanilli fraud, 179
Millman, Robert, 187
Mills-Peninsula Hospitals ad, 101
Milwid, Beth, 266
Minischiello, Lisa, 215
Minneapolis Star Tribune, 289
Minority Report, 202
Mirabella, 309
Mirabella, Alan, 107
Mitchell, Emily, 252
Moet & Chandon, 40

Molnar, Alex, 48
Money, 239
Monge, George, 25
Montana, Joe, 162
Montgomery, M. R., 166
Montgomery Ward ad, 100
Monthly Labor Review, 269
Moore, Christin, 247
Moore, David, 292
Moore, Lisa, 228
Moore, Mary Tyler, 15
Moores, Eldridge, 213
Morgan, Jill, 149
Morris, Edmund, 27
Morris, Jack, 304
Morse, Melvin, 198
Morse, Rob, 75
Morse, Roger, 217
Mortimer, John, 149
Moses, Edwin, 167
Motamedi, Beatrice, 270
Motoring Accessories, 224
Moyers, Bill, 9, 130
Mozart, Wolfgang, 130
Mugabe, Robert, 87
Murray, Cathy, 219
Myerson, Arthur, 307

N

Nachman, Jerry, 143
Nadel, Dr. Ethan, 156
Nader, Ralph, 20
Naipaul, V.S., 133
Nathan, Leonard, 302
National Aeronautics and Space
    Administration, 221

National and International Religion
    Report, 209
National Association for the
    Advancement of Colored People,
    262
National Association of Home
    Builders, 239
National Candy Wholesalers
    Association, 116
National Center for Health
    Statistics, 74, 124, 243, 247
National Center for Health
    Studies, 242, 251
National Centers for Disease
    Control, 258
National Council of Churches, 203
National Crime Survey, 65
National Enquirer, 145, 146, 147
National Examiner, 145
National Exercise for Life
    Institute, 154
National Geographic, 221
National Institute for Occupational
    Safety and Health, 266
National Institute of Business
    Management, 280
National Institute of Environmental
    Health Sciences, 125
National Institute on Drug Abuse, 288
National Institutes of Health, 121
National Jewish Population
    Survey, 210
National Lesbian and Gay Health
    Conference, 112
National Lesbian and Gay Help Foun-
    dation, 124, 126
National Opinion Center, 234
National Scrabble Association, 235
National Sporting Goods
    Association, 167

Nature, 213, 220
Nau, Jean-Yves, 231
Navratilova, Martina, 176
Needleman, Jacob, 206
Nelson, Sharon, 128
Neuwirth, Bebe, 8
New England Journal of Medicine, 114, 123, 126
New Joy of Sex, The, 288
New Kids on the Block, 302
Newmyer, Ron, 71
New Product News, 105
New Scientist, 216
News Extra, 146
Newsweek, 68, 77, 116, 206, 238, 290, 311
New York Times, 68, 110, 136, 159, 216, 228, 237, 239, 275, 303, 310
New York Woman, 274
NFL Players Association, 157
Nicassio, Joe, 255
Nicholls, Richard, 151
Nicklaus, Jack, 167
Nicolelis, Nancy, 276
Nielsen Marketing Research, 107
Nielsen Media Research News, 205
Nirenstein, Jim, 78
Nixon, Richard, 47, 89
Nix, Shann, 246
Noah, Yannick, 178
Noden, Merrell, 42
Nofi, Albert, 273
Nolte, Nick, 12
Norflett, Janet, 16
Noriega, Manuel, 8
North American Conference on Christianity and Ecology, 208

North, Ollie, 1
Northway, Don, 291
Northway, Margaret, 291
Northwestern National Life Insurance Company survey, 268
Noth, Chris, 190
Nugent, Ted, 119
Nureyev, Rudolph, 21
Nussac, Sylvie de, 21

O

Oakley, Robert, 81
O'Boyle, Maureen, 193
O'Brien, P., 243
O'Connor, Cardinal John, 203, 208
O'Connor, Sinead, 182, 303
O'Connor, Ted, 277
Office of Technological Assessment, 267
Ohio State University, 73, 101
Okie, Susan, 65
Older Women's League, 267
Olsen, Billy, 174
Omni, 215
Opera Motors, 298
Orange County Register, 41
Oregon State University, 220
O'Reilly, Jean, 207
Ort, Eric, 77
Osborne, Jeffrey, 189
Osgood, Charles, 37
Ottiker, Marie, 47
Otto, Barbara, 266
Outdoor Retailing, 156
Overholser, Geneva, 64
Ozaki, Robert S., 85

P

Pacific Dessert Company, 291

Paganini-Hill, Annlia, 122

Paglia, Camille, 257

Paige, Woody, 158

Palliser, Charles, 150

Parcells, Bill, 162

Park Engineering, 225

Parks, Gordon, 19

Partnership for a Drug-Free America, 74

Parton, Dolly, 305

Paterson, Katherine, 150

Pauley, Jane, 279

Pawlawski, Mike, 163

Pear, Robert, 67

Peck, Scott, 207

Pella Windows and Doors ad, 101

Pener, Degen, 113

Penland, James, 113

Penn, Sean, 191, 264, 305

Pentagon, 36

People, 191, 264, 315

People for the Ethical Treatment of Animals ad, 119

Pepper, Robert, 194

Perkins, John S., 22

Perlman, David, 111, 126

Perrine, Valerie, 119, 311

Pesci, Joe, 262

Peters, Dee, 52

Petit, Charles, 62, 230

Phelps, Robyn, 247

Philips, Julia, 135

Philips Lighting Co., 223

Phillips, Wade, 178

Pigout Barbecue Restaurant, 298

Pike, K. M., 127

Pimental, David, 119

Pinochet, Augusto, 301

Plager, Bob, 165

Plant, David, 204

Playboy, 248, 273, 306

Player, Gary, 172

Plimpton, George, 134

Pogrebin, Letty Cottin, 12

Pollitt, Katha, 132

Popcorn, Faith, 252

Popov, Gavril, 82

Popular Science, 224, 226, 237

Population Reference Bureau, 82

Porter, Joel, 48

Post, Jerrold, 38

Povich, Maury, 194

Powell, Colin, 138

Powell, Mike, 167, 174

Powers, Roger, 93

Poyner, Jim, 96

Prappas, George, 69

Pratt, Larry, 64

Presbyterian Church, 201

Prescott, Peter, 133

Priest, Max, 6

Proaps, Linda, 135

Progressive Grocer, 105

Punch, 103, 112

Putnam, Sandy, 235

Q

Quayle, Dan, 79, 173, 277

Queenan, Joe, 22, 132

Quinn, Martha, 312
Quintanilla, Michael, 40

R

Ragowsky, Mark, 154
Raitt, Bonnie, 304
Ramo, Chet, 213
Ramstad, Jim, 64
Raphael, Sally Jesse, 193
Rappaport, Julian, 266
Raspberry, William, 11, 73, 138
Rather, Dan, 13, 307
Ratliff, William, 65
Rauter News Service, 224
Ray, Edward John, 106
Ray, Judson, 62
Reader's Digest, 39, 41
Reagan, Hazel, 42
Reagan, Nancy, 4
Reagan, Ronald, 23, 27, 37
Reagan, Ronald, Jr., 22, 263
Reagan, Russell, 238
Recording Industry Association
  of America, 188
Redford, Robert, 11, 189
Redgrave, Lynn, 12
Reed, Willis, 160
Reeves, Dianne, 263
Reid, Brenda, 246
Reinisch, Dr. June, 245
Religion in American Life, 209
Renisch, Dr. June, 117
Reno Gazette, 292
Republic of the Marshall Islands, 39
Reuters, 287, 306
Reynolds, Barbara, 205, 243

Reynolds, Burt, 2
Reznikov, Ilya, 90
Riccard, John, 17
Rice, Charles E., 49
Richardson, Robert, 151
Rich, Frank, 136
Richman, Alan, 137
Richman, Tom, 251
Ridker, P.M., 120
Ries, Al, 280
Rigby, S. J., 47
Rind, D., 222
Ripken, Cal, Jr., 177
Ripley, Alexandra, 134, 143
Rivera, Geraldo, 3, 132, 306
Rivera, Neftali, Jr., 36
Roach, Mary, 254
Robbins, Alan, 97
Robbins, Harold, 140
Roberts, Cecil, 276
Roberts, Cokie, 48
Roberts, Julia, 6, 184, 314
Roberts, Vera, 140
Robinson, Haddon, 204
Robinson, James D. III, 104
Robyn, 310
Rock, Barrett, 214
Rock, Chris, 182, 240
Rockerfeller University research, 225
Roddenberry, Gene, 194, 289
Roddick, Anita, 97
Rodin, J., 127
Roe, G., 305
Rogers, Joseph Lee, 258
Roland, Jon, 222
Roof, William, 51

Rooney, Andy, 164, 303
Rooney, Mickey, 262
Roper Organization, 105, 243, 245, 272
Rose, Judd, 184
Rose, Pete, 155
Ross, G. G., 220
Rossi, Marie, 35
Ross, Ronald, 122
Roszak, Theodore, 186
Rowen, Carl, 75
Roy, Prannoy, 218
Ruff, Robert, 58
Rukeyser, Louis, 97
Rundgren, Todd, 218
Runnels, Tom, 153
Ruplenas, Robert, 26
Russell, Kurt, 306
Russell, Mark, 77
Rutledge, John, 84
Ryan, Nolan, 173, 174
Ryan, Pat, 163
Ryder, Winona, 8
Ryun, Jim, 173

S

Saab ad, 99
Saaberdra, Louis, 181
Sadik, Nafis, 85
Saenz-Nagrate, Frederico, 46
Safire, William, 24
Sagan, Carl, 51, 215, 223
Saint Laurent, Yves, 5
St. Omege, Troy, 33
Sales and Marketing Management, 55
Salk, Dr. Jonas, 250

SallieMae ad, 214
Saltznin, Ellin, 253
Samms, Emma, 18
Sample, Joe, 188
Samuelson, Robert, 66
Sanders, Charles A., 229
Sanderson, Scott, 154
Sandoz, Marianne, 33
San Francisco Chronicle, 291, 309
San Francisco Hospital Association, 127
Sanson, Stephanie, 219
Sanyo, 229
Sapp, Carolyn Suzanne, 129
Sarandon, Susan, 12
Saroyan, Wayne, 37
Sasser, James, 67
Savage, Fred, 302
Sawyer, Diane, 277
Schapira, David, 128
Schmookler, Andrew, 109
Schrage, Michael, 54
Schroeder, Patricia, 35
Schwadron, 105
Schwartz, Joe, 272
Schwarzenegger, Arnold, 17, 183
Schwarzkopf, Brenda, 44
Schwarzkopf, Norman, 43, 44
Schweitzer, Paul, 83
Science, 109
Science News, 227, 230, 231
Science Teacher, 128, 226, 227
Scorsese, Martin, 185
Scott, Jacqueline, 50
Seagal, Steven, 207
Sealey, Peter, 106

See, Carolyn, 203
Segal, Marian, 123
Sellah, Rev. Rabboni, 20
Selleck, Tom, 183
Selvin, Joel, 308
Senate Aging Committee report, 110
Setron, Marvin, 83
Shani doll promotional material, 240
Shapiro, Jeff, 34
Shapiro, Laura, 150
Sharp Electronics, 98, 229
Shaw, Bernard, 42
Shaw, Dougliss, Jr., 230
Sheldon, Sidney, 142
Sheridan, Phillip, 125
Shields, Brooke, 13, 16
Shields, Mark, 49, 70
Shmilova, Olga, 209
Shrgrue, Dan, 218
Shudin, Viktor, 92
Shuman, Howard, 50
Sid-Ahmed, Mohammed, 51
Siegel, Bernie, 120
Siegel, Mo, 280
Siemens Corporation, 235
Sietsema, Tom, 236
Sills, Judith, 245
Silver, Joel, 307
Simic, Charles, 138, 139
Simon, Elsie, 67
Simon, John, 133
Simon, Neil, 147, 264
Simpson, O. J., 158
Sinatra, Frank, 22
Singer, Isaac Bashevis, 149
Singleton, John, 186

Skypager ad, 99
Sloan, Mark, 41
Small Business Administration, 269
Smart, Pamela, 305
Smart, William, 13
Smeal, Eleanor, 276
Smith, Hendrick, 88
Smith, Jeff, 197
Smith, Liz, 26, 244
Smith, Lonnie, 177
Smith, Michael, 95
Smith, Page, 239
Smith, Patricia, 227
Smith, Steve, 165
Smolowe, Jill, 81
Snead, Elizabeth, 229, 257
Snider, Mike, 122
Snlow, Skip, 76
Snow, Carol, 139
Snowden, Lynn, 166
Somers, Suzanne, 16
Sommeral, Pat, 9
South African National Party, 310
South China Morning Post, 51
Soviet Defense Ministry, 302
Spalding, 156
Spanbauer, Tom, 129
Span, Paula, 309
Spaulding, Douglas, 93
Specialized Bicycle Components, 232
Spencer, Felton, 169
Spender, Stephen, 139
Spock, Benjamin, 13
Sporting News, 159
Sports Illustrated, 155, 253
Sprint ad, 101

Spurrier, Steve, 162
Stack, Peter, 187
Stallone, Sylvester, 4, 7
Stamos, John, 15
Stanford University, 117
Stanley, Robert, 25
Star, 144, 146, 147
Stark, A., 221
Starr, Maurice, 262
Star Tribune, 208
Stasio, Marilyn, 131
Steel, Danielle, 140
Steele, Shelby, 59
Stegner, Wallace, 56
Steinem, Gloria, 258
Stern, Gil, 255
Stevens, Barry, 214
Stevens, Ted, 271
Stewart, Rod, 306
Stirling, Ian, 216
Stone, Andrea, 72
Stone, Merlin, 201
Stone, Oliver, 303
Stores, 96
Stothard, Peter, 68
Strand, Mark, 139
Strauss, Robert, 90
Strawberry, Darryl, 210
Streifer, Phillip, 305
Sturdivant, John, 267
Suddeutsche Zeitung, 217
Summers-Orlando Sentinel, 63
Sun, 144-145
Sundberg, Walter, 203
Sununu, John, 27
Sussman, G. L., 127

Sutherland, Keifer, 180
Swayze, Patrick, 261
Swedish Academy, 139
Swertlow, Frank, 189
Swital, Carisia, 201
Switzer, Barry, 168
Switzer, Robert, 288

T

Talbert, Melvin, 208
Talent, David, 223
Taliq Corp., 224
Tampa Tribune, 40
Tan, Amy, 147
Tan, Roger, 32
Tarpinian, Greg, 271
Tass, 90
Taylor, Elizabeth, 240-241
Taylor, Humphrey, 117
Taylor, Paul, 240, 246
Technology Review, 105
Tekna, 226
Television Advertising Bureau, 100
Terry, Randall, 198
Thermoscan, Inc., 232
Thomas, Clarence, 75
Thomas, Isiah, 173
Thomas, Karen, 242
Thomas, W. Ian, 208
Thompson, Roger, 5
Thomson, Thomas, 51
Thornburgh, Dick, 62
Thronton, Sarah, 278
Thurmond, Strom, 66
Tiegs, Cheryl, 6

Tinoco, Eduardo, 63
Tipler, Frank, 202
Tokarz, Karen, 10
Townsend, Robert, 9
Toyota, 228
Tracy, Edward Austin, 9
Travers, P. L., 196
Trebelhorn, Tom, 266
Tredgold, Jeff, 108
Trillin, Calvin, 78, 132
Trotta, Liz, 6
Trout, Jack, 280
Trudeau, Garry, 288
Trump, Donald, 28, 98, 315
Trusov, Fydor, 90
Tsongas, Paul, 83
Tsounis, Alexandra, 47
Tsuruda, Koichiro, 215
Tubbs, Alan, 67
Tucker, Mary Evelyn, 200
Turner, Lana, 7
Tutu, Desmond, 197
Tweed, Shannon, 265
Twenty First Century International Fire Equipment and Services Corp., 225
Twiggy, 192
Twohy, M., 131
Tyson, Mike, 169-168

U

Uchitelle, Louis, 56, 234
Uhlenberg, Peter, 244
Ullman, Tracey, 53
Union of American Hebrew Congregations, 203
United Bible Societies, 195

United Methodist Church, 201
United Nations, 84
United Press International, 35
Unser, Al, Jr., 175
Updike, John, 134
Urban Institute, 273
US ad, 100
U. S. A Dry Pea and Lentil Council, 99
USA Today, 52, 62, 103, 141, 157, 204, 245, 251, 271, 287, 306
U. S. Department of Agriculture, 231, 244
U. S. News & World Report, 50, 93

V

Valenti, Jack, 88
Valvano, Jim, 162
Van Arc, Joan, 304
Van Buren, Abigail, 1, 112, 137, 248
Vancouver Media Foundation, 118
Van Damme, Jean-Claude, 16, 261
Vanilla Ice, 151, 191, 305
Van Meter, Jonathan, 189
Van Peebles, Mario, 185
Vargas, Marilene, 257
Verducci, Tom, 165
Veronis, Suhler & Associates, 180
Viking Stoves, 99
Vincent, Marjorie Judith, 10, 252
Vishniac, Ethan, 223
Visser, Lesley, 160
Volkmer, Harold, 66
Volkogonov, Dmitri, 89
Vonnegut, Kurt, 132, 140
Voodoo To You, 225

W

Waddle, Tom, 158
Wade, Terance, 309
Waite, Armond, 186
Waldrop, Judith, 60
Walford, Ray, 115
Walk, Bob, 165
Walker, Chip, 238
Walker, Constance, 287
Wallace, Amy, 86
Wallehinsky, David, 86
Wall Street Journal, 43, 83
Walsh, Claire, 254
Walsh, Joe, 182
Walsh, John, 201
Walt Disney World, 179
Walters, Selene, 27
Warner, Jim, 175
Warren-Smith, Paul, 84
Warwick, Dionne, 7
Washington Post, 95
Washington Times, 311
Washington University study, 213
Wasserman, 102
Wattenberg, Ben, 97, 193
Wattenberg, Dr. Lee, 116
Watt, Tom, 165
Watzlawick, Paul, 4
Wayans, Keenen Ivory, 193
Wayne, Stephen, 67, 68
Wayzata Technology, 218
Weaver, Sister Mary Martin, 15
Webb, Peter, 214
Weekly World News, 144, 146, 147
Weir, Robin, 23
Weiss, Bob, 170

Welch, Edward, 236
Welty, Eudora, 147
Western Temporary Services, 259
Whetstone, Brad, 110
White, Daniel, 217
Whitehead, Sir John, 86
White, John Paul, 174
White, Willye B., 17
Wickam, DeWayne, 10
Wieseltier, Leon, 257
Wilder, Douglas, 257
Will, George, 55, 59, 76, 88, 265
Williams, Cynda, 3
Williams, Leona, 78
Williams, Marjorie, 17
Williamson, Marianne, 242
Williamson, Richard, 163
Williams, Pat, 176
Williams, Susan, 6
Willie, Dr. Charles, 244
Willington Morning Star, 207
Willis, Bruce, 8, 261
Wilson, Barbara Foley, 245, 246
Wilson, Flip, 160
Wilson, Glenn, 155
Winebaum, Jake, 105
Winfield, Dave, 175
Winfrey, Oprah, 12, 133
Wingard, Deborah, 124
Wirthlin Group, 56
Wittkowski, Bernard, 103
Wolcott, James, 14
Wolfe, George, 182
Wolfe, Sidney, 111
Wolfe, Tom, 130
Wolpe, David, 200

Woodruff, William, 96
Woods, George, 111
Woodward, Joanne, 250
Woodward, Kenneth L., 15
Work in America, 268
Workman Publishing, 288
World Almanac, 255
World Monitor, 226
World Tie Corporation, 226
Worthen, John, 141

Y

Yakovlev, Vladimir, 88
Yale University study, 272
Yanayev, Ganady, 90

Yard, Molly, 243
Yee, Albert, 224
Yeltsin, Boris, 92
Yergin, Daniel, 96
Young, Andrew, 274
Young, Elaine, 179
Young, Sean, 304
Your Church, 195
Yuanreng Hu, 83

Z

Zajonc, Robert, 120
Zeibert, Duke, 88
Zollo, Peter, 240
Zucconi, Vittorio, 63